For my lighthouses: Maxine, Ava, Jessica

Acknowledgements

To the parents of my liver doner, thank you for this second chance.

Raymond Weber, for being the very first to tell me I was missing my calling by not writing.

To the nudging family, friends, and fans who persisted in telling me to write the book.

My musical family, for teaching me and humoring me. I love you guys.

All those who took me in when I was a hot mess, opening their front doors and kindly watching the shit show unfold in disbelief in their living rooms.

My family, by blood and not. We sure had a wild roller coaster ride together, didn't we? For that, we are bonded above and beyond.

Todd, for being my first musical partner in crime when I was a newbie bandleader, sticking through my faux pas, never judging, always believing.

My sisters Esther and Marisa and my nephew Galen, all inspirations.

My first voice coach, Vincent Roppolo, without whose nurturing care and training I would never have believed I could be a singer.

Stephen James Walker, for being my soulmate during the most difficult years of my life.

Anders Osborne, for giving me the opportunity to get straight.

My sober sisters, for sticking together while we were kindly getting our asses kicked together in sobriety boot camp.

The staff at Cumberland Heights, especially Mary Cowan, for believing in me, just me, for the sake of me.

The New Orleans Musicians' Clinic, for being heroes and saints to a wild bunch of half-broke horses called musicians.

Ochsner Hospital, for saving my life.

All of the talented, smart, kind people in the world who have taken their precious time to share their lives with me.

The higher force up there, who must have had a good laugh with the Greek panel of the gods, laughing at this mortal dancing in her red shoes through every predicament and landing *ta-da* precariously on her toes every time.

My father, without whom this journey of absurdity, bewilderment, torture, awe, joy, severity, and music would never have happened.

And especially Paula Underwood Winters, for taking this whole pile of chaotic writing and making it a real solid in hand piece of big fish truth for you, readers, to ponder over. She is the angel sent.

Also especially thankful for Angie Joachim, for reading and rereading my words and providing editorial insights on a home-schooled child's first book.

A special thank you to pianist and New Yorker Alan Kamen, for being here from the beginning of my musical stint as a bandleader and as a real friend through thick and thin.

Jeanne Vidrine and Kellye Bolton-Kendrick, thank you. I know you know.

Always love, always light. To those who don't believe they can, I am here to tell you loud and proud, standing on the count of nine and a half, oh yes you can!

Preface

The small pueblos of Northern Mexico are desolate, arid places. Scrubby, leafless trees are about the only vegetation and freezing cold in January. These were the performance territories for the Mexican circus we traveled with.

We were five adults and four children living in a school bus and small van. One day while Ingrid and the other children were getting introductory training in tightrope walking and balancing a pole on one's chin that would later support a stack of dishes, I was approached by a man who lived in the pueblo and asked to paint a sign on his truck.

All the men in the circus were sitting outside around a fire to keep warm. We parked the truck to be lettered close to the fire. But it was still so cold, the brush kept falling out of my hand. After several frigid hours I completed my job and headed for the bus to warm up, passing the small van where David was resting. He was near death after being bitten by a rabid dog.

"Max, where is everyone?" he asked as he looked out.

"I don't know," I answered.

"Can you make me a bowl of oatmeal?"

"Sure," I answered.

We had a wood burning stove in the bus. The rule was to keep a fire burning at all times so people could come back there and be warm. There was no fire, no people, no stack of wood to build a fire.

The few lone willowy trees in the distance would have to be my source. Several trips had to be made to gather enough scrawny branches to build a fire that would sustain cooking oatmeal. But at last the fire came to life.

Now for the oatmeal. No water! The pueblo had a well that was a hole in the ground covered by a board. I had to lie flat on my stomach on the freezing cold ground, pull up the bucket and throw it with all my might into the hole. Only it was made of wood and every time I threw it, it landed on its side and floated. Eventually, I managed to get enough water to fill the jug.

I started back toward the bus when David poked his head out of the van, obviously agitated and in a very irritated voice greeted me with "WHERE'S THE FUCKING OATMEAL?"

Welcome to The Big Time...

Maxine Pearlman

(Ingrid's mom)

Contents

Acknowledgements v

Preface vii

Contents ix

The Daisy 1

End of One Journey 2

Heads Up 6

Red Glitter Polish 9

A Ballerina Dream 11

San Francisco 14

My Mother, Maxine 19

My Irish Dad, William David Maloney 21

The Work Group 24

Half Famous 26

Energy Fields 29

Easter in Mexico 31

Cahill at Bat 33

A Song for My Brother 35

Mr. Scotty Moore 38

Feliz Navidad, Gringo 39

A Buddhist in Orizaba 40

¡Viva Mexico! 41

Tengo Ganas 42

New York Dreams 43

Introducing The Flying Neutrinos Family Band 44

The Foraging Kind 53

Tantric Sex and Other Oddities 55

"Sign her. She sounds like Julie London." 59

Lost Innocence 65

White Picket Fence	67
New Beginnings	70
Never Lived Alone	72
Ghetto Gatsby	74
Dearest Ava,	77
The Little Bulldog	79
Pool Sharks and Chess Strategies	81
Ode to Melvin	83
Rhythm of the Rain	84
Shotgun Sundays	86
Love Letter to New Orleans	91
New Orleans Musicians' Rights	93
The Paper Trail	95
Letter to the President of William Morris	97
How It Feels	99
French Quarter Kid	101
Jackson Square: Ground Zero	103
The Art of Writing	106
Performer	109
My Voice	111
The Tree of Jazz	114
Louis Armstrong	115
Storyville, Teddy Riley, and Cutting Chops	116
Uncle Lionel	117
Red Roses, Ferraris, and Reality	118
Without Music	120
Stevie Wonder	122
Music Warriors	123
Security	124
Ten Cents in a Mansion	125

A Rainy Sunday	126
An Hour in the Life	127
Dear Ava,	129
Majestical Man	131
Ragtime Talks	133
Circus Lights	134
Lady Zipperette	136
Jefferson Parish Prison	140
Sex Dungeon, Personal Belongings, and Extortion	147
Dear Jimbo,	150
Angola Prison Rodeo	151
A Reading	152
Peter Pan Hero	153
Dear Ava,	154
Tourette Syndrome	155
San Juan Airport	157
Drop 'n' Roll	158
Sea Legs and Ships	159
Airports and Planes	161
Iceland and Clothes	162
Dear Mamacita,	164
Norway	168
Dear Ava,	170
Norway to Greece	171
Dear Mamacita,	173
An Aesop's Fable Come True	174
Really?	175
Irma Thomas	176
Billie Holiday	178
Edinburgh Jazz Festival Headliner	180

Dear Mamacita,	184
Dear Ava,	185
From White Flight Land to the Bayou	186
The Mayor of St. Bernard Avenue	188
Fabulous Flora	189
Bicycle Thieves	190
Dear Amanda,	191
Asphalt Jungle	193
Miss Sarah's Domain	195
The Temptress Hotel	199
College Try at a Dating Ad	201
Black and Mild	202
Body and Soul	203
Beaten with a Broom	204
Behind the Red Picket Gate	206
Ingrid's Book of Etiquette	208
Upstanding Citizens of New Orleans	211
"Isn't It Pretty to Think So?"	213
A Day in the Life	214
Viva Las Vegas	216
White Girl	217
Blurred Lines	219
Dear Jessica,	222
The Turning Point	224
He Saved Me	226
Happy To Be on This Journey	227
Transitions	228
Bitchin' Birthday	230
Porch Watching	231
Mr. Hudson	233

An Unusual Massage	234
"It's a Boy"	236
Always Late, Early	238
Food for Thought	239
Namaste, Newbie	241
Listen	243
Lady Charmaine	244
Going the Distance	246
Raymond Weber Jr.	248
The Soundtrack of Your Life	249
Summer in New Orleans	251
Cone of Uncertainty	257
Hurricane Zeta	259
Make a Wish	260
Fairy Godmother	262
Gay Brothers	265
One Year Sober	267
Contender	270
Messengers of God	272
God, Religion, and Church	274
Merely a Mortal	276
MELD Score	277
What These Eyes Have Seen	280
As the Hospital Turns	286
Rodger That	290
Gratitude Letter	291
Road Trip	293
Hurricane Ida	294
Whipped Cream and Cherries	297
Ambassador of Love	298

Mortality	299
There Is No Ending That's Not Also a Beginning	300
The Drinking Game	304
Meet Me Under the Chime Tree	308

The Daisy

There's a daisy,
Where the wild wind blows,
Sun beats down
Through a sidewalk crack it grows.

Its innocent beauty,
Strong as a weed,
Solitary figure,
Alone, observing.

I sit on the stoop,
And look at the crack,
There it is
Looking back.

Mirrored I see,
Not a rose beauty,
Clipped and groomed,
But a rambunctious spirit,
Left out of the room.

Strangers trod by,
On their trudging way,
Me and the daisy,
Lackadaisically sway.

In the asphalt jungle,
Lies a little seed,
Climbing from the mud,
Hearty, wild, and free

End of One Journey

How the fuck did I end up in the ICU — at Christmastime in 2019 — with Stage 4 cirrhosis of the liver?

I stared at the ceiling, halfheartedly wondering why everybody visiting me looked so sad. I wanted to take a Polaroid shot of their sorrowful faces; looking at my family and friends, I thought, what's wrong with *them*? It seemed like a funny scenario, with my visitors leaning over me, so dramatically morose. In retrospect, knowing I was a few days away from death, it wasn't funny at all.

I had two choices. Take the path of death or get my crippled body up and check out at the front door. Opting for what seemed like the harder choice, I crawled into a wheelchair, knowing no one was going to give me a ride home. The hospital ordered me a Lyft and gave me a walker.

I agreed to go to rehab for a month beginning two weeks from the hospital release date. I had been in the ICU for almost two weeks.

My eyes and skin were yellow from jaundice, and my leg looked like the Elephant Man's. I sat in the wheelchair outside the hospital entrance, freezing with a little snuggle blanket with Christmas trees on it wrapped around my head that my mom had given me. I was feeling so alone and beaten down.

The question, after reflecting hard, for hours and days, was whether it was time to let go. But I knew deep in my heart I wasn't ready to say goodbye yet.

Also, there was the realization that my dad was up there somewhere. He would kick the shit out of me if I didn't get up on the count of nine and a half and fight for my life. *By the hangnail,* my mom always says about me. And she's up, folks, for the next round, ready to be beaten in the ring of life some more.

Twenty-eight days away from death in the ICU, 28 days in rehab, 28 days in Intensive Outpatient Program, two years of isolation due to Covid that included hospital visits for all kinds of random infections and procedures. The one thing that was always consistent was a big needle in my arm, drawing blood.

* * * * *

I was the most enthusiastic dreamer and go-getter in the entire world.

With force, hard work, and the belief that I could make The Big Time happen, I walked the streets of New York City, certain that if played correctly, traditional jazz (trad) could again become the rock 'n' roll of its time, like in the 1920s.

And somehow, I did it with my band, The Flying Neutrinos. We were a complete success story come true. Billboard charting, world gigs, recording catalogue in film, golden reputation, press, sponsors. The whole package.

However, I trusted people who kept ripping me off. We charted #9 on Billboard's Jazz Charts, but we were not getting paid by the music labels we were signed to. I couldn't seem to make any of my band members happy no matter how much I gave them.

I came back home to New Orleans to play music for the joy of it, but I also found a whole shit show of musical dysfunction after learning what professionalism is and should be. I found myself becoming mediocre in my professional performance standards. I was selling out to low-paying gigs to support my family and pay for utilities and food.

* * * * *

In 1998, I married Clyde, a phenomenal talent in photography. We met and fell in love among a circle of New York City contenders in art, photography, literature, and music. Our tight-knit group of friends was sprinkled generously with a fairy dust of exuberance; we all rose in stature together in our artistic pursuits. After Clyde and I topped out in our respective fields, we decided to move back to New Orleans. Following a botched photo shoot with trumpeter Terence Blanchard for *Vanity Fair*, he decided he did not want to be a photographer. (In New Orleans at that time, the industry suffered from mediocrity.) The professional developer had reversed the negatives, and the deal was blown. After our child, Ava, was born in 2001, Clyde decided to be Mr. Mom, and I would thereafter be the money-maker.

Clyde has a lot of beautiful qualities. He can be sensitive and is capable, intelligent, detail-oriented, and a great father. However, in retrospect, I believe I married someone who was my polar opposite. I felt his way of looking at the world was often pessimistic. That gradually started to affect my more cheerful demeanor and my self-esteem. Once he was comfortable in the marriage, it became clear to me that he did not consider me an equal partner.

I became very unhappy. Clyde didn't always participate in many family activities. I did not want to give up on my family, so I stayed put, but I found myself feeling increasingly miserable and trapped. And I pacified myself with alcohol. Prior to that, my drinking was limited to social events with Clyde. We began to separate emotionally.

We had no structure. There was no allotment of chores, no game plan, no order. To entertain himself, Clyde played video games for hours. To entertain myself, I would sit on the couch and watch a movie alone while drinking half a bottle of tequila. Predictably, our marriage continued to deteriorate, even though we tried counseling. We were two unconventional artists trying to build a family during the days following Hurricane Katrina (2005), and it became too much for the both of us to bear.

I always put Ava to bed, and I made sure breakfast was made in the morning. We both did our share with taking her to school and picking her up; I did this even while playing gigs till 3 a.m. Clyde seemed to have difficulty adjusting to the schedule of a young child and at that time opted not to do much socially. For me, this was painful because we had previously done everything together wholeheartedly. Even holidays blended together year after year until the patterns that we were in made me feel stuck. I imagine he was also feeling quite stuck. I got burned out, and my drinking became a daily habit.

When our marriage eventually imploded, my drinking inevitably became the scapegoat. I lost my home and my daughter. The insurance on my car was removed without my knowledge, which led to an expensive lien being placed on my license that took me five years to pay, and in that time, I couldn't drive. I was left nearly penniless. Clyde and his parents seemed to feel that in the interest of protecting Ava, this approach was justified. I now understand that my alcoholism hurt the people closest to me, and for that I will be making amends for a long time. But alcoholism is an illness, and I deeply wish a more compassionate approach had been taken.

I had experienced too many trials and tribulations in my strange, unusual upbringing to let that rejection break my spirit. Many say I'm stubborn. How am I still here? I never give up. Ever.

Every leg of my recovery was a long pilgrimage emotionally, intellectually, and physically. It takes many struggles to really heal. Just when I thought I was happy, clear to begin a fresh new life, something would get in the way, such as needing a liver transplant in July 2021.

Some days I felt devastated about what I did to myself, my family, and my friends. I also felt terrible imposing a million dollar hospital bill as well as taking a liver someone else could have used. I don't know if the carefree spirit I once had will ever come back. I look in the mirror and I see a girl who trusted the world. Overall, I think she was right to do so. At times, I think she should have had her guard up.

Clyde once said, "Your fans think they know the real you, but I know the real you."

Who is "the real me"? A dirty boat freak child who's trying to pull one over on everybody to convince them that I'm normal? Maybe. A lonely dirty kid making dreams to live in? Maybe. A boot camp child who never had a fun childhood? Maybe.

I learned a lot in rehab. We are born unique in God's eyes. You are you for a reason. You are special because you are you. To try and pretend otherwise is a disservice. That freed me from all of the years of not feeling good enough. It's been a long and hard dirty road that extends wide and far.

Heads Up

On December 30, 2019, vocalist Debbie Davis of The New Orleans Nightingales and Pfister Sisters sent the following email:

Dear friends,

It's with a heavy heart and no small amount of apprehension that I write this. Ingrid is in UMC Hospital where she has been for nearly 2 weeks after suffering a seizure and an aneurism brought on by advanced chronic liver disease. She is currently unable to walk on her own due to a hemorrhage she suffered in her leg that caused swelling which has only recently begun to abate but is not yet resolved. She has detoxed in the hospital and has been diagnosed with advanced cirrhosis. Her liver function is severely compromised, complete with jaundice, and there is no indication of when or if her liver can function again on its own.

Medically speaking, her liver has a 52% chance of failing in the next 90 days, even if she stays sober. Assuming her liver doesn't fail, and she stays sober for 6 months, she'll qualify for the transplant list. From there, there's no way of knowing how long it might take to find a tissue match. And, at any point along the way, her health could take a turn for the worse. That is to say, there is no best case scenario.

I found out about this situation a few days before Christmas and, while I couldn't reach her directly, I got as much information as I could from people who had been to see her. This is what I know: The first few days were rough, with hard DTs, sedation, hallucinations, memory lapses, lost days, and difficulty differentiating present from past and fiction from reality. She seems to be lucid and comprehending things as they happen now, but her denial and need to rationalize her addiction is still very firmly in place.

Sophie Lee, Jayna Morgan, and I visited her today hoping to let her know that she is loved, that the people who love her are worried and want to help, and that the decision to live and fight and change is hers. She acknowledges that she can never drink again, but she says she won't go to rehab even though she has no reason not to. She wants a "mentor" to help her stay sober, but she doesn't want to go to AA because she doesn't fit in there.

As it stands now, her plan for recovery is to get out of the hospital and not drink anymore while living with her boyfriend who is also an alcoholic who is also not going to drink anymore. She is different from other people who drink so she doesn't need what they need and she can just stop. Anyone who has lived with an addict in their life knows this maneuver all too well. As we all know, the decision must be hers. If someone else can convince her, I hope they will try. As far as I'm concerned, if she has any chance at survival at all, that's the only one there is.

It is no secret that Ingrid has been on a downward slide for a while now. It's also no secret that she has burned more than a few bridges on her way down. I don't mean to put myself or this information in the middle of anything else you may feel about Ingrid. However, it was important to me to let you know, as her colleague and friend, that she is very sick and may in fact be dying. She has not been given a release date, as of yet (honestly, I'm hoping they keep her there indefinitely).

She's supposed to only have 2 visitors at a time but they didn't enforce the rule when we were there. She was caught a little off guard when we showed up, but I know she was glad to see familiar faces who came because they actually cared what happened to her. No matter what she decides to do or what she's equipped to do next, I only hope she finds some peace in her heart. She deserves that much.

I'd like to respectfully request that you keep this information confidential. There are many people holding one grudge or another against Ingrid who might take a ghoulish satisfaction in her suffering. All of this will become common knowledge soon enough, but for now, the least we can do is keep her from being the object of scorn and ridicule. Ingrid may be a little pissed at me for telling y'all, but I'll take the heat because I know at the heart of things, there is love among us and that's what counts. I hope you'll help me protect her from those who might be less than kind to her in this dark hour.

I wish you all love, luck, good health and prosperity in the new year and hope that we all have reason to celebrate and share in each other's good fortunes.

Your friend,

Debbie

* * * * *

Dear Debbie,

Thank you for letting the New Orleans community of musicians know about Ingrid's medical status. I hadn't realized how bad her situation is. Her decision to not go to AA is an indication that it won't work for her because she's still not ready. Besides, I have a friend who has gone to a few different AA meetings in New Orleans and he found them to be sad and unsupportive.

Anders Osborne started a foundation called Send Me A Friend, which is strictly for musicians trying to get sober. I think it's a sponsorship program that looks more like what Ingrid is asking for. I can message Anders in confidence and ask how to get her the help she needs. Also, the Musicians Clinic offers

$25 therapy sessions. She's had such a tough time of it the last few years. Once her dad passed, I could see a change in her and that was even before she started The New Orleans Nightingales project. I don't know if she's been seeing a therapist since her split with her ex, but I can't even imagine how she's dealt with being separated from her daughter.

When I get back in town, I'm going to pay her a visit. If any of you would like to join me, let me know.

Margie Perez

* * * * *

Hello, all.

Just an update.

Ingrid checked herself out of the hospital on Monday evening. She is currently living back at the place on Franklin Ave. near St. Claude that she shares with her boyfriend, who most of you know is also an alcoholic. She still has limited physical mobility due to her unresolved leg issues and her prognosis is unchanged. As far as I know, she can be reached by cell phone, though she has yet to reply to my texts. I suspect she doesn't want to talk to me because I pushed the subject of rehab and wouldn't let it drop during our visit in the hospital. I am told that Anders Osborne was going to try to get her to go to a meeting yesterday but I'm not sure if that happened or not.

It is my opinion that, if she doesn't go to rehab, she has no chance of surviving this. Even if she does go, she may not survive it, but going to rehab will give her the skills and tools she will need to change her habits and her frame of mind and fight to stay alive (and will also keep her sober). Right now, she is going into battle with no weapons expecting to slay a dragon that has already done everything short of killing her outright. If anyone thinks they can get her to hear them, now is the time. Odyssey House has a brand-new facility on S. Broad Street and will take people on Medicaid or with no insurance for 28-day inpatient care to clean up and figure out how to build a new life. I don't know if we are looking at calendars or clocks, but time is definitely running out.

I love you all. I will keep updating.

Debbie

Red Glitter Polish

There I was, five years old, sitting in the middle of the wide, bright, sunny, open, hot desert, wearing a thrift store tutu, plastic barrettes, and red glitter nail polish on little toenails sparkling in the sun. All by my little self, waiting for my parents and their psychological work group to finish their long meetings in the dry goods store they rented and lived at in the dusty small town of Gerlach, Nevada.

The winds blew sand and brambles across the dirt roads of the town, which held a railroad track, water tower, bar, restaurant, and empty worn playground. I played on the monkey bars until my fingers blistered. I sat under the huge water tank, the only shade in town. Then, after the meetings, my mom and dad and I would go to the restaurant for a cold orange sherbet and apple pie a la mode. Slot machines rang, cold air conditioning filled the dark bar smelling of whiskey next door, and the jukebox was always playing old country songs.

Every week the book mobile would drive through town. As many books as allowed were checked out and read voraciously, quickly leaving an empty void until the truck returned again to deliver stories from many other lands.

The small yellow plastic record player burned a hole in the few records I had: *Rambling Rose, Blueberry Hill, Yellow Submarine.* It was a lonely existence trying to occupy myself in a small town that didn't seem to have any kids.

Dancing through the dirt streets in my tutus, knocking on trailer doors, trying to sell junk for spending money, going with my mother to the hot springs at the base of the mountain that was an hour walk each way on a quiet, dusty, empty road.

My dad showed old black and white movies on a big projector screen in the back of the store once a week for the townspeople; Charlie Chaplin, Buster Keaton, King Kong. My father's gypsy tribe would stay for a while until my dad called a leave and we were on to the next adventure.

Cheap hotel rooms in San Francisco. Red glitter polish. Mexican circuses, red rhinestone glitter polish. Homemade rafts up and down the Mississippi River, no matter how muddy or dirty, red rhinestone glitter polish. Flickering sparkles in endless hot, bright, sunny locations. I would paint my toes with as many coats to get all the glitter and miss, painting my skin as well. Maybe it was a sense of security, as red lipstick had become in my adulthood. I told myself, everything's gonna be alright, and it always was.

There was always an adventure around the corner to be found. Whether it was kids on street corners playing or discovering a pet mouse on the river and adopting it, or dumpster diving to score a baby blue ball gown with rhinestones after Mardi Gras that was a couture fit for a nine-year-old and worn 24 hours a day and slept in.

Once, when I was nine, an old lady at a marina in Florida whose office I was passing time with, staying cool while eating Cheetos and drinking a root beer, said with pity and concern, "Ingrid, underneath, your nails are filthy. No one will take your seriously if you present yourself like that." Back at the homemade paddle wheel houseboat, I coated the nails with red glitter polish immediately since we didn't have a shower or a bath. And so it went, growing up in all the solitude and daily unknowns, I was always hopeful that magic would appear by wearing the red polish. And it always did.

A Ballerina Dream

From the time I first saw *The Red Shoes*, I was sold on the magic of dance. I studied every piece of film I could, read every autobiography I could, learned the language and the positions. I auditioned for New Orleans Center for Creative Arts (NOCCA) when I was 15 and was told I was too fat to be a dancer by the ballet mistress (who was an old fat lady herself). It was devastating to me. So, I became anorexic between the ages of 15 and 18. I starved myself from 145 pounds down to 113, from a size 10 down to a 6; I lost my period for three years and stunted my growth. It became mental torture to think about eating half of a yogurt all day long. My mind was so sick about calorie counting. It dominated my thoughts.

I so much loved all the ballet dancers and their stories, from the free movement style of Isadora Duncan, to the uniqueness of Vaslav Nijinsky, to the short, tight choreography that Balanchine created for Gelsey Kirkland, to the elegant lines of Suzanne Farrell, to the spectacular story of Dame Margot Fonteyn. I was always intrigued by how bodies intertwined into patterns, from the simplicity of a Jerome Robbins pas de deux to the grand kaleidoscope of sparkly multitudes of Busby Berkeley chorus girls.

I also became enamored with choreography, which led to a dream to have Bob Fosse as my mentor. I created routines, such as one to "Chattanooga Choo Choo" for my little brothers and sisters to perform on the streets and routines for the chorus girls in the Mexican circus. I also created routines in exchange for a six-week modeling class in Veracruz, Mexico.

After the NOCCA audition, I decided to audition for the Can Can Cabaret on Bourbon Street. I got the job at the age of 15. The dance captain, Mary Jean Jaeger, took me under her wing and taught me all about what I needed to know, from combination changes and counting properly to posture, breath, core, and attitude. Next thing I knew I was dancing the can-can on Bourbon Street, doing a kick line, the chair dance from *Cabaret*, and some modern dance to Grace Jones' rendition of "La Vie en Rose." I was making $10 a show, three shows a night, which I used to paid for my braces. The kick line is not an easy endeavor, and the more kicks I did, the more I wanted to just lie down and die.

My father used to cry over my choreography to "New York, New York," or the way I moved to express a piece. When I told him I wanted to sing, he told me I should stick with dancing; I would never be a singer. Well, the reason he thought that was because we were all newbies when we started the family band and he had no idea that there are keys that work for certain voices. No one knew enough to know I was singing notes that were high enough for Minnie Mouse.

My dad would give his military dance classes outside of the school bus on the side of the road in Mexico or Texas or wherever we were on a given day. That consisted of separating the top half of the body from the bottom half of the body and the whole body. All my brothers and sisters were lined up, and he would count 1234, 1234, 1234, 1234, and we would have to make up any steps or moves that we wanted to, and when he said, "switch to lower body, upper body, whole body," we would all just switch positions. Some of us adapted well, but one of my sisters wasn't naturally gifted in dance and had absolutely no interest in the family band, so she did a little fan dance over and over; my dad used to get so mad at her, like she was doing it on purpose. It just wasn't her calling. She also played the drums, or, if she preferred, as my dad said adamantly, she could do kitchen duty in the bus, because we all had to pull our weight.

I incorporated all of my moves of ballet, modern jazz, Broadway jazz hands, kicks, splits, show stuff, and I danced on street corners with my family band for years. I don't know how I had the guts to do that. But people loved it and it was a showstopper and a money maker.

When we were in Cape Cod, we performed in front of the Town Hall every single day. One day, producer Vincent Roppolo, who was putting on a production of *A Midsummer Night's Dream* at the Provincetown Playhouse, asked me to play Puck. The play's concept was a mix of Grecian Nijinsky and Kabuki makeup. He asked me to sing my part because he realized I couldn't act or pull off Shakespearean verse, so I started singing and he said, "Do you know you sound like Billie Holiday?"

He told me I should be singing, and he taught me all of the tools I needed to learn to be a good singer: breath control, projection, diction, keys, posture and stance, and imbuing every word with meaning. These were all the components that made it possible for me to go to New York and become a singer who was taken seriously.

An old tourist in Provincetown once told me that dancers have a shelf life and singers can be in a wheelchair singing until they're 90. He was right.

After auditioning for everything from Alvin Ailey to Broadway shows to Radio City Music Hall's Christmas show, I realized I was too far behind in formal training to be a competitor in that way. Also, the fact that I was not being hired as a singer by all the bands I would sit in with in the jazz world made me decide to start my own band. At age 20, I began a new chapter, singing, bandleading, and writing songs. With ownership of The Flying Neutrinos also came the responsibility to walk the streets and make opportunities happen for the band.

San Francisco

Noonie Padoonie was my nickname when I was a child, used endearingly but rarely. My father would also call my mother Boopsie. It was the three of us sleeping in an old-fashioned hotel room and living bohemian lives in San Francisco. It was a free-spirited life of a four-year-old wild child, wearing 1,000 plastic barrettes in my hair and lingerie, running barefoot through the halls. I was the poor version of Eloise.

I remember my dad and my mother during those days. They seemed happy together and with their individual responsibilities, as well as united as a family. My dad had Irish rogue good looks with the palest blue eyes; they were like the sunniest day. They would go to a place no one could ever go with him in his thoughts or his dreams. My dad lost his two front teeth in boot camp when he was 14, and I remember whenever he would laugh, he would cover his mouth with his hand. He would laugh with his whole body and his eyes would water up. It was so contagious we couldn't help but laugh, and we didn't even know why we were laughing. That's how happy a guy he was.

My mother looked like the raisin box lady — at least that's what I told everybody. She was so exotic to me in every single way: her face, her laughter, her openness to take me everywhere from the park to the library and on little adventures throughout the day. She was very exotic, gypsy-like, with her wild hair and her olive complexion. She was more reserved; she had a beautiful smile with a lot of serenity.

In the mornings in North Beach, I would go down to the hotel lobby and entertain the desk clerk with cartwheels and curious questions and read her books; I'd just have social time with her. It was a grand old hotel with red shag carpet, high ceilings, clawfoot bathtubs, long drapes, and neighbors who were artists or characters who had lived there for many years.

The hotel once held a lot of glory. The elevator was the old-fashioned kind. You had to close the brass gate and push the buttons in a certain manner to make it even move. I was too busy running up and down the halls all day visiting people to have any time for mischief. One lady in particular, who was my mother's friend from down the hall, used to give me bubble baths and paint my nails in red glitter polish. Boy, was that the life. What more could one kid want? I would go to the dark murky coffee shop with my father and keep myself occupied with the jukebox while he played chess and conversed with the elder statesmen. I remember it had a lot of wood detailing, and the smell of coffee was so thick it was like walking into a foggy day. The jukebox was my favorite. *La Bohème*, *La Traviata*, Nelson Eddy and Jeanette MacDonald, Al Jolson were all playing constantly.

Apparently, according to my grandma, we were so poor my mother carried me around in a drawer when I was a baby until we could afford a crib. Our life was perfect when I was a little girl; I don't remember being unhappy about anything at all.

My mother let me be a free spirit, but my father told her to watch me carefully because I was the kind of person who would try to fly. He said my half-brother Cahill knew exactly what his limits were, and my half-sister Mandy never tested the waters of what was possible. My older half-brother and half-sister were wounded and gentle souls; they lived with their mom, Eileen Cahill Maloney, who was a reporter at the *San Francisco Progress*. Whenever I spent time at their apartment, they completely spoiled me with vanilla wafers, hanging me upside down by my ankles, yanking my hair, making me laugh, and just being silly together. Mandy looked like my dad. She had twinkling blue eyes and blonde hair and was built with that Irish stockiness that could break anyone's neck if they messed with her or her tribe. Cahill had blue eyes and blond hair as well, and I thought he was so handsome. He had this particular crooked smile that said trouble. My brother taught me how to play baseball and pool, and he and my sister would take me to the parks and run up and down the streets of San Francisco like we were wild and free horses.

My mom loved to go to bookstores and get lost in the spiritual section, which I thought was so boring. Action, adventure, the dream, the glory of being on stage and entertaining people far outdid any spiritual reading aisle in my little girl's brain. Who wouldn't want to wear tutus all day long and dance and dance and dance and cartwheel and laugh and sing and watch all the people's faces smile with joy and you were the one who did it? Wow, that was it.

By age six, I was an avid reader, reading anything I could get my hands on in the library, from *Grimm's Fairy Tales* to *Aesop's Fables* to you name it. I loved any books that were a set or series and never seemed to end. Getting to the end would make me sad to say goodbye as if to a friend with an empty space waiting for a new series of books to get lost in again.

At night, in our big fancy faded-glory hotel room, we would watch old movies together. Musicals, gangster movies, literature, any feature movies that were on, but they were always black and white ones and those were the go-tos. John Garfield was my father's favorite, Judy Garland was mine, my mom never really said who her favorite old-time movie actor was, but she watched all of them. We had not a care in the world. Every day was a sunshiny day of adventure waiting to happen outside the front door. This was The Big Time for a kid.

While my mom, dad, and I were living at the hotel in San Francisco, my friend and I would jump up and down on the beds watching a big old TV that had three channels to change. One day we had a wild little party watching Sammy Davis Jr. sing "The Candy Man." We thought we were at a rock concert and promptly broke the TV by screaming, yelling, and banging the screen for him until it exploded in sparks and died.

My dad would take me with him sometimes to European-style coffee shops. I had to be quiet and behave myself. The jukebox became my best friend. "Rhinestone Cowboy" and "Hot Time in the Old Town Tonight" were my favorite tracks. The jukebox had real records that moved mechanically on to the rotating player. It was fascinating to watch in detail.

We had a good life together in my five-year-old mind. I was allowed to do anything I wanted as long as I didn't hurt myself. I did pretty well until I jumped off a chain link fence, flapped my wings to fly, and promptly landed *plop* on the concrete. I still have a scar on my knee to show for it.

My father was my pal who took me to triple feature movie theater outings that held lots of chocolate, buckets of popcorn, and Coke.

And then one day, my dad decided that he wanted to save the world. We moved to the Bay Area, into a peanut truck in the driveway of the teacher for a work group called Messages from Michael. My dad wanted to start his own work group, so he took this opportunity to learn some psychological tools. His days were not as free anymore, but that was okay. I found drawers to go through, makeup to wear in the big house on the hill to explore, while people came together for meetings to talk about past lives, do the Ouija board, and discuss mankind's suffering. I don't remember seeing my dad too much after that, except when we were sleeping in the peanut truck at night. I would be at the foot of my mom and dad's bed and watch his red cigarette light suck in and suck out like a little fluttering butterfly. My father adapted to this new routine quite quickly.

While my father was rounding up the troops and making his master plans, I continued to go to the library, eat Froot Loops by the box, and jump on people's waterbeds. There weren't any kids my age, so that was where I started to learn to be alone with my dreams in my head.

When I was 12 years old, my dad and I formed a silent pact to be partners in the search for The Big Time. Every time in my young adulthood I wanted to leave the hardships of the group, he would say, "You can't leave now, The Big Time is right around the corner." Which led to more struggles, effort, and labor without the glory of the stage or the money and spoilage.

Where did the concept of The Big Time start? It drove me for my whole life to get to that place of glory. My father said he had the best childhood ever, running wild in the streets of San Francisco while his mother gambled and his father was "an inebriated butcher." I felt like my dad epitomized Rosebud in *Citizen Kane*. Everything he ever did was to try to achieve acceptance from the world. When he was not given unconditional love, he shrugged his shoulders and moved on like the nomad aborigines that he admired, toward brighter horizons.

My mother, on the other hand, didn't care about The Big Time. She truly loved my father. She came from a secure middle-class background in Brooklyn. She was raised properly, went to college, and won awards for her intelligence and her artistic talent. When she was in middle school, Barbizon wanted to sign her to be a fashion model. But she followed my dad through all kinds of adventures that she enjoyed, with an open mind to learn how to be free-spirited like him. I do believe she was really happy the first batch of years, until the group started. She wasn't into open relationships or saving the world or building a raft or starting bands or living with strangers, but she did all of that out of love for him. She painted signs to bring in money for food and taught the others to paint as well.

Unlike my mother, my father never really had any official schooling. But he was extremely intelligent, and when he applied the techniques necessary to accomplish a goal, he did it creatively, uniquely, diligently, and impeccably, with a little crooked twist. He found items that were intended for other uses but easily put them to use for his purposes. Henceforth came his raft, which was built from trash, garbage, oil barrels, and discarded wood.

The desire to be normal never really occurred to me until I was a young teenager. Going to school, living in a clean home, having friends to do things with, going to social events — it was like a dream that couldn't happen to me. Most kids didn't even know how lucky they were to not be traipsing the streets, sitting on street corners with holes in their shoes, sleeping on hard floors, and earning your keep at an early age, or "doing for duty." Even more complicated, I was learning how to build rafts, listening to required hours of psychology meetings, and existing wherever I was at the time, whether it was the muddy side of the Mississippi River, in the middle of nowhere, in Mexico, or somewhere I didn't speak the language. Of course, I never understood what those kids had to go through, because I wasn't one of them. But on my side of the fence, their lives seemed pretty lollipop special. They even got allowances! I brought that up to my father once and he agreed, and it lasted for a few weeks until the money was needed for other things like food or gas.

The gift (and the curse) was that nothing was ever the same. We went to bed when we were tired, we ate when we were hungry, we explored a new town when we got there, we read a book when we had a battery for the electric lantern, we learned about the constellations when we didn't have anything else to do at night.

I remember those days in San Francisco as being a happy little family. My dad seemed happy, my mom seemed happy, I was happy.

My Mother, Maxine

(aka Mamacita)

Somebody up there gave me the perfect mom. She has always allowed me to just be me, fine-tuning along the way, reprimanding me for my mistakes with respect, and accolading my successes with selfless enthusiasm. She chose an impoverished bohemian lifestyle with my father to have time to grow spiritually and artistically while allowing space for adventures with him.

Because of that choice, there wasn't any money. She always made sure I had diapers and a pair of shoes. My mom put no expectations on me to be a person she had made plans for. She gave me complete freedom and trust to make my own choices, even though they may not have made any sense at all or been the wisest at times.

She knew she had, was, and is still instilling values that formed my moral compass. Her harsh, quiet word was taken seriously. While her one attempt to spank me (and missing the mark because I stepped to the side) was infuriatingly hilarious, I did more than deserve whatever she dished out, which was rare.

She is my best friend, mentor, and a shining example of a great human being. We talk every day about many subjects and laugh our heads off. A lot of my friends have adopted her as their own mom and all always ask how she is. She is my Wonder Woman.

I love you, Mom. Thank you for everything you have done for me so selflessly. And as the cycle continues, I hope to be able to do the same for my daughter.

*****

The Day My Mom Caught on Fire

Our little tribe, called the Work Group, was all about boat building, psychology, and music.

My father found a large oyster dragger boat on the Long Island shore. It was grounded in the mud, full of barnacles and smelling like salty oily sea water. It tipped to the side when the tide was out because of its massive hull. It was old and falling apart. The group of about 15 people put in a diligent effort to fix it up and make it nice, preparing it for our maiden voyage, destination unknown.

I was six years old when I was allowed to go to school. I loved it. Sports, reading, learning, and kids galore. I didn't know yet that I looked like a freak with a crooked bowl cut and thrift store plaid skorts. One night after school, when the Work Group finished working on the boat for the day, we all celebrated with a dinner lit by kerosene lanterns. The main cabin was ready to be inhabited after a lot of bitter cold winter days and hard labor. I remember there was a big Persian rug, a luxury in our world. Wet boats are not hospitable to old rugs.

We all packed in and ate some sort of stew. My mother walked over to the sink that did not have running water to refill the kerosene lantern. There were big white candles lit above her on the shelves surrounding the sink. She had her back to me, and I watched in the shadows as one of the candles fell on top of her hands, then quick as that, her big puffy hair was on fire like the burning man.

Everyone, in shock, jumped up and went into full action. My father threw her down on the carpet and rolled her in it back and forth until the flame was put out. Cahill, who was a baseball player, was so full of adrenaline he threw me out of the cabin door and I flew across the deck, almost flipping over the rail into the low tide, sharp oyster bay of mud.

I don't remember much after that. The next morning, I was allowed to go in and see my mom in the little bedroom area. Grey winter daylight was coming through the little port window on her. She lay very still in the dark, small room. Both of her arms were wrapped completely in white gauze. I had never seen my mother helpless before. I didn't know what to do, so I sat quietly.

A few days went by, and she seemed in better spirits. She was putting black teabags on her burns, which helped heal her and avoid scarring.

Since that event, I have always feared fire and the power it holds.

My Irish Dad, William David Maloney

(aka Poppa Neutrino)

My dad's side of the family was primarily Irish. My great-grandma lived in the Redwood Forest. When I was a little girl, we would visit her. Up the long stone stairs to her house in the clearing of the woods. I would play in her old garage with the antiquated porcelain dolls that, in the style of the turn of the century, held my grandma's head of carrot red curly hair on their heads. She played waltzes on the upright piano for us. While I was lost in the beauty of her dolls, with sunlight shining through the windows of the murky garage, she would hobble out and bring me mandarin oranges in a can. Those were special days.

My dad's first marriage was to an Irish journalist named Eileen Cahill. Apparently, he was related to the Jack Daniels legacy, according to the book *The Happiest Man in the World*, by Alec Wilkinson, a writer for the *New Yorker*. Their children, my half-siblings Mandy and Cahill Maloney, were both gone too young, but they were spunky spitfires full of life.

As corny as it sounds, "When Irish Eyes Are Smiling" would bring tears to my dad's eyes.

When we moved to Manhattan as a family band seeking The Big Time on the streets, my dad met Father Pat of the Irish Catholic Church at 10th Street and Avenue B in the drug-infested East Village. He took us in, and we ate, communed, and dialogued on a family level because of our Irish roots. Father Pat made the national news for being the source that transferred money and guns for the IRA.

I love my heritage.

Irish people are survivors with a sense of humor. The Irish and African Americans were instrumental in rebuilding New Orleans during different periods. I find it very interesting that a lot of the African American community in New Orleans have Irish surnames.

I'm proud to have in my bloodline anybody who can live off of potatoes and a hunk of butter and be a survivor. One of my closest friends and a former neighbor, Sinead Rudden, is from Longford, Ireland. When she and her honey got married, I was invited to perform in a castle and experience Ireland in a way that is worthy of a movie.

*****

When I was a child, I didn't think in complexities; I thought, I love my daddy. All I wanted to do was spend time with him. In my child's mind, I was like a dog waiting for its owner to give it a pat on the head. I would wait and wait patiently until there was a moment to be attended to and go for a milkshake, go bowling, take a walk, take a drive on a moped, talk about things, or dance together.

My father had such a busy life trying to save the world and its people that I often got left behind. I know he didn't mean harm. I don't think it even went through his brain. He came from the streets with no structure, and his mom was only 16 years old when he was born. She had him accidentally with Louis, a movie usher. His birth certificate said, "Lack of prophylactics."

According to my father, he couldn't have had a better childhood, sleeping under gambling tables, running around the streets of San Francisco, finding adventures. As he grew into a young man, big trouble ensued. He got caught hot-wiring and stealing cars, and he ended up on a spiritual journey starting with his discovery of the Beatniks in North Beach in the 1950s.

How could he have known how it felt to be a little girl? He was a complex person. He was set on a game plan, and anything that would take away from that, including me, should no longer be part of the program. But I was part of the program because I was a kid and I had nowhere to go. As children, we were trained to fear and respect him. At the same time, he was my father. He disciplined us with boot camp precision. He wanted us to be strong mentally, physically, and spiritually. We were trained as little warriors. He taught us how to play chess, how to fish, how to build boats, how to paint signs with my mother, how to think, and especially, how to understand that we had to navigate this difficult world with the right tools in order to attain our goals. He just didn't want to play "doo-doo" kids games as he called them.

Those were his fine-tuned psychological workshop ideas that helped the mind and its process of critical thinking become stronger and clearer. He was a serious man, although there were moments when it was so unbelievably hilarious to be with him. One of the best ones happened when I was ten years old. We took a moped down a dark highway road in Florida to go and get food for the boat. Halfway coming back, the moped broke down. My dad tried to fix it in the dark on the side of the empty highway. When he did, precariously, he didn't want to stop.

I was running alongside him barefoot. How he got the moped running was by running alongside it like Barney Rubble barefoot. I started laughing so hard I doubled over, then my dad started laughing so hard too, with his missing teeth showing and without free hands to cover his mouth. It was a moment when there was no wall. He was not my commander, he was not my teacher; he was my dad, and we were having the best time ever. He brought hotdogs and peaches to add a creative touch to the communal dinner party at the marina.

When I was four, my father was busy hanging out with the elder statesmen beatniks. When I was six, my father was busy building boats and learning tools of psychology. When I was 11, he started the family band. That is where we really had something in common that we could work on together. We were a team for The Big Time. We walked the streets day and night looking for opportunities. We were bonded. We were pursuing that big dream for both of us. It made me feel special.

Then came my young adult years when I started my own band. It was problematic after that because my father never wanted to surrender leadership. He knew it was the right thing to do; let me go fly as a parent should do for their child. He couldn't seem to stand by without inserting his very dominating two cents. Who was I to block him as he kept asking me who knew more about running a band?

He permeated the internal workings of my band, from telling me how to boss my players into musical subservience to doing it himself from a seat in a packed audience. Yelling at the trumpet player to stop covering up my vocals. Telling my guitarist to relax his anus. Some guys quit because of his interference. I was actually flying, creating my own band, making opportunities for us because of all my hard work.

My father acknowledged my success and wanted to help improve upon it. It was suffocating. Yet, I didn't have the strength to put my foot down and tell him to mind his own business. We had walked so many roads together. I had taken over the big steps alone in Manhattan because he chose to focus on his rafts.

He constantly told a Vaudevillian Jewish joke that was a little too true to life. "When do you let go of your kid?" said the old Jewish mother. "When you're in the grave." Not even then. He still haunts me today with bittersweet memories.

He finally found peace before his passing in his solitary existence, with friends and followers living their own lives as well. Love, serenity, surrender, the best conscious preparation to depart this earth without anger, frustration, or fear.

I loved him deeply and still do. He did great things for many people. Who can negate a life well-lived on one's own terms? I miss him terribly. No one can ever fill the codependent relationship we had with each other.

The Work Group

My father was a larger-than-life Elmer Gantry character. When I was six, my father founded the first incarnation of the Work Group. He started with different prototype designs from the Salvation Navy with the concept of building paddle wheel showboats from scavenged items by the Mississippi River from wood, oil barrels, and foam. The concept was to help people who were serious about changing their lives for the better.

He was always a seeker of wisdom. From reading the *Sufi Stories* to triadic work and a series of many other tools he learned about various psychological work group techniques throughout history; from Christianity to Buddhism to the works of a particular Sufi named George Gurdjieff.

When he was a young man, my dad went to the Baptist Seminary School in Dallas-Fort Worth. In his studies he discovered that Gehenna was literally the burning garbage dumps outside of Jerusalem and that there really was no Hell. If someone was misbehaving, they would be ousted to Gehenna for eternity. My father was so excited at the idea that he joyfully told his teacher. He was promptly kicked out of school by the headmaster.

We lived in the peanut truck in the driveway of a big fancy house in the Bay Area owned by Beverly, one of the leaders from the Messages from Michael work group. Our little family nucleus continued somewhat normally for a while. I went on library outings with my mom while my dad was an apprentice of sorts. I was left to my own devices in the big house.

My ground zero haven was BellaDonna's room. BellaDonna was the most glamorous person I had ever seen other than my mom. She wore blue eye shadow, long thigh-high brown suede boots, miniskirts, and a bob and was always stylishly put together. She was my new idol as a fashion queen. While she was at work, I would go into her bedroom, try on her clothes and makeup and jump on her waterbed. Sometimes I'd sit on it and watch cartoons with her husband, Will, who was Mr. Silly Fun. BellaDonna wasn't too happy when she came home after a long day at work and saw the condition I had left her closet and bedroom in. I remember her scolding me. No one had ever done that before.

Slowly, my dad was getting his sea legs and recruiting the first incarnation of his Work Group. Those core people were the foundation of the adopted family that helped raise me alongside their own upcoming tribe of little doppelgängers. We are all still unified today.

Things started to change. My family wasn't just the three of us anymore. My dad didn't have time for me or my mom. He was completely immersed in creating the Work Group. He recruited a little group of people from Beverly's group to join him. BellaDonna and Will accepted, as well as Beverly's daughter, Nickie, who later ended up running away with Will when the group became too insane for him. There always were more women than men in my dad's regime, making it a matriarchal tribe. Cahill's significant other, Priscilla, and a few others from Beverly's group signed on as well.

The Work Group's first mission was to go to Omaha, Nebraska, to build a showboat made out of oil barrels tied together, stuffed with liquid foam as hulls and a big square body of a structure made of wood, finished off with a massive rotating paddle on the back of it. The goal was to float it down the Mississippi River to New Orleans. My dad loved New Orleans so much. A bohemian utopia. He took my mom there and then it became home if ever we had one.

Slowly, my mom started to lose the one-on-one relationship she had and treasured with my father. She believed in him and supported his dream. She put aside her own need to be the only woman in his life and allowed other women into her treasured domain of her relationship with my father. She was willing to compromise what she had with him alone to allow in a lot of strangers. She was okay with the concept of the Work Group until the open relationship rule came into play. As my dad immersed himself fully in the teachings and raft building as the leader, we just fell by the wayside as a family. I was left to my own devices with strangers babysitting me in campgrounds with spiders and nothing to do. My mom loved me and my dad. She wanted to be with us. But she couldn't take any more of the dynamics that were going on, so in 1984 she moved to San Antonio. The separation from me broke her heart.

That pattern of learning to entertain myself alone in foreign places became quite normalized over the years of growing up. The transition from what it was to what it would become was a big void of unknown with no routine at all. I was in the last chapter of a sentimental storybook, and at the beginning of a dark, murky Grimm's fairy tale.

Half Famous

We were living in little boats in Florida when, at nine, I discovered Elvis Presley and Marilyn Monroe. My father, in his alternative rent-free boat-building life, had many different ideas for boats to live on. They were all homemade except for the Oyster Dragger and the little boats. Independent housing became a need after many different people coming and going were upsetting his individual freedom. We were in each other's faces and spaces all the time. Pooping overboard in an open-air boat with bare butts mooning the world didn't seem like much of an upgrade to me from the private port-a-potty wood box room on the showboats. The perk was you could look down on the water while you went and watch your feces float down the river like a sailboat.

On that Intracoastal Waterway journey, my dad decided that we should all have our own little boats. Of course, at that age, I couldn't be responsible for my own boat, so I lived with him on a larger open-air motorboat. It was fun.

We had a husky then who lived on our boat, and my dad had the only battery-operated TV in the Work Group. He and I would watch movies and eat candy at night once we had anchored somewhere offshore for safety from land pillagers. One day when the group was having a really long work session, I watched a biopic saga on Marilyn Monroe. I was completely taken with this orphan who blossomed into a starlet and who became so idolized while still remaining a confused, lost, lonely child. My heart went out to her.

I could relate to that dirty orphan girl's feelings of loneliness. It made me idolize the idea of being adored, loved, and accepted as the solution to the problem. She was my second idol after Judy Garland. My mom took me to see *The Wizard of Oz* at the Saenger Theatre when I was four. The sophisticated old theater with long red velvet stage curtains, the stars in the ceiling, the organist who played during intermission, and the saga of poor Dorothy on the Yellow Brick Road were mesmerizing.

My mother thought maybe I was Frances Ethel Gumm reincarnated, since once in a bookstore I was hypnotized by a book of photographs of her. Judy was the Raggedy Ann to the glamour of being the Barbie Girl incarnate. I became Marilyn Monroe. I studied every photograph and book on her in every library where I was dropped off. Perfecting Marilyn's eyebrow lift facial expression with every quarter photo booth in every five & ten and bus stop in every town, the smooth detail workings of becoming Marilyn were taking hold.

Unfortunately, a ten-year-old dressed in a platinum grey wig, a thrift store white *Seven Year Itch* dress, and goops of cheap red lipstick wasn't cutting it. I was still a dirty barefoot urchin trying to cram feet into high heels that blistered. At that age I didn't care what anyone thought of me when it came to expressing myself. I would hop off the boat and doggy paddle or wade to shore wearing my Marilyn garb around any town, wet and smelling of seaweed with eau de stinké dog. Marilyn stayed for years with me as an alter ego personality figure I could lose myself in to feel special.

During the same window of time, my dad became friends with a man who owned a trailer in a trailer park. In the mind of a calculating kid that equaled a shower, air conditioning, free refrigerator access, and TV. The mother lode jackpot. The gentleman wanted to travel with our little fleet, so while they were out boat hunting, I was allowed to stay in his trailer alone.

One day a movie called *Love Me Tender* came on. The second Elvis' face came on screen my pinpoint focus zoomed in on the most innocent face I had ever seen. That was it. I was in love for the first time. The next few days my family had to put up with my singing "Poor Boy" a million times. Not knowing the verses, I became a broken record, repeating the chorus to the point of annoying everyone around me. Another demigod to dissect in the libraries for a girl's alter ego wisdom. I held on to every detail of those two people's lives, making them my own little imaginary family. Reading paperback books from the thrift stores on Elvis' last drugged days in Graceland written by the Memphis Mafia to drawing in pencil my best art piece yet, the classic photograph of Marilyn nude. I gave it to BellaDonna's parents for Christmas. We were staying with her sister, Darla, for a while.

Once again, I was dancing and singing to Marilyn in Darla's house, with her record player, turning from Broadway hits to The Beach Boys, dressing up in her clothes and makeup to entertain myself in the house alone. Downstairs the Work Group painted signs or held their six-hour meetings with my father, meandering through multiple ideas that made no sense as they danced tied together with an imaginary string that held many pertinent subjects. There never seemed to be a closing statement that came full circle to the opening one.

I looked in Darla's mirror in the bathroom one day and saw a bunch of pill bottles. Thinking of Marilyn Monroe, I wondered what they were like. I was too scared to try them, but I opened them and looked at the pink and white capsules, wondering what they held to entice my idols to go down the rabbit hole. The two gentle souls who were so talented, so delicate, who died at such a young age completely enraptured my heart. I adopted them. These two symbols still somewhat hold the spell they cast on a lonely young child.

The first famous person I ever saw in person was Richard Gere. A talent scout found the family band performing on the streets in the French Quarter. We were signed up to be local performing talent for the street scenes in his 1986 film *Mercy*. The whole world of filmmaking was new to all of us. Our call time was early in the morning. We ended up in the cast talent holding tank area in a restaurant patio on Bourbon Street with all the other street performers, from snake handlers to our friends David and Roselyn and all the kiddos. Playtime for a bit of solace. Autumn and Stormy were fun to play with. They knew the art of finding ways to entertain themselves quietly while playing the grownup waiting game. Arlee, a young adult professional, was preparing for her moment to shine. By the time we were called out to Bourbon Street very late at night for the scene, they could barely stay awake.

My dad was getting mad with the production company for having the gall to make us wait so long and there was a lot of tension in the air. I had been in high anxiety mode for days thinking about being in a scene with Richard Gere and what I would say to him. Silently rehearsing pretending to be Miss Cool while inside my heart was pounding through my stomach and throat.

We were set up in the middle of Bourbon Street in the middle of the night with the whole filming crew and the bright blazing circus lights shining down on us. Richard Gere was uneasy about crowds. I saw him standing there nervously watching us perform. I was the first one to catch his eye in the crowd, which sent him into a panicked expression as he caught my eye catching him. We locked a look. He froze. Someone in the crowd caught sight of him too. It started a wave of recognition that almost caused a stampede on him. He ran down the street like a crazy man past the drunken freak show party while the film crew immortalized the scene.

Fast-forward a year, while I was waiting excitedly for the movie to come out, there was a big surprise. My mom and I went to see the movie together. I could barely contain myself with the thought that I was actually going to be a movie star. The results were extremely... disappointing. After filming all day and night, our big screen debut was a far-away shot of Richard Gere turning down Bourbon Street giving us a glance and what the audience saw was a blob of black and white figures clustered together, playing in a sea of insanity.

Energy Fields

Our first trip to Mexico as a family and group was when I was nine years old. We took trains all over Mexico all the way down to Merida and Campeche, sleeping on train station floors, washing our clothes on rocks in the rivers with the local villagers, and camping out in the yards of villagers who were kind enough to host us with the very little they had. We were intriguing and entertaining to those families.

We were something of a freak show to all the kids in town who were hanging in the tree limbs and watching us set up camp. We had divisions of labor where a couple of people would set up camp, and another person would find the local corner store or mercado if it was still open. I was not a happy camper. In fact, I was a big brat.

In the train station at the Mexican border my dad made us give away everything we owned except for a couple changes of underwear and clothes. I refused to get rid of my books and journals. Being a picky eater who thought homemade macaroni and cheese was nasty, I would only eat the Kraft kind. Eating whole beans out of a pot, stinky cheese, and fruit that got quite damp and mildewy from the heat was unacceptable to a girl who loaded up chicken fried steaks, mashed potatoes, and biscuits.

The first time I spoke a Spanish word I was desperate to go to the bathroom. My father sent me into a bar where women and children were not allowed and left me to my own devices to figure out how to ask for the bathroom. The door said "Dama" so I just kept saying "Dama, Dama, Dama" to the bartender. I guess he thought I was crazy because it means lady. Henceforth, I became immersed in the Spanish language and culture of deeply kind and generous people with a unique sense of humor.

Back to that village.

While my mom was trying to hammer tent stakes into a mud-packed yard, I kept annoying her to the point of driving her crazy. My dad decided it was lesson time. He took me outside the wood fence of the house. Under the streetlight standing in the sand, he got a big fat stick and drew a three-foot circle around me, then stepped back. Of course, I was crying. He said, "You see that circle? That circle is your energy field, and nobody is allowed to enter your energy field without your permission. Do not enter anyone else's energy field without their permission."

I kept crying, but he thought I got the point. He put his hand over my shoulders, and we walked down the dirt road to the plaza downtown and got bottles of Coke. Then we sat on a bench in the dark. Once he had made his point, he was a happy guy. He said, "You see the soldiers? They may be walking around the plaza, but they're not going to come into our energy field without our permission."

Well, they did. They put handcuffs on my dad, put both of us in the back of their pickup truck; surrounding us were soldiers with machine guns who took us to jail. By happenstance, they drove by the yard where my mom was setting up camp. My dad yelled from the back of the pickup, "Max, we're going to jail!"

She didn't know where it was, so she started running behind the pickup truck as fast as she could, arriving at the jail about a half an hour after my father was interrogated for being a child molester. Someone saw him lecturing me and I was crying, so they turned him in. Needless to say, I never forgot the energy field message.

Easter in Mexico

The whole family had been hitchhiking all day long on the broken asphalt highway deep down in the middle of Mexico. Three kids and five adults, hot, tired, sweaty, and hungry. At the end of the day the family came to a smaller highway leading off the main one. It was a one-lane road even more broken up.

We hitchhiked into the small pueblo, convened in the plaza as usual, and waited while my father figured out the next move. He was speaking Spanglish with the Mexican locals at the corner store and seeing what was in town. He came back and told us in a strange, animated way, after seeing a TV in a restaurant, that there had been an assassination attempt on our American president. He heard there was a beach on the small road, so we bought some small snacks, rolls, smelly Mexican cheese, fruit, and water, and continued to hitchhike down the road toward the beach.

It was my tenth birthday. I was kind of disappointed that the whole day was spent hitchhiking in the middle of nowhere, with no one around, just sitting on the side of the road watching those weird airwaves move the concrete when there's too much heat.

The sun was starting to slowly go down in the sky when we got to the beach. When we arrived, we couldn't believe what we were seeing. Hundreds of families were on the beach swimming, barbecuing, laughing. Mariachi bands strolled the beach selling their songs for pesos, vendors selling fruit on sticks. It was a grand party out of nowhere.

The kids took off our stinky socks and shoes, rolled up our pants, and jumped in the salty ocean, where we splashed and played. It didn't matter that the bands weren't coming to sing to us directly, and it was a little sad we didn't have the money to buy the cotton candy sticks, but I felt so lucky to be a part of a huge Easter celebration with so many people happy that I felt like we all were having the grandest birthday party for me.

Watching on the outside looking in can be an interesting view. Looking at the backs of musicians in gold brocade cowboy suits playing for the family I wished I was part of. Something was better than nothing, I told myself as I snooped around the outer circle, trying to get myself invited to the party.

It started to get cold and dark. Sandy, salty, tanned families packed up their wet towels, umbrellas, and picnic baskets. They went home, I guessed, to brightly lit, warm homes where hot dinners, showers, and comfy beds awaited them.

My dad didn't want to camp out on the beach as a solitary group so far away from any kind of help if banditos came along, so we hitchhiked in the dark to somewhere safe and set up camp for the night. Safe locations were usually a friendly family's backyard, the outskirts of a Pemex gas station, or a train station floor. Sleeping with sand and salt everywhere from booty to toes for days is pretty annoying. But it left evidence that the mirage experienced was blink-eye real.

The next day we hitchhiked down to the next unknown adventure beckoning from the solitary, hot, quiet, bug-ridden, sugar cane field-lined, black cracked asphalt, two-lane road.

Cahill at Bat

I was 11 years old when we went on a family bicycle trip. There were four children and six adults traveling from San Francisco to Tepic, Nayarit, Mexico. Cahill was invited to try out as a pitcher for Fernando Valenzuela's home team.

My dad, with his master salesman skills, sold my brother's dream to every restaurant and motel on the journey through Mexico with a small article that had been printed in black and white, telling them that if my brother got the spot, we would repay them.

Our family ate hearty meals and slept in clean beds. My brother practiced at every roadside rest stop. I was his catcher, as was my dad. Cahill taught me how to catch the ball, control it with two fingers, look where you wanted it to go, and throw it with spitfire projection to the glove. I watched him do sit-ups and jog in preparation. Under the headlights at truck stops, he trained with discipline as best he could under the circumstances.

Sadly, the pressure of the tryout was too much. The breaking point happened in Tepic. I wish I knew what Cahill was thinking. I was too young to ask, but in retrospect, I understand why he was drinking before each tryout. Apparently, self-sabotage runs in our family. The bike trip came to an end, as did my dad and brother's relationship to pursue baseball as a family unit. My dad and mom's relationship ended soon thereafter.

My mom was painting a sign for a Loncheria Betos in downtown Tepic. The family who owned that restaurant called me *Guerita*. It was my dream at that age to own a diner. Behind the counter, the mama was making a *raspado*, shaved ice with sweet milk and coconut. She asked my mom, "Why don't you let her stay here?" My mom didn't want to let me stay there, but my dad said, "If this is what she wants..." He looked at me directly as he was about to leave town a few days later and said, "**Always** give more than you take and you will have value. And **always** behave as if someone up there is watching you."

Those next three months I lived above the diner, sharing a bedroom with the restaurant owners' 16-year-old daughter, Sandra, who looked like a Mexican Priscilla Presley. She taught me about music, style, and class. Her dorky brother, Beto, 11, took me around the corner to a parking lot where 12 boys and girls congregated to play every day.

Cahill died in 2013. After a long estrangement, we had just begun reconnecting after my dad's death. Shortly after, he was admitted to a hospital with a stomachache. Three weeks later, he was gone due to Stage 4 stomach cancer.

A Song for My Brother

Hey you,
Where y'at?
You died so quick,
I haven't processed
The loss of your life yet.

Now
As I watch the Saints
Play Atlanta,
You come to the forefront of my mind.

You.
I loved and admired you so much.
My big brother.

Always teasing,
Yanking my pigtails,
Hanging me upside down
By my ankles,
Telling me not to stick my hands
In your pockets,
Then when I did,
With your wry smile,
You watched me
Get cut with your razor blade.
"I told you so," you said.

Mr. Charming.

You.
Teaching me how to pitch a ball properly.
Hand placement
On the ball,
Every finger
Controlling the direction,
Eye contact
To the precision point,
Fire attack

To the trajectory, called a strike.
Low ball, high ball, curve ball.

You let me be your pitcher at nine years old
While you prepared for your Major League tryouts.

CRACK! with the wooden bat.
BAM! in the leather glove.
Run and collect the ball
In some small random empty baseball field
Of the South.
Just you and me.

You.
Aggressively and destructively
Pursued the Major Leagues
As an ambidextrous pitcher.
The golden card for success.
Our dad was your coach.

Why were you so scared to succeed?
Why did you get drunk the night before every audition?
We all traveled
As a family
On bicycles and in vans to support you
Because we believed you could win.
What happened?

I miss you.
And I miss our sister Mandy.

I remember how you taught me
How to play pool.
Back shot,
With arms behind back and booty on edge of table
To make the awkward angled move.
Pre-planning your chess moves
With the placement of balls blocking the pockets
To win the game.

A parallel to life's chess game.
You were so much like Dad,
It must have been unbearable
To constantly fight with him.

What were your demons you never shared?
I wish I knew.

Thank you for taking the time
To be a big brother to me.

Tell Dad I say "Hi."
And please make amends with him
For the next go-round...
That would be healing for both of you.
He loved you so much.

I wish you'd had more time here.
53 is too young to die.

All my love for you, Cahill Maloney.

Mr. Scotty Moore

I learned how to paint signs from my mom and dad at age 11. Right before the family band was incarnated, the family was traveling through small towns in Texas. Krishna Dasi, a 21-year-old German Sonya-sin who became a follower of my dad's psychology, and I went out selling signs together. She was dressed in orange and smelled like India. We sold a job to paint a sign on a big brick wall at a used car sales lot. We painted fast and hard with large, shadowed letters as the sun was setting.

What did we do with the profits, my dad was wondering, and where the hell were we at bus bed call time? We knew we would be in big trouble for being late. We were spending our profits on all the Elvis Sun Sessions cassettes in the small corner music store on the same block as our sign job.

We explained what we did. My dad gave us a hall pass with a toothless smile and said, "That's my girl." That night, I lay in my small plywood space (two school benches yanked out) and listened all night long, watching the stars out of the little school bus window, in awe of Elvis, guitarist Scotty Moore, and bassist Bill Black... "Mystery Train," "I Don't Care If The Sun Don't Shine," "You're Left, I'm Right, She's Gone," "Milk Cow Blues," "Trying To Get To You." When WWOZ radio in New Orleans did a tribute to Scotty Moore, who died in 2016, I listened to all the Sun Sessions tracks.

Scotty had helped guide Elvis on how to attack the phrasing on his vocals. Elvis wanted to be a ballad singer.

One of my guilty pleasures is to cold call my underdog idols when I'm in their hometown. James Burton, Tony Joe White...When I was in Memphis, I called information for Scotty's phone number a few years ago and called him.

He answered the phone and we had a solid conversation about music. Kind. Talented. Real. Thank you, Scotty Moore. It's amazing how music can take your mind off wanting to just pull the sheets over your head. "When It Rains, It Really Pours."

Feliz Navidad, Gringo

My sister Jessica always said when you're down to a can of beans, that's when you become your most creative.

How lucky we were to be given the freedom to be ourselves. Raised in a family that stated, you can. The roads taken and the price paid to be allowed that freedom included walking, biking, and sleeping on train station floors to pay the dues.

It was almost Christmas. One night, in Mazatlán off the Malecon, my dad sent me solo into a Mexican bar, where no women were allowed. At 14, with a spittoon, after mustering enough bravery to be a street performer, I walked in alone, wearing our uniform dress of black and white. A *borracho*, an older Indian Mexican, asked me to sing "Feliz Navidad."

While my family of munchkin talents waited outside, I sang his request, shaking my jazz hands and stomping out Fosse moves in the dark murky bar lit by Christmas lights. He turned his back from his bar drink, gave me his full attention with his pockmarked face, and on completion of my singing, he gave me a thousand peso note.

My father couldn't believe how much money I walked out of the bar with. We had the best Christmas meal as a family in the school bus we lived in.

A Buddhist in Orizaba

When I was 18, my dad sent me down to Mexico to support a Mexican family in Orizaba, Veracruz, by painting signs. They were the cooks in the second Mexican circus we traveled with. He was finishing his raft in Provincetown and winter was coming. He was planning on coming down to get the family.

I lived in a hut with them, where we all slept on the mud floor together. The husband beat his wife into passivity, the grandfather was a roaring drunk, puking in the outhouse every morning, and the kids were sweet but dirty and hungry.

I was named after Ingrid Bergman. My middle name was Lucille, which, while we were in Mexico, morphed into "Lucia" because people there had difficulty pronouncing my first name (the hard "G" gave them trouble). Thereafter, to honor the kindness of the Mexican people, I kept "Lucia" as my stage name.

I painted signs, taught English lessons, and started a dance troupe that performed in the local discos. Whatever money I made went to food for the tribe. While I was there for a batch of months, in that window of time, I met a gentleman a couple of years older than me who was a Buddhist. He was a solace during those lonely hard times of trying to do right. He took me on a challenging hike to the top of a mountain. We ate at a good vegetarian restaurant; he gave me wisdom I have shared with many over the years when others were looking for answers. He and I were pen pals over the years when I moved back to the states. He truly was a friend in an hour of need.

We lost touch for 20 years. Then one morning he reached out. He said he had been trying to find me under my maiden name for a long time. We talked for an hour on the phone in Spanish about how to make our daily rituals. As I was reconfiguring my life, it was the perfect gift.

Gracias, Roberto Rosario de Pacheco.

¡Viva Mexico!

Walking the cold, grey, windy streets in Mid-City New Orleans during Covid, looking for a place of solace to read and stay warm while a mechanic checked out my car, I smelled it a block away. Corn tortillas and *Huevos a la Mexicana*.

An immediate flood of memories came rushing through my body. I was riveted by a deep nurturing instinct to eat a solid hot meal, listen to Spanish music, and be transported vicariously to a country that held so many bittersweet memories of coming of age from nine to 19 (intermittently). Inside Taqueria Guerrero I ate a big hot meal made with mama love. Sitting there and seeing the authentic posters, flags, and Mexican *paletas* in the freezer box brought back all the years of playing on Mexican street corners, traveling through pueblos with Mexican circuses, living with inviting families, going to *mercados* for fresh-squeezed orange juice, taking dirty trains and street buses, camping on beaches and in people's backyards, laughing Mexicans of all ages, drunk clowns, and bars that didn't allow women or children. Double feature Mexican movie matinees with hundreds of kids throwing popcorn across the theater at each other, church services where women must wear a skirt or dress and a lace doily on their head to show respect to God.

I wished so badly I could go back to Mexico. The place where, as poor as it is, the people are kind, good, honest, and hardworking. Besides, where else in the world are you woken up at dawn to crowing roosters, blaring mariachi music, and joking while each family member prepares for their duties that day? Who sweeps their front dirt yard? Who else yanks kids' hair into perfect braids with rose hair oil and irons their school uniforms impeccably? Who else has three generations living together with a toothless grandma putting everybody in their place while she peels and prepares dinner that early? So that morning with a full belly and a nurtured heart... I thought, *¡Viva Mexico!*

Tengo Ganas

Tengo ganas de ir a un pais Latino. Me encanta la cultura de Los Latinos. Siempre una sonrisa. Siempre amor, no importa dinero para ser feliz. Siempre frijoles y arroz, tortillas hecho a mano con queso del mercado. El regalo mas especial es un jugo de naranja fresco del mercado. No me gusta como juele menudo.

La cosa que me encanta mas de mi tiempo en Mexico fue la musica y los circos. Viajamos con dos. Aprendi a poner vasos arriba de mi cabeza en un acto llamada "Acto de Los Equilibrios." Espero regresar un dia a Mexico, Puerto Rico o Cuba. Me hace daño que este presidente no trata Los Latinos con respecto. Despues de Katrina, si no fue por Los Latinos trabajando muy duro, este ciudad no pudia ser fuerte otra vez. Respecto y gracias por hacer este mujer fuerte y chistoso.

New York Dreams

Japanese designs in thrift stores,
Kaleidoscope prisms of light on skyscrapers,
Rooftop poetry read with tears through smiles.

Hudson River winds blow cosmopolitan hair,
Exotic Spaniard palate tapas.
Jazz players jam their soul into two chorus solos.

Window displays with eye candy dreams,
Doorman through the buzzer hears you sing.
Oooooh, oooooh, when will the chocolate money come through?
Glamorous, black-swathed fast-footed creatures
From many lands with places to be,
Manhattan buzzes with activity.

Serious faces with dreams to acquire,
Racing to futures before they expire.
Dreams pass by every corner where vagabonds lay,
Maybe they came here once to have their day.
Handsome beauty groomed and grown,
Serious faces lost in thinking zones.
Beehive of activity, toiling away,
Desiring to live the dream.
The sun also rises to a haven,
Full of schemers with practical themes.

Introducing
The Flying Neutrinos Family Band

The skyline loomed majestically ahead of us. We drove past large factories in New Jersey. White, yellow, and grey smog filled the air, creating a haunting look to Manhattan. The kids looked at the amazing view from the back of the vehicle.

I had tickles in my stomach. I could not wait to get to town and find some action. It was 1987. The band had been preparing to get to that point since it began six years prior. I was so excited to hit the concrete with my dad, the way we had done together in New Orleans, Mexico, and every other little town along the way. This was the big one we had talked about. This is where the dream could really come true.

We drove through the Holland Tunnel and right into the extremely busy Garment District. It was a very hot summer day. We circled around for blocks and blocks, waiting patiently while my dad tried to "feel out" the right spot. Finally, we parked near 7th Avenue and 39th Street.

The family changed into our black and white outfits in the dark, brushed out our dirty hair, and grabbed our instruments. We marched out of our clown truck single file, led by my dad to the magic "money spot": Broadway.

As per routine, we formed a semicircle, this time in front of a large statue of a man with a sewing machine. Facing thousands of people marching by at lunch hour in their well-dressed suits, we set up the spittoon, metal folding chairs, sousaphone, saxophone, trombone, drums, accordion, and washtub bass. The kids put on their tap shoes. This all happened quickly. No dillydallying or someone would get a yelling.

We were ready to take the first song order from my dad. He called "Try a Little Tenderness"; we played it in the slowest, saddest tempo known to man. I danced my slickest breakdance moves, and the passersby kept walking.

We played for a long time. It was so hot. A few people with perplexed faces dropped some money in the hat. We played for a few hours, packed up, then went to the local deli to count our money, eat a snack, and make a plan.

The deli was hot and steamy with yummy smells of Chinese food sold by the pound in the lit buffet area. We had cereal, rice cakes, peanut butter, canned soup, and brown rice in the truck, so we were only allowed to purchase a drink or a single snack. Everything was so expensive. Munching on a dry bran cookie without a drink, I counted change with the kids in the group. It was good math practice for us. The grown-ups counted the bills.

Dad was out hitting the streets, figuring out where we were going to stay that night. We couldn't all fit in the station wagon and we couldn't camp out in Manhattan. He came back a little while later and said we would sleep in Penn Station. It was busy and brightly lit and he felt we would be safe for the night.

We left the vehicle safely parked on a dark side street and marched ourselves and our instruments into the train area of Penn Station. We set up camp in a tight circle and placed our maces, fire extinguishers, and machete knives in an accessible place.

We had slept in many train stations in Mexico and had felt safe and fine with the idea. The only difference was that other Mexicans were doing it too. In Mexico, we were the intriguing Americans and it didn't seem too weird. This was weird.

We were the only people setting up camp on the benches in the center of Penn Station. The police came by and said we could not stay there. Dad stood to the side with them and explained our story, whatever that was, and they agreed to let us stay one night only.

"Make 'em say 'No' three times," Dad would always say. "It's the salesman's pitch, and if they say 'No' the third time, you know they really don't want it."

My stepmother, Carolina, who had married my dad in 1987, walked the kids to the bathroom to brush teeth and use the potty. Then we tried to sleep and finally, under the bright fluorescent lights and heat, we fell into an exhausted, sweaty, dirty, and stinky dream. We woke very early with sore bodies and bad breath. We sat disheveled on the benches and waited for Dad, who was already up and out looking for the next move.

He came back, said it was raining outside and that we would play in the subways. I was very disappointed. I had hoped to go up from the streets, not down, so this was very humiliating news. I even told my dad I wouldn't do it and he said, oh yes, I would.

We marched through the train station in single file looking like the street hillbillies we were. I had my big washtub bass on my back bumping into the thousands of people filing by like an organized ant pile. They kept bumping into me, and Dad kept yelling at me like it was my fault. I was so mad.

We hopped into the subway and zoomed over to Times Square. We were in the heart of Broadway, only below it. During summer in Manhattan, the subway felt like a hot blow dryer and smelled like dirt, urine, and must. We got off the train and set up under the sign that said "Times Square," across from a little flower store and dead center between the crosscurrent of people running every which way to catch their trains.

We placed our backs against the wall for safety, keeping the youngest kids within reach. We set up to play some New Orleans jazz with our newly discovered "backbeat," taught to us by the Andrews, a legendary New Orleans musical family.

Dad counted us off, and we went into "Bourbon Street Parade." We played an ensemble chorus up front together, then my cousin Todd went into a lead trombone solo, and Carolina played a sax solo. I dropped my bass stick, went to the center of the "stage" and danced like I was flying. I kicked my leg in the air, hit my head thanks to my flexibility, then I ended the chorus with a split on the dirty floor, and we played the out chorus.

When we finished, a miracle had happened. There was a full audience standing there applauding and putting lots of dollar bills into the dinged-up spittoon. Wow. How exciting! We played a full hour set and then took a break.

Dad let Todd, my sister Marisa, and me walk around the area together as long as he could see us at all times. We walked over to the grey flower stand and newsstand and bought a pack of gum with some of the change Dad had given us. We talked to the people who worked the stand. They were very nice.

We played our usual round of sets that day and after a few hours packed up our instruments, tip jar, chairs, and drum shopping cart and made our way out to Times Square. As we exited the subway through the hustle and bustle, we felt fresh air and Broadway excitement. We went to the nearest deli to count the money. It was $400. Jackpot. That was the most money we had ever made in a day. In New Orleans we would make between $100 and $200 at the most.

Dad gave us a grand toothless grin and said we were going to celebrate our "big win," so we could order anything to eat at the deli that we wanted. This deli was super fancy and clean and had an endless buffet of exotic foods. We kids looked at each other with a big smile and grabbed a big plastic container and made our own individual special dinner with dessert and drink.

Dad ate his favorite starch dinner with a Diet Coke and a Dove Bar. He had just quit smoking after 40 years because he wanted to be a singer. He went cold turkey and took up eating four Dove Bars a day. After his dinner, he hit the streets to figure out where we were going to stay for the night.

The rest of us slowly savored our delicious dinner and watched the marquee lights of Broadway slowly go on as afternoon turned to evening. It was so exciting to be in the middle of it all. We kids imagined where all the people were going and what we would do if we were one of them with the luxury to be entertained. We all agreed going to the movies would be it for sure.

Dad came a while later and said he found us a room about 15 blocks away. Hot and tired but excited at our win for the day, we achingly marched past the Broadway lights into the dark side streets to a small old hotel with a neon sign that said "Hotel."

One person checked us in at the dirty white fluorescent-lit lobby, got our little metal key with the green plastic tag that held the number, and somehow snuck all the rest of us with instruments into a little room with one double bed. We made makeshift beds in the corners of the room. I chose the closet and pretended it was my own little room. I looked out the window at the neon hotel sign and thought it looked familiar. Was this just a cliché like the old movies we watched? No, this was actually THE hotel from the movie *Big*. I recognized it and became very excited that I was actually in a famous hotel. Even though it was the scene where Tom Hanks was terrified of being alone with gunshots outside, I still believed this was destiny, and our destiny was about to change for the better.

We all took baths and got cleaned up, turned on the TV, flipped around and found a movie called *Cabaret*. We got comfy and laughed at our adventures and settled down to watch a movie that would then change my life. The dancing excited me so much I almost couldn't sleep. But sleep I did in my closet as the rest of my family slept in their little self-made nests. I felt happy, I felt excited, I felt safe. I couldn't wait for the next day to get back to the subways to dance and try out some of the moves I had witnessed on that little old-fashioned black and white TV.

We spent the next few days playing in our magic spot with the same results. Dad felt confident that this was consistent enough to set up shop in a nicer space. He found the Hotel Carter on 44th Street, half a block from Broadway, with our favorite little deli on the corner and the *New York Times* office across the street. Two blocks down were X-rated movie theaters and prostitutes; two blocks up were classy Broadway shows and elegance. We were right in the middle.

We rented a suite at the Hotel Carter. It had two whole bedrooms, a bathroom, and a little kitchenette. Top floor! Even though the décor was very 1970s with brown polyester with burn holes in the bedspreads and the carpets were dusty and stinky, we felt we were certainly living the life. The kids even started getting spending money. Allotments went out to each individual for food and necessities regardless of age. We were all working and we all got an equal share.

I was given free time to go out and explore. What more could a 17-year-old girl want? I went to the movies with the kids as we dreamed about. We went to museums, I studied about ballet at the Library at Lincoln Center, and then I hit the streets at night with my dad to seek out opportunities for the band in clubs and theaters, and with promoters.

It was all instinct on Dad's part. He put his feelers out and we would go with the flow. It would always start with a bagel and coffee in a diner or the deli in the heart of it all. Then we would walk by all the theaters and down Restaurant Row. There was one club called the Red Blazer Too that he felt was the jackpot. If we could get in there, all of Broadway would come in and see us play.

The owner happened to be an Irish drunk who didn't seem to know whether it was night or day, but he was kind enough to let us sit for free and hear the big band music playing there. We never did get a gig there, though it is where we met several key musicians who introduced us to the New York City club circuit in areas other than Broadway.

Dad always said I wasn't going to be discovered walking down the street; he said I was a pretty girl but not beautiful. He said deserved opportunities came by walking the road, doing the work. And that when one had truly walked the road, another would see that solidity, could not deny it, and would not be able to take that away from him. So we kept walking the road, but to no avail. Dad promised it would happen and that was a guarantee.

Dad and I went to the *New York Times* office and explained how important this family band was and why the paper should do a major story on us. They didn't get it. We went to the *Village Voice* as well. They didn't get it either. I knocked on booking agents' doors on the days when we weren't playing. In my long socks, pink high-top tennis shoes, long folk skirt, baggy sweater, with a bandanna around my head, I proceeded to explain to them without a resume or recording how wonderful we were. They were all kind but noncommittal.

By default, I think the outfit kept me safe from the standard "So you want to be in show business, kid? There's something ya got to do..." scenario.

We continued to perform in the subways. We gave our all every single second. Performing with "desperate enthusiasm" was how we were described. I believed so hard and so did Dad. We wanted this so badly. The press said we were like the Addams family who drank something weird and ended up in Preservation Hall.

Why my dad wanted it, I wasn't sure. He had always loved the press. He was a big ham. I knew what I was born to do and wanted to feel that complete freedom of life on stage.

The rest of the family did their best for different reasons, but they didn't really care about The Big Time the way my dad and I did. Marisa didn't want to be the "housekeeper" as was threatened if she didn't play the drums. How else was she to earn her keep? Todd was a natural talent and easygoing personality who truly loved playing music and learning about his craft. BellaDonna was there for the Work Group and making sure the kids had some sort of fun along the way. Carolina cared about the Work Group and loved my dad and supported his dreams. Priscilla was there for the work, although I think she truly did enjoy playing the sousaphone.

We evolved to performing in front of the Broadway theaters before showtime to the waiting audiences. The money wasn't as good, but it was fun being in front of the lights if not yet behind them.

We met an old man who played this circuit as well. His name was Reuben Levine. He played the violin and told dirty vaudeville jokes. He was in his 70s and played the violin quite well when he wanted to, but he felt the money wasn't there, so he would just start a song and then stop and tell a joke. He did pretty well with the audiences. We loved him and he loved us. We adopted each other and he became our "Uncle Reuben." He showed us the tricks of the trade, such as how to sneak into the second half of a Broadway show, how to buy stolen goods, and most important, an ongoing argument with him and my dad, the timing of comedy.

Reuben lived in a little hotel on 48th Street. He had a room that was filled from top to bottom with his stolen items and porn magazines, with only a little walkway from the door to the bed and bathroom. Even the bathroom had supplies that fell off the back of the truck. He couldn't see very well, so I never knew why the magazines were there.

He would always bring little presents for the kids. He gave me a pink spaghetti strap sundress with a fruit pattern all over it. It was the nicest dress I had ever owned. He knew everybody on Broadway, and they all loved him. He introduced us to everyone he knew: Howard Bielsky, a keyboardist who taught us proper scales and some ear training, all the people who worked at Colony Music, all the characters he knew.

Reuben also did his shtick in a little restaurant on the Lower East Side called Sammy's Roumanian Restaurant. He invited all of us one night to come and eat Jewish food while he entertained the audience. We tried to eat chicken livers, bread with chicken fat poured out of syrup servers, and seltzer water out of a spray bottle.

Dad asked me to get up and dance to Reuben's music. While Reuben sang, I twirled in my pink dress around the uptown socialites who came in slumming for a one-of-a-kind experience. It probably was one of the more memorable performances for them I am sure, but for me, I constantly seemed to be twirling in between plastic-coated tables.

I swore to myself, no matter what, I would never give up. Ever. Remember. Remember. Ever.

As summer 1987 progressed, we were settling into our new life of wealth up North. We had our routine of playing music for three to four hours a day. We had our music practices as a group and as individuals. Carolina homeschooled the kids. The adults had Work Group sessions.

Not much was happening with contacts or expansion for the band, but we were meeting people who had been contenders at one point or another. We met Charles Ward, the last living Ink Spot. He gave Carolina singing lessons. We got to know the street breakdancers, who were very nice and taught me some moves. Marisa learned some drum maneuvers from the bucket players. I mean, even Hall and Oates saw perform. We were featured in a major PBS segment by a documentary filmmaker named Victor Zimet.

Slow but steady. Walk the road.

The kids were not thrilled about this life. Marisa didn't want to play the drums and my father screamed at her a lot to get her to smile. Todd was always being yelled at for forgetting his tap shoes or not using his brain. My sisters Jessica and Esther were only four years old and being dragged around the subways and streets, playing maracas and bongos out of time.

Tension was building. Dad was constantly on me about being anorexic and getting me to cram a muffin down my throat instead of nibbling half a yogurt and vegetables. He yelled at me about my dancing, how I wasn't feeling the music or keeping the time within a four/four count. I would run off steaming mad and then realize I had nowhere to go, so I would come back and try to understand what he was saying. Then he would be happy that I got it and we would go and have a make-up soda together. Priscilla and BellaDonna were both the subject of Work Group meetings. Carolina was mediating those meetings. We were all mediating the meetings on each other. You had to walk on eggshells with my dad if you had a problem with him; you had to really think about how to word it clearly so when he received his "photograph" or picture of himself, he could truly understand it and "accept it, reject it, or need time to think about it."

After a month at the Hotel Carter, the Korean owners tried to kick us out because of the New York tenant laws. After 30 days we would have had the opportunity to attain rent stabilization, and of course they didn't want that to happen. Dad played his warrior chess game and went out and befriended the Guardian Angels, a nice street gang that wore red berets and helped people. He asked them for help. They agreed to strong-arm the owners into letting us stay. But it was to no avail, and we were aggressed on even more by the owners and their cohorts. We packed up our little bags and washtub bass, said goodbye to the heart of Broadway, and moved into a teeny railroad apartment by the railroad tracks in Hoboken, New Jersey, home of Frank Sinatra. I watched the twinkling New York City nights from the back window facing the railroad track from that point on.

We continued to commute on the subway and play our spots, but it was getting hotter, and performing spots were getting tighter due to a program called Music Under New York (MUNY), which we auditioned for, were accepted into, and limited by because spots were allocated.

The final straw was when some crazy person started torching subway attendants in the token booths. Dad decided it was too unsafe for his kids and it was time to hit the road.

We worked harder above ground, saved more with joint savings, spent less, and with a little time we bought a big truck that was used at one time to sell candy, chips, and other snacks. It didn't have any windows. It was one big, hot, dark aluminum box. We painted it blue. It cost $500 and it ran.

What to do, where to go, what was next? Dad meditated, contemplated, and psychically dreamed. He dreamed of the Pilgrims. He thought it meant that we should wear Pilgrim outfits and we would be highly successful. We didn't like that crazy idea. He finally decided we should go further up north into the country. It would be safe and cool. We packed our few things and loaded up into the truck. As Dad started up the truck, we all sat on the floor in the dark and waited for more information on where we were going. Nobody knew, not even my dad.

New York City was over with. I was heartbroken and mad. We had worked so hard. I had worked so hard. I was confused about whether to stay or leave. Leaving terrified me. I felt betrayed. We hadn't reached The Big Time. I felt my dad had given up and let me down. He was my buddy, my partner, my teacher, and my father. So many things mixed up in one person who didn't have the time or patience to be linear.

He was "random" and was going to live "his" life with no regrets. When I was grown, I could live mine and be glad of it. No looking back and wishing for a Disneyland fairytale of the past. Only childhood boot camp, getting my ass kicked and being glad to move on forward. He made that loud and clear, saying it so many times. Yet, he was so generous with his efforts to do grand things for the kids when he wanted to. And then he was on to the next thing. He included everyone, but on his terms.

We left town and drove north, stopping at many roadside rests. Dad reviewed the map, and the kids ran around with Auntie BellaDonna making up fun games. We performed in dead little downtown neighborhoods for change along the way. Somewhere after the first few days, Dad knew his vision of Pilgrims wasn't about us dressing like them, but a message to go where they first landed.

So, in August 1987, off we went to Provincetown, Massachusetts.

The Foraging Kind

When I was a young girl, with my Peter Pan tribe, we kids were told to go out into the woods and collect firewood. We had done this in Mexico for the wood burning stove in the school bus. We also did it in the cold snowy woods of Roxbury, Connecticut. Woods surrounded the little George Washington style house where we found ourselves. The house, which was down the road from Dustin Hoffman, had been provided by two millionaires who worked for a Russian shipping company. They had discovered us and picked us up off the streets of New York City. They paid for everything. Training, lessons, rent, whatever we wanted at the grocery store, a passenger limousine, and spending coin for the kids. All this was to provide an opportunity to tour Russia as a family band once we had a polished act.

We lived for eight months in that house, making granola and yogurt, and baking bread to stay fed. The house even had a stream in the dirt basement to keep milk cold. While foraging through the woods, we would always find and see interesting things. Deer close up, turkeys, old vintage bottles, weirdly shaped sticks, and the freedom to bitch and moan with four other munchkins about how unfair it was that the kids had to collect wood in the middle of a freezing, tree-bare, snowy winter. But hey, we were hunters searching for vital survival heat.

I'm pretty sure my dad always had to have it his way, by the number of times he aborted opportunities that required diplomacy and democracy. Our relationship with the Russian millionaires was no exception. My dad got into a fight and canceled the plan to go to Russia just as the cold fall started. He thought one of the millionaires was trying to pull some action on Todd. It was chess war.

After the Russian deal came to an end, the family band spent the winter and spring in New York City walking the asphalt jungle with my dad, once again searching for another Big Time opportunity. I cold-called the *New York Times*, theatrical agents, jazz clubs, and pounded the pavement. With a lot of sweat and psychic hunting, we got gigs at the Village Gate and a feature article by Chip Deffaa in the *New York Post*.

My father taught me how to be a persistent seeker of opportunity. *If you want it, go out and get it.* A valuable lesson imprinted into my system for adulthood. The band would not have been possible without my pounding the pavement and the boardwalk of Atlantic City for opportunities to grow musically and pay the bills without a day job.

During Covid, in 2021, I looked out the back door of the Gentilly house I was living in at the fall leaves blowing. I realized, if I stayed there in that dormancy, nothing would ever change. The house, the neighborhood, the city, me. Maybe that's okay. Many people were okay with that. It was up to me.

After my liver transplant, I felt like a war horse put out to pasture. I had been trained to acquire the goal with the dopamine of success pounding through my brain, reminding me that I was a winner. There are no words to describe the gratitude of having a home, food, and the little extras that make one feel like a queen in any other impoverished country. But the dormant hunter needed to be activated again. I couldn't accept every day with the same routine, numbing my mind with the same mundane activity.

How was I going to spend my irreplaceable time? Squander it on the nothing? Maybe the monks knew something I didn't. Every minute, every hour, every day, ticking away until they're not. What did I want to fill my new bank account with? What kinds of memories would go into the savings account of my mind?

The fire in the pit of my stomach was just an ember in recovery mode. But once the licking of wounds was complete, the conquering would begin anew.

Tantric Sex and Other Oddities

When I got my period at age 11 on a Mexican train from Tepic to Houston, I thought I was dying. Mexican trains are the absolute worst. Shit is smeared everywhere, there's no toilet paper. I found a piece of somebody's brown paper bag left and tried to do something with it. When I told my mom what was happening, she told me with a hug that I was a woman. I cried so hard in her arms. I didn't want to be a woman.

Growing up in an isolated tribe, dating in a social world was nonexistent. I got my first French kiss (from a boy) at age 12. He was an 18-year-old Mexican I had a crush on. Just thinking about it made my stomach flip flop. I was living with my mom then in Tepic, Mexico. She always went out of her way to make a social and school life for me to experience.

My dad reiterated over and over how this was his life and he was going to live it the way he saw fit. When we were grown up, we could live ours the way we wanted. Within his matriarchal tribe, the kids were very carefully watched over. No one was allowed to even kiss anyone without a six-month AIDS test. We didn't even stay in a town more than a few weeks, so boys were out of the question.

At 17, I fell head over heels for Ricardo, the multitalented son of the owner of the circus. He had big, dark, serious eyes that burned through you above his ninja mask. We kissed behind the stage curtains. We really liked each other a lot. He had machismo and that made my stomach drop. I loved watching him juggle bowling pins with his cousin Carlito while balancing on a unicycle or motorcycle in a big metal pen going round and round, faster and faster, doubled with his other cousin, Rolando, or doing the clown act with his dad, or flying on the trapeze. There wasn't anything he couldn't do. I told my dad about my feelings for him with respect to his six-month test rule. He took me for a walk through the dirt road pueblo and asked me what I wanted more, The Big Time or Ricardo as a boyfriend. Of course, I wanted both.

He explained that my dating the son of the circus owner would complicate the dynamics of our business relationship with them. I respected his request. It was unbearably painful to see and ignore Ricardo. He hated me for it. I would wait till the show was over to watch him in the shadows or stay on the sidelines to see him perform. We left the Circo Hermanos Bell after a few months anyway. My dad got into a fight with the owner when he didn't get his way and we left to start our own circus, taking with us Suavecito, the old drunk clown, the mute ninja, and a couple of *trabajadores*. We played every plaza, and like the clown car, we all slept in the donut delivery truck in a line that rolled over at night in unison, as there wasn't any more room for bodies.

When we lived in Connecticut, my dad, Todd, Priscilla, and I commuted into New York City in the limo as well as lived in it while we played music on the streets and in the subways. The money we earned was for the group expenses. Survival was the priority. A social life was not. I wasn't really interested in sex. My mind was too occupied with dance, music, choreography, reading, playing drums, and maybe a pen pal or two.

The whole time we were in Roxbury, the only friend outside the group I had was a Mexican girl named Norma. My stepmother saw a little article in the local paper about her being an exchange student and made the connection for me. You would think that at 19 I would have been a little more advanced in my social life. Nope. We were too guarded from danger. The library or a movie was the apex of fun.

At a certain point my dad thought I needed a sexual partner. He tried to connect me with Jack, a member of the Work Group who was 35. The three of us had a meeting. I felt embarrassed and absolutely not interested in having sex with someone I wasn't attracted to. He was like a big brother to me. So my dad moved on to a young Jewish guy, Larry Feintuck, who used to come see us play at the Village Gate. He was nice, funny, and clumsy. We went to a few jazz concerts and ate at some Jewish delis. When he tried to kiss me, I moved to the side and he almost fell down. I told him I just wanted to be friends. He said he had enough of those. The one great thing Larry gave us was a unique original song he wrote, "I'd Rather Be In New Orleans," which became the title song for our first album. The irony was that he had never been to New Orleans.

There we were, my dad and me, selling books at night on Sixth Avenue in the West Village. Books are the only thing you don't need a license to sell on the street. My dad and I were, as he would say, "shooting the shit." He started talking about tantric sex, which I had never heard of. He learned this when he was young and sleeping with somebody's wife. I wanted to shrink into the sidewalk.

"First the man puts his flaccid penis inside of you, both of you lay very, very, still until one of you feels something. Then you let that feeling take over and start to build and build until he ejaculates." I never asked him for advice, especially not with massive numbers of people walking by us, some looking at our book collection for sale.

"Ingrid, there are people you would never imagine who are absolute gems. It just takes a little chiseling to get to the brilliance of their being."

My dad kept referring back to Larry. I kept trying to imagine chiseling away at him the way an Aesop fairy tale would talk about the silver glint of a prince trapped in the curse of a bear put on his head. I just didn't see it at all. It was too personal to tell him how many sex acts I had silently witnessed in the group while being confined to tents, trucks, and boats. I watched in a dark tent one group member give a blow job to another and then drink milk out of the group milk carton and hand it to me next.

Sex was discussed openly. It wasn't taboo. The problem was it was impossible to meet someone I liked and had a chance to get to know. I finally lost my virginity at 20. It was awkward and painful. Having your cherry popped is no ice cream sundae.

The problem with open relationships is that people get hurt. I didn't know any other way. I started seeing three guys at one time, each of them aware of the others. They tried honorably, but it put an immediate wall of discomfort between each of us. I don't like hurting people, but I don't like being suffocated either.

I've been loyal in the three major, committed relationships I've had. I've also been a ho-ho when I was a free agent.

I once got a hall pass after the fact from my boyfriend of five years. The band went from Manhattan to Las Vegas to play a two-week run at Caesars. While there, I saw a photograph of a man I thought was a young Elvis. That night he came to the gig with a bunch of rockabilly kids. He was dressed in a gold lame suit; 1957 Elvis with violet eyes. I am a sucker for an Elvis lookalike. They came to California with us. He and I sat on top of the Hollywood Hills looking at the sign. On my last night in Vegas, I banged him on the floor of our hotel room while my manager was asleep on the second double bed. She was a deep sleeper. I told her about it the next day. When I got home, I told my boyfriend, who also looked like Elvis, what I had done. He got really sad and asked why I would do that to him. I said, "Honestly, because he looked like Elvis." He thought about it for a moment. And then he said, "Oh, okay," and that was it.

Fucking and sucking are not even close to as good as a gentle juicy kissing session, in my opinion. I know my dad and mom meant well, but there's a book that is quite educational, *Sex Tips for Straight Women from a Gay Man*, that gives qualified lollipop tips.

After becoming single following 16 years of marriage, it was a stroke to my ego to get hit on again. New Orleans has the strangest hit lines I've ever heard. Especially at bus stops. *You think I need a hair trim?* Um, look closer at his forehead, honestly, nope. *You sure? How 'bout my neckline?* Again, nope. *You married?* No, I have a boyfriend. *We can share...* Very blunt statements that at first make you wonder if they're messing with you. *You want to fuck?* I don't even know you. But they're not joking. One guy told me he lived with his grandma, who actually turned out to be his older wife.

Another time, I was seeing an Adonis specimen of a man for about a year off and on. He was so funny and nice. A fitness trainer. I thought he might be "The One." We were hanging out in my rental room at 3 a.m. and the phone rang. His phone was facing up and there was my good friend's name on the screen. "Do you know her?" I asked. He nervously said he had to go. So I called her from my phone and asked if she knew him. She told me he was her live-in boyfriend of five years. "Don't worry," she said nicely. "You're not the only one."

While we were married, my husband said he could picture me with a Black guy. While we were together, my Black boyfriend told me he could picture me with an old rich White guy. I can picture myself with someone who doesn't think he's all that and a bag of chips. Only then, maybe I'll scare him with presenting the idea of Tantric Magic.

"Sign her. She sounds like Julie London."

When I was 22, my father signed over The Flying Neutrino name rights to me. I was going to lead a new incarnation under the original band's name. My father was both my mentor and my problem. If it wasn't for my father, I never would have walked the road to music. That way of approaching going after what I really wanted in life would not have happened without him. He was the family bandleader. He felt that we never would have made it if he wasn't there advising me on what moves to make. He could have been right.

I had been walking the streets of New York with Todd for approximately four years when we finally got signed to Fiction Records, The Cure's record label, in 1995. It was The Flying Neutrinos' first official signing under my leadership. Chris Parry, an Englishman who founded Fiction Records and discovered Robert Smith (of The Cure), had offices in New York City and London. Fiction was affiliated with a parent company, Universal Music Group, for distribution and marketing. It was Chris who exuberantly compared my voice to Julie London's.

Chris was based in London and Jonathan Daniel was his A&R man in New York. Jonathan was friends with my friend, musician John Ceparano (Jet Set Six), who introduced Dae Bennett, Tony Bennett's son, to us. Dae became our producer and advocate. He even brought Tony to our shows at Windows on the World. Tony was a funny, high-class gentleman. We all sat in a circular booth with him on our breaks and listened to his stories about Billie Holiday and his dirty jokes.

John and I were always walking at night, looking for club opportunities and figuring out how to get a record deal. He brought Jonathan to our weekly show at the Rodeo Bar on East 28th Street. I was so excited. All of the hard work performing in stinky little clubs that paid nothing, where people only cared about cocktails, was all worth it to get to that point.

Robert Smith came to one of our shows at Coney Island High in the East Village with his tribe led by Chris. In between our sets, he asked if I would teach him how to swing dance. All I wanted to do was stare at his mouth, which he had lined with orange lip liner. He was so shy. I gave him a dance lesson at side stage. Quick-quick-slow, quick-quick-slow.

From the time that we signed with Fiction, we were officially the little home team rock stars of New York City. The retro swing movement was in full swing. Somehow our band landed in a group of other retro swing bands. My original plan was to show the youth how traditional jazz was the rock 'n' roll of its time; that it was by the youth and should again be for the youth.

We were getting to know the Squirrel Nut Zippers, getting to be close friends with Royal Crown Revue, playing double bills with Lavay Smith and her Red Hot Skillet Lickers, and talking business with Scotty Morris, the bandleader from Big Bad Voodoo Daddy. We were all in a very small clique that toured all around the country, having 3 a.m. hangs after gigs. It was the life!

The problem was that all the major labels seemed to be merging into one conglomerate all at once. Just as we were about to be signed by Bob Krasnow with MCA, after months of negotiations, he retired when MCA and Universal merged. We were still signed to Fiction. It was Fiction's responsibility to make sure our product was being distributed and marketed, but Fiction was too small to be able to do that alone. It needed a parent company to handle those functions. Tommy LiPuma went to work for Verve Records and took us on. Verve was thus going to be Fiction's parent company. But, after months and months of waiting, there was no new record, so it came down to trying to verbally enforce the contract that had been agreed upon, which stated that the label would finance an album within six months of signing us. Did we want to sign the Verve record deal?

Through Fiction's negotiations, we had made *The Hotel Child* with Verve without having any paperwork on file. Tommy produced the album on good faith and got paid $60,000. Al Schmidt engineered it. I was fortunate to get the very best A-team players for the album. Guitar player Matt Munisteri's songwriting talent was the power behind the album. I also had Todd Londagin on trombone, Dan Levinson on clarinet and sax, Jon-Erik Kellso on trumpet, Michael Hashim on sax, Will Holshouser on accordion, David Berger on drums, and Matt Weiner on bass.

All the pieces and parts were there. We were the kings in our town. In addition to our regular weekend gig at Windows on the World, we played private events for the likes of Sting, George Soros, Christie Brinkley; we opened for Tony Bennett and Porno for Pyros, we played the Enit Festival. Every single big opportunity was being opened up to us. Fiction Records was paying out of pocket for us to open for major acts.

The Flying Neutrinos' first European tour piggy backed The Cure's tour simultaneously, which meant we crisscrossed their dates and hung out with them in Paris. We were scheduled to play all high-end clubs in every city from Ghent to Copenhagen to Paris. We played Ronnie Scott's in London, a hippie commune in Copenhagen called Freetown Christiania, and a really odd rodeo bar in Paris for two weeks. We received the very best press, including a full front-page feature story in Ireland, yet we never even played there! Fiction Records had put us on a major tour without an album to sell. Our debt to them piled up. Normally a record label recoups its cost before it pays artists any royalty money. It was the label's mistake, but I was financially responsible.

I moved to **New York City** when I was 20. It had taken six years to position us to have the right team to navigate a bidding war with Big Time labels coming into play. That's a long marathon to hike in the streets of **New York City**. I walked the streets looking for clubs to get the band booked into, I walked the boardwalks with my first manager, Casey Kennedy, to acquire that first consistent chunk of change by working six-week runs at the showboat casinos. It took a lot of gumption for me to get composer Marc Shaiman and festival producer George Wein's home phone numbers so I could harass them about opportunities for the band. I put so much foot into the pavement and I lived in so much chaos.

I was trying to learn how to be a bandleader, grow as a singer, learn the networking etiquette from the top of the top elite, charming them but not ending up in a position of having to fuck them. None of this was an easy feat for someone who came from the streets and whose weakest skill was organization.

I had two female managers who took the ball and ran the full field nonstop: enthusiastic, creative believers. Casey was first. Teal Camner was second. They were extremely different in their approaches trying to get The Flying Neutrinos to The Big Time. Casey was not in the profession, but she was a go-getter and she knew how to high-ball wealthy music lovers to the point where they believed we were worth what they were shelling out. She believed in us. Teal was (and still is, as of the writing of this book) in the business. She was an aggressive salesperson with so much enthusiasm and belief in the band that she charged through every obstacle until the goal was accomplished.

After years of arguing with my dad about the way music should be played, we finally landed on big contract negotiations with labels, managers, and booking agents (the trinity of success). The contract offer with Verve Records was on a platter in front of my face. The very thing that I had come to **New York City** to conquer, right there to take and own.

But it all came to a screeching crescendo halt. My father dominated my world so much that I allowed him to overstep his bounds with me, the band members, and any person who came with a possible opportunity to achieve a higher status quo.

I allowed my father to be my musical and business advisor. I gave him and the group ten percent of my money. That helped sustain the family when the boat was docked at Pier 25. Certain members of the group took on bookkeeping and secretarial roles to help the band move forward. I would have preferred to lead my own band and make my own decisions about what I wanted and how the contract should be written with the least amount of rampage possible from an industry that is known for thievery. I didn't have the guts to really put my foot down with my dad. I was young. I was learning how to lead a band for the first time. With all of the years of being told, "You can't leave now, The Big Time is right around the corner," he made me feel I couldn't make it without him, that I couldn't do this without his help. He was there to scream from the audience when he felt any band members were playing too busily and taking away from my vocals. He also had issues with players who did not play traditional jazz the way he thought it should be played. He bullied musicians into stoic submission. He was there to navigate the chessboard moves of my career.

On one occasion, he wanted me to sign a management deal with a mafia boss who had a crush on me but who wasn't in the music industry. "Money can buy anything," my dad told me, without understanding how that guy wasn't the right one to sign a management contract with. Another time, he was there when I was offered a deal with Harry Connick Jr.'s management. They only wanted me. My dad said, "Are you going to dump your teammates who brought you here?" I turned it down. Right after that, some of the guys started having attitudes; they wanted more money from the record deal than I was able to give them. One by one, they started leaving the band.

But this time, I thought, was it. The team that had brought us this far — Fiction Records, Jonathan Daniel, Tommy LiPuma, Dan Cleary (Natalie Cole's manager), Verve Records, Harry Connick's management, a five-album record deal — was going to jump ship if the deal wasn't signed. I procrastinated making that massive stress-laden decision. Sign the deal and take a chance to possibly move to the next level, or call it a day?

All the while, my father was never present at any of the meetings with those high-powered people. He was merely a silent boss. He and I took many walks through Manhattan talking this through. He did most of the talking. I slipped in my commentary. That was our dynamic for years and years. Walking the streets of New Orleans, Mexico, **New York City**, feeling out opportunities.

My father was a master salesman. He could persuade a man to give him his wife. I wanted to sign that deal so much. It was my choice, my signature, my name, my responsibility, my grand opportunity, that I had spent six years working so hard for. All of the cheap stinky bars, subways, streets, weddings, you name it, this was the chance of a lifetime to be a real world stage platform artist. The culmination of those factors would never happen again. There were a lot of people on my team who were counting on this deal. My band, my managers, the fans who believed in us. Fiction Records made it clear that if I didn't sign the contract with Verve, they were done with me. I spoke to my trusted inner circle in length about what to do. "So what, they don't make creative control clauses anymore. Do you really think they're going to make you record something you don't like?" "Do you really have to have final say?" "You can always renegotiate." "You can't always get what you want..." said a friend who was an A&R man. He knowingly smiled. I looked confused. "But if you try sometimes, well, you just might find... you get what you need." In other words, *sign the deal.* What about the clause that stated that Verve had first right of refusal if any of the band members were to leave? The guys didn't want that, or they wanted to be paid more in the advance, as well as more points in the royalty deal. There weren't any more points to give. They knew that. Managers took points too.

After having made a record without the contract signed, none of us made any money at all. Getting paid for our recorded work was at stake too. My father begged me not to sign away my creative control. He said they would sap my soul and I would turn into another addicted entertainer. He promised there would be more deals. And they would have creative control. I should not trap the guys if they wanted to leave. I was so torn. I was damned if I do... I couldn't not take my father's advice. It would have felt too much like going against the grain of him always being right. It pained me physically to make the call.

I was standing in front of the Gramercy Tavern. Ten years earlier I had danced like a dork in Gramercy Park with the family band, on that same block. It was distinctively memorable that day because my dad was insistent that I would be an emcee for the band. I thought I would pass out speaking to an audience. I was so against it I sat in the airport limo we owned. But he was adamant. So I got up and said the punchlines to some stupid jokes and the audience laughed. Then I became a golden child in his eyes. I wanted to **always** be a golden child in my father's eyes.

I told Verve Records I was not signing the deal. I chose not to sign, because I had listened to my father. That was the end of the band trying to attain a standing position in the history books. From then on, we were just a party band for hire. No more managers or entertainment attorneys. No more networking resources from higher-ups in the business that I had gotten to know.

Marvin Katz, Elvis Costello's lawyer (who later became mine), took me to a lot of networking lunches. That was where all the bigwigs gossiped about Big

Time industry secrets. He introduced me firsthand to all of them and told me who they were. Marvin was very serious and very happily married to a woman he respected. He told me one day, honestly but quietly, "You're going to be a big star." But he jumped ship as well. The whole pyramid of power people all knew each other. If one's on board, they're all gung-ho. The second that first risk-taker who believes in you drops out, they all do.

Dan Cleary was managing me at the time the deal fell through. He was nice, but he made it clear that he couldn't accomplish anything without a team. With the lack of my one signature, I was dropped by everyone.

Around that time, I had fallen in love with Clyde. I asked him, "Should we stay in **New York City** or move to New Orleans?" There was nothing happening in **New York City** for him as a fashion photographer or for me as a contender anymore. I got pregnant, and we packed our belongings and our two Boston terriers into a vintage cherry red VW bus that kept catching on fire and breaking down. We moved to New Orleans less than a year before 9/11. All of the glory was left behind in a trail of gasoline-scented smoke chugging down the I-95 heading south.

Lost Innocence

New York City used to be The Flying Neutrinos' playground. After years of walking the streets, the good got going and we were little rock stars for a long minute.

The World Trade Center was our home base. The raft where the family band lived was a few blocks away, and Windows on the World was our performing residence for a good while. The twin tower holding the club on the highest floor swayed slightly with the breeze. It was the gig to have. We were young, life was one big fun adventure where we were all for one and one for all, marching the Yellow Brick Road to The Big Time under my newbie band leadership.

On New Year's Eve, all of those somebodies and those who thought they were somebodies were prancing around with toothy smiles and martinis. It was the IT place to be. The swing crowd, the Wall Street crowd, the East Village freaks, the socialites, and the Staten Island mafia.

Our entertainment lawyer's office was two blocks away from the World Trade Center. On September 10, I went there with my new little family to sign off on some contracts. The next morning we were on Candlewood Lake in Connecticut, watching in disbelief as the whole tragedy went down.

Was this the war of the worlds? It was inconceivable.

I was booked there to play a private event September 29; employees who were like family went down with the imploded horror. How close, but how far away we were from Ground Zero. So many were there on the wrong day, at the wrong time. How did destiny decide that was their day? It could have been me and my band or my family.

That day spearheaded the end of our innocence as Americans. That incomprehensible event took away the belief that everything would always be okay. Then came Hurricane Katrina and multiple world disasters. War. Covid. Riots. Chaos. More hurricanes, more fires, more exposing of beloved figures we had never thought of as predators.

My sister Jessica is a journalist. She was on the runway on a plane headed to Ireland that day, sitting next to a suspicious person who was asking her very strange questions. Jessica worked as a reporter for *The Tribeca Trib*, which covers Lower Manhattan. For a 9/11 anniversary issue, she interviewed a firefighter on the day Bin Laden was killed. He showed her all of the Mass cards he carried in his hat every day from all the funerals of fallen heroes he had attended since 9/11. That firefighter happened to be my love interest in my first music video, "Cry."

Many years later, I was hired to perform for an event to benefit Katrina victims that was produced by the wives of some of the firefighters who died in the towers. The widow who was my contact said, "We understand what they are going through, we know how to help. No one can understand except for the ones who have lived through it."

We are living in a world that has become survival of the fittest. Yet, in that dirty mud still lie so many pure lotuses called all of us, who keep trying to fight the good fight and who believe in the goodness of people.

White Picket Fence

I thought I wanted a white picket fence, literally as well as figuratively.

My whole childhood I begged my parents for a normal life; to go to school and have friends.

I dreamed of it my whole life. And Clyde gave it to me, albeit in an unusual way. I was the breadwinner and he was a stay-at-home dad for most of our marriage. That was okay with me. It made me feel good that I could take care of my family.

Clyde came from an affluent Republican, Catholic, Marine Corps family, who had a postcard perfect life. Coming from the streets of New Orleans, I was intrigued with the whole family and their ability to have the kind of pristine order to their lives that I lacked. Clyde was a handsome man with proper training, but he was also spoiled. Of their own accord, my in-laws paid for Ava to go to private school and indulged the family with nice dinners and summers at a charming 1920s cabin on Candlewood Lake in Connecticut. Their generosity was enormous. It was also controlling. For example, I was not considered when deciding on what private school Ava should go to.

Clyde's parents co-signed on our house in New Orleans, but along with the down payment, I paid the mortgage until Katrina. Our house took major damage and we received insurance money, which Clyde used in part to build two studio rentals in the front of the house. I was not consulted when Clyde rebuilt our house into his dream home, something I wanted him to have. (All I wanted was a Mexican style bathroom, which I never got.) He worked hard on the house, took the profits I made from CD sales, and supplemented that with his parents' financial contributions. By himself he started to turn a huge old Victorian triple lot shotgun into a home while I worked. It was an odd twist of fate that Katrina destroyed and also gave rebirth to a unique new home. The house was a huge utopian compound in the middle of Mid-City in New Orleans. From then on, that rental income covered the mortgage and produced a profit that went toward repaying Clyde's parents.

I was glad that our family was going to live a better life. I put in all my time and money, which was good then with my work. I made $18,000 on one gig in Connecticut that funded the car Clyde wanted. Another time he wanted a 1954

Mercury. I spent my Katrina clothing insurance money on that instead of buying new dresses.

Clyde built the dream I had wanted. The unwritten terms that came with it were suffocating. Lack of communication, lack of participation or, when required, doing so only begrudgingly. I suspect he was probably depressed. During the period when we were separating, I was told by his mom that I was lucky to have lived there all those years rent-free. I got no thank you for having supported her son for 14 years.

A trip to Disney World was a prime example of our patterns as a family. Clyde would participate for his mom and Ava's sake, but he'd be so miserable, I would have to create an imaginary happy bubble to get through it. This went on for years, including at holiday gatherings. As a child I was forced to participate in unhappy family events, but as an adult, I was usually inclined to leave such events. I internally acknowledged that our family was not a happy one, but I also hoped with time, maybe it could be.

Clyde's mother would create a proactive fun plan for Ava's and our sakes. (Like Clyde, her husband didn't care to participate unless he had to.) We ate nice dinners when they came to visit, they gave expensive gifts every Christmas in Connecticut. It was an ideal life in the eyes of someone like me, who had never grown up with any order or cleanliness. I loved Clyde for being a structurally solid foundation. He made me feel cared for, at least theoretically. He went out of his way to make contracts for my shows, cook gourmet meals, and drive me to my gigs. He even checked the ingredients on my face cream to find out why I was breaking out.

He was great at details.

I am not.

He came from a conservative family.

I did not.

He went to private school. I did not.

He took me to his parents' saltbox house in the beginning. We were alone there. He walked me to the back of the big pond with swans in the backyard, turned around with me to look at the large, perfectly manicured property and said, "This is it." I looked around as he said that and felt a sense of calm.

I've never cared about money. It's just paper and short-term power. We're all going to die without it. He was trying to impress me. It was impressive. But I had seen so many luxurious homes and related to so many people in high places at that point, I wasn't so wide-eyed at the thought of marrying money. The truth is, I loved him. He made me feel safe. Why would I have a child with him otherwise? In fact, the money made me uncomfortable. Despite my hard work, I could never give my kid anything as special as the traditional "White Christmas" and all the presents on her list like they could, which, as she grew older, became much more expensive.

The money controlled Clyde. He wanted it from his parents and was on his best stoic behavior to get it. He was obligated to do whatever his parents wanted. He told me, point-blank, that his dad was not going to give me my half of the house profits as community property law in Louisiana mandated. He wanted to make me pay for my drinking.

* * * * *

Clyde built a white picket fence home and I had no say in any of it as his partner. Not the road trips, not things we did together as a family. I felt that his attitude was predominantly "It's my way or the highway." I had been an exuberant, proactive wild card acing The Big Time in New York City for a while, with no clue about how to be a "traditional" mom in a normal home. All of the things that had happened in my young adult life were by my choice and leadership. Clyde didn't understand that. He was just living his normal routine as he had before, but with a kid in the mix, which seemed to make him grumpy. Because of his cold, detached upbringing, he didn't have the capability to love me as I thought real love should be. Maybe I was being unrealistic. To me, it's not the money. It's having a best friend to experience life with.

We were living my dream of a relationship in New York City for a few years during the beginning of our marriage. We had friends, laughter, creative projects, and adventures, even if only a day trip to Coney Island. My idea of a white picket fence changed when it was materialized, making me feel trapped in a box. The idea of just existing in a house together year after year was maddening. I was proactive when it came to my career, but when it came to Clyde, my way of showing love was to not make waves and let him have his way.

I take ownership of the fact that I chose to drink. That said, I believe if Clyde would have just said once with true meaning in his heart that he truly loved me and asked me what I wanted, maybe things would have been different. The unconscionable cruel verbiage that came out of his mouth was like artillery shooting my being down. *He must be right.* Because that's how I already felt about myself.

I take responsibility for my actions. At the time, I allowed myself to be a victim behind a white picket fence because I truly wanted our family to thrive. Unfortunately, the will of our ways took us into separate directions.

New Beginnings

In January 2015, on a cool, grey day that felt like fall, Clyde somberly handed me a large manila envelope without saying a word as he walked out the door. Sitting on the couch, I quietly opened it. The papers inside were an official divorce contract and an eviction order. I had 30 days to remove myself with my personal belongings. I was shocked that I could be evicted from my own home; after all, I had put a down payment on it and supported the family in it for 12 years. It was the house my mother had checked out for us, in the city I had brought Clyde to. His best friends were people I introduced him to. We lived in the neighborhood where I had grown up. *He wouldn't be here without me having created this world for him, and now he wants to eject me from it! This can't be possible.*

Clyde had never communicated with me to let me know he had decided the marriage was over until I received that envelope. *Sixteen years later and a wonderful kid and this is how it ended?* There are three sides to the story — mine, his, and Ava's. Each of us had valid complaints.

I frantically called and met with at least seven lawyers. All the same, I had no rights to the house, as it was in Clyde's parents' name. Neither Clyde nor I had credit. I didn't have any official paperwork on file stating the house was half mine. We bought the house in 2002 for $152,000. I had put $7,500 down from my record label advance. A few years after I was evicted, it sold for $420,000.

Clyde's parents, who are extremely wealthy, gave me back my $7,500 and nothing more. Clyde had a big metal storage unit plopped down in the driveway on January 23, the anniversary of my dad's death, for our close neighbors to see. I did not put a single thing in it.

Prior to that, I hadn't left of my own accord, because of my daughter, and I never gave up on the hope that our relationship would change for the better with time. I still did my mothering and money-making duties. But I was unhappy with the way I wasn't considered, and the dismissive way Clyde spoke to me. I drank a third of a fifth of tequila every evening. I felt just disposable in the end, really. And to add whipped cream and a cherry to my misery sundae, he had a new girlfriend move in a month after I moved out and married her a month after our divorce was final.

Where was I supposed to go with $1,300 to my name, with rents having tripled post-Katrina? A friend owned a few shotgun houses in Gentilly and offered me a discounted deal for a few months to get on my feet, with hoeing and raking included in my rental chores. I didn't even know where Gentilly was or anyone who lived there. But it was a house with a door that locked, a roof, and heat, air, and water.

I asked my fellow Nightingale singers and their husbands to help me move on their day off. Clyde and my daughter were not there. He had locked the bedroom door with the valuables, and my friends and I packed up 14 years of my life there in four hours. I was shaking so much I thought I was going to have a heart attack. One friend gave me an anxiety pill. After we all tossed as much as we could into their family SUVs, the place looked ransacked. Who had time to clean up?

Two dogs, a journal collection, a dress collection, sound system, music book, photographs, my daughter's bed (which I had been sleeping on for three years), a TV, and a couch. That was all I left with. The only thing I took of monetary value was a little black and white painting by Ron English that Clyde and I had bought with the last of our money at CBGB in New York City when we first got married: a young, naked Marilyn with Mickey Mouse boobs.

The last thing to happen in that home before I left was a Nightingale walking me to the bathroom and asking which electric toothbrush was Clyde's. I pointed at it, not having a clue why she asked. She took it, turned it on, and proceeded to deep-clean the toilet bowl with it for about two minutes. That was one of the weirdest, meanest things I'd ever seen anybody do. I felt terrible, but I saw that she was making a mission statement for me.

Shortly after I moved out, Clyde started a new life with another partner. My daughter didn't want to be a part of whatever was about to go down. I didn't blame her. Clyde had created a safe haven for her. To his credit, he is a great dad. And the neighborhoods I lived in post-divorce would not have been safe for her.

I faced a new beginning in a new world I was totally unprepared for. In my life plans, I never, ever imagined any of the events that ensued would actually be my reality for the next six years. I had never lived alone in my life. I was terrified.

My old life had ended on Clyde's terms. My new life started on my terms, for better or worse. That's when the real dumpster fire began.

Never Lived Alone

Never lived alone. Ever.
Solitary silent confusion.
Keep order.
Random or structured?
Both.
Make sure the floor is swept and dishes are done.
Raft life has not trained this girl too well,
But she's learning.
Sorrow, loss, anger.
Forget emotionality, activate.

Complete exhaustion
Go. Do. Be. Activate.
Can the body heal itself?
There is an imaginary but real arrow of pain
Shooting through the front of my heart to the shoulder blade.

Choose your words carefully.
"Fuck."
I don't know anything.
I thought fair equals fair.
Nope-sy.
Feeling utterly screwed over.

In Gentilly
I walk four blocks daily
To the Brown Derby ghetto grocery.
Omar the Israeli owner is kind.
He makes sure there is Perrier for me.
Overly nice porch sitters
Saying hello with kindness.
My body walks silently through the calming sunshine
With dignity and nothingness.
Why and how does one get ejected from their family and home
With silent cruelty?

Closing the day of my birth,
I walked to the Elysian Fields bus,
There was a majestic sunset on Royal Street
I sat on someone's stoop for a few moments reflecting
A homeless man walked up
He was surprisingly intelligent
We talked for a half hour.
He fell on hard times.
Six kids.
Our personal worlds are one paycheck away from being homeless.

As I lie thinking,
With my two lovable doggies,
Contemplating how to be
sustainable, generous, forgiving.
I wonder,
Where is all of this leading to?
No one is exempt from life.
I don't know how this month's bills will be paid,
but they will.
And they have.

I miss my baby girl.
Who's becoming her own person.
The heavens are showering blessings on me.
I'm listening.

Yesterday in the glorious sunshine
I took my second motorcycle ride.
The first one was with my dad when I was four.
The clouds are billowing,
The sun is bright.
Water salty and oily.
Life is magical.
Hopeful, trusting,
With eyes cautiously open.
Alone in Gentilly

Ghetto Gatsby

I woke up early — 9:30 (for a musician, that's early). It was getting hot. Where was the coffee? Walked the dogs per usual. Who designed these long three-block streets in Gentilly without trees? There's just one tree on the corner and the dogs were nearly dying.

I hate showing my legs. I'd finally resorted to shorts and Walmart wifebeaters to stay cool. I sat under the tree, sweaty, with sorrow in my heart. I watched the world around me objectively. If you really look outside of your own four walls, you'll see life more clearly.

A gorgeous woman drove up to the house kitty corner from where I was sitting. She was wearing a white Gatsby hat and white 1950s dress, and she drove up in a junker to vivaciously greet the person standing in front of the house. I watched precariously, not wanting to violate her personal space, but she saw me, sat on the porch, and engaged me with her eye contact and body posture. It was just what I needed to get moving.

I hustled back home, mopped, and washed dishes and doggies.

I wanted to see and talk to people I knew after that hard work and solitude all day. I hailed the Elysian Fields bus to Frenchmen Street in an effort to not wallow at home alone. I didn't want to have a wild party, just a real meal and familiarity. When I left dinner, I spotted a vulnerable woman sleeping in front of the old Cafe Brazil with a dog that looked just like the one from *The Little Rascals*. I asked her if her "baby" needed water. When she realized who I was, she teared up. She said my music helped get her through battered women's shelters and she was about to have an adventure by hopping a freight to Montana the next morning.

Every night in Gentilly there's a train whistle that blows so hard. It inspired me to write the first song for a new recording even my cowriters had not heard yet. I put my arms around the woman and her dog and I sang it for the first time a cappella. She cried hard.

I wished I could tell that woman in the white dress on the corner how her impeccable demeanor changed my game that day and therefore changed someone else's life that night.

Can you hear that train calling
Calling through the night
Can you hear that train moaning
It gives me quite a fright
Can you hear that train blowing
Blowing with all of its might
Can you hear that train blowing
Calling you with its invite.
Ooooohhhhh
Oooooohhhhhhhhhh
Oooooooohhh
Come with me tonight.
I don't know what's lying in the future
I don't know anything at all
I don't know what will be coming
Want to hop on that train whistle call.

"Wanderlust" by Ingrid Lucia, 2021

*****

Where's the Red Lipstick?

I spent one morning digging trenches for tomato plants in exchange for part of the rent. While in a complete dirty sweat, I got a call asking if I could come down one block and sing to a family member who was bedridden.

Despite being hesitant to sing a cappella – and impose my stinkiness on someone – I said yes.

She was a lovely Italian American woman. I sang a few songs I thought she could relate to, and then asked her if she had a request. She said, "Can you sing *Do They Play Jazz in Heaven?*"

I told her that it was me on the music video and audio recording. She sat straight up in her bed in the dark hospice room and said adamantly, "Where's the red lipstick?!"

*****

Mr. McKenzie's Chicken

I walked in. It still looked like the donut shop it used to be. It's now called Chicken in a Box. On the wall is an award for Culinary Excellence from Tulane. Waiting for my order, a handsome young man walked up to me, leaned on the Coke machine, looked me directly in the eyes, and asked, "Are you married?"

I said, "You're blunt."

He said, "I'm single."

Taken aback, I asked, "What are your hobbies and interests?"

"Driving by the lake and eating fine food," he replied as he pointed to the counter.

Thanks for the ego boost, Mister. And the meat pie and mashed potatoes were really good. I recommend them!

Dearest Ava,

When you were a baby, in the backseat of the car, Grandpa told me I should scream at you in military action. To pacify you. I would not. Driving that old white Cadillac, you in the baby back seat, him in passenger, I explained. I would never pacify your voice. Even if it meant you screaming. As you did for years.

You were a rambunctious, physical baby. Do you remember how mad Dad would get at the inability to control you? All of his screaming at you on the pile of sand in Mississippi with Grandma and cousin Hannah to witness? You never wanted to sit still at the dinner table in your highchair. Ever.

With all of the gigs around the world I played from London to Los Angeles with carefully chosen babysitters I picked, from Aunt Jessie in Los Angeles to Grandma Maxine in Jackson, Mississippi, while bringing you with me because I loved you so deeply, I really wanted you to see the world.

I made extra labors to make sure you were there with me to witness how beautiful the world is. I always believed in you being allowed to speak your voice no matter what.

I tried my very best, Ava, to not let you down.

First birthday party with ponies I paid for with my hard sweat and voice, I wanted to spoil you as was never done to me. I've been working like a musical monkey since I was ten years old. It was my dream and path I knew when I was four years old and first viewed *Gone With the Wind* at the Saenger Theatre with my mom.

Remember going to see "Dora the Explorer" there together?

It's been a hard road, but worth the journey. Some people struggle so hard to find their way in life. Some know the word from the beginning. That gift to know is the curse and the blessing. I was given the gift. You are the greatest experience I've had in this life, apart from performing. I wish I could believe in unconditional love with a partner. I do still hope for that gift.

There are moments of light with someone like Dad. For a moment there is a light that is inexplicable; that has only happened four times in my life, to experience when there is a connection to God. I call those moments "Star Eyes."

Birthing you was the most breathtaking "Star Eyes" I've ever experienced in my entire life from all of the journeys I've been through.

Life survival seems to take hierarchy. The only constants I can acknowledge in this life are being somewhat in control of creating and the gift of you, which has been missing.

For me, you are the biggest gift of all.

And my own self ownership of the skill sets I have worked really, really hard and toiled for, called my voice, word, and wild card ideas to try and make this world a better place.

Your text really upset me today. I truly appreciate you being open to share your word and truth. If there's ever a right as an American after our forefathers have worked so hard for that privilege, it's the bravery and freedom to share your truth without being hanged.

There are many band-aids in one's life. You can choose to avoid the subject material problems at hand. I choose to be the owner of my own ship. To navigate the waters of self-responsibility, creative work, and a little pleasure. I don't do drugs or even take aspirin or prescription medication. I've cut down my band-aids quite a bit with the choice to focus on writing, music, and curated relationships.

I've never fallen down. I'm standing like a warrior with good people on my team who, for whatever reason, believe in me. And I, more than any song I write, I try to help, fighting step by step to survive each day, and believe in YOU.

I will always love you more deeply than my best writing attempts and dreams to write the masterpiece.

Mom

Alone in Gentilly

The Little Bulldog

She humbles herself, every day.
Etiquette is her mindset display.
She has muscle mass
That could kick your ass.
But she refrains.
Class is the name of her game.

Every day,
This little bulldog watches and looks,
Discerning each situation.
Has she read
The AKC manners books?
Never once attacking,
She snubs her nose to negative ways.
She's a lady.

When it's time to play,
She'll be your clown all day.
Rolling like a dead cockroach,
Doing the Mexican hat dance,
She looks you in the eyes,
Acknowledging a festivity chance.
Her core is tough.
I've learned so much from this little soul.

Wise and silent,
Always, with eyes discerning,
Stubbornly stating
The direction she is yearning.
What the heck.
You like slumming
By fried chicken bones on the shadow streets.
No-uh.
Staying alive is our mantra.
Hello and greet.

I love you, Allie.
You've taught me a lot.
How to be set in your ways...

And not ask a lot.
Your beauty catches every hero's eyes,
You are an angel,
I'm lucky to have you in my life.
Snore, snore, snore.
Or as she states,
with her little French Bulldog nasal passage;
Sing, Sing, Sing...
Love begets hate.
She makes peace ring.

Pool Sharks and Chess Strategies

I went to Frenchmen Street with my bestie Renee Shaw, who said that divorce is contagious. Her story came two months after mine. She went out of her way to be a real friend. When I was living in the ghetto, in her kindness, she took me under her wing when not many did. She brought me a big bag of Christian Dior products, as she has worked for that company for years. We both got our community property closeouts from long marriages one day apart. She was married for 35 years, and I for 16. We decided to bond for an evening.

Frenchmen Street had turned into a continual carnival. It was nice to be allowed in front doors by my lifetime tribe, but it was disturbing to see fancy bodies spending their money on overpriced cocktails while not caring about the talent standing in the windows playing their hearts out. It's a violation. So, we diverted.

We walked into the R Bar, a prominent hipster bar with a pool table and a really great old-school DJ, a few blocks from home. The youngish man holding the pool table asked me if I wanted to play. My brother taught me how to play pool. *You visually line up the balls geometrically, you want to shoot into the hole, then place the rest of your balls to lock and stabilize the pockets so if your enemy can make the ball, yours goes in with it by default, heightening your power. Never give your opponent a shot option. And you must make a powerful spread break properly.*

Pool is a chess game.

I won three games straight with a wonky stick. Two against a gentleman from Brooklyn, a smart young man who was in New Orleans for a convention to change gun laws in this country. Then walked in some of the oddest characters I'd seen in New Orleans, and that is saying a whole lot. John Waters meets New Orleans. A butch woman with a sweaty wifebeater and a dressed-up young man who looked like a tennis player asked if we were ready to play doubles. Mr. Brooklyn, who I beat twice, signed up. The woman was so aggressive, she played her shots physically and mentally like Jackie Gleason in *The Hustler*. They wanted to bet money, but I don't gamble. She was a cocky rooster with perfect hits on every ball regardless of how it was aligned, efficiently coming in for the kill.

Claire was her name; I shook her hand, allowing the tension to release before we were done with the game. She loudly said she didn't like ice cream cones because she didn't suck dick and was lactose intolerant. Quite a memorable phrase.

I focused my mind so intently because I didn't want to see a collective of big egos win the game. Me and Mr. Brooklyn won the game. Offense. Defense. And the offense had to walk away. Sometimes it takes a gentle hand with focus to offend and knock the balls in. And sometimes it takes a gentle hand to hit the white ball in a place where the offense doesn't have a shot. Game won.

Thereafter, Mr. Brooklyn, Renee, and I had a long conversation about each state's gun laws. He shared his lobby group's position on strengthening gun control laws. We need that activism in Louisiana. Apparently, our state is the hardest one to crack.

* * * * *

When we were kids, my dad used to make us play chess against each other for five dollars a game. Strategies of life. When to be on the offensive or defensive with pre-positioning and thinking. He taught us well, but as a child I couldn't see the moves. His chess board is the only thing I own that he treasured and used often in his own journeys.

Todd talked to me about his perspective on playing. His young son, a bunch of years ago, kicked my butt and I had to cough up $20 toward a new bike on a bet. With the wisdom my cousin gave me, I had been checkmating my ex-husband-to-be quite a bit. The look on his face made me laugh so hard. He put on the Bobby Fischer documentary and ten minutes in said, "Oh no, you're not watching this," in realization that he was giving his opponent ammunition.

I think if we all learned chess strategies and applied them to life across the board, there would be fewer losses by default.

Ode to Melvin

I ran in the summer heat with my roommate and her daughter, ten-year-old little Miss Delia, to catch the 4:25 p.m. bus. We were dressed up in our retro swing outfits to go to my gig at DBA, a music club on Frenchmen Street. We sat with the rest of the hot, agitated locals for an hour and 20 minutes, waiting for a bus that never came.

Essence Festival, an annual African American music and cultural event in New Orleans, was no excuse. The gig started at 5:30. At 5:20 the three of us stuck our thumbs out with our ten-dollar bill.

A huge tricycle motorcycle pulled over. Melvin, a senior motorcycle cowboy, offered a ride. I hopped on. Three would have been a bit precarious in one extra leather luxury seat. It took them another two hours to get to their destination. Melvin turned up his soul stereo to a song about loving your grandma. The wind was blowing and we were living the dream. I held my gig bag tight. It was the most fun I'd had in a long time. What an angel.

We played with a stellar lineup to a loud chattering audience. I talked about the end of a musical era in New Orleans with the guys over dinner. Watched the next act struggle through a loud talking audience. *It is time for a change. Not sure what that is yet. There's no future in this.*

I was up at 7:30 a.m. to go hear Deepak Chopra speak at Essence Festival's empowerment seminars at the Convention Center. As I waited for the bus to come, I wondered, Where are you at this hour, Melvin?

Rhythm of the Rain

Pounding, pulsating,
Thunder, dark grey
There isn't a song to explain
This rain today.
Mood set, early morn,
Shall we go with forlorn?

No, I say to myself.

Vaudeville lights plugged in.
Two dogs snoring
In rhythm's hymn.
Listen to nature's voice,
Breathe and release,
Silence and violence,
Whoosh, silence, whoosh.
Release.
Bam.

Thunder's low voice
Boomingly speaks.
Roooooaarrrr.
BOOM.
Pounding rain.
Grey.
Who's in charge of this show?
Explain.

Breathe.
Prepare.
To take on this murky day,
With a dare.
There's a new song brewing.
Today's the day to lock it in.
Mission statement.
Beans have been soaking,

Time to put them on the stove.
Brown rice,
Here we go...

Justification day,
For the creative zone.
"Let's Get Lost"
To get found and own.

Breeze blowing,
Rain pounding,
Clouds in disarray.
Today is the day
To activate.

I hear a melody in the rhythm of the rain,
It sounds like a sway,
Hard, soft, consistent, contained,
Nature's voice to understand.
Listening,
Feeling, the grand...
Rhythm of the rain,
rhyTHM of the rain,
RHYthm,
Rhythm of the rain.

Shotgun Sundays

Songwriting

Titles usually come first. Sometimes the muse flies by, if you catch her, a song happens in five minutes, as in "Put The Radio On." Dream state messages come rarely: "Hello Sunshine, Goodbye Blue." Some songs take years for the last verse to show itself: "Honey Child" "Let Me In."

Writing for other artists creates a new archetype to create images around: "The Game" I wrote for Lena Prima could never be mine. Co-writes are the most wonderful. John Fohl, Roland Guerin, Chris Adkins: each brings a new perspective on chord choices and lyrical power.

Sometimes a song comes from a hook, as in a lick trumpeter Mark Braud might play as part of a wooing style. Duke Ellington would do that quite often: "Cootie's Blues."

Friends and family unknowingly expressed:
"You're Not The Only One" was inspired by my daughter.
"When Does The Party End?" drummer Gerald French would always ask.

Thousands of titles on napkins, paper bags, sketch books. The ones that call out are the ones that become born in the now. I'm still searching for the one that becomes great art, that becomes religion.

* * * * *

The Mask

Whether it's putting on makeup or an attitude, we all have a mask we wear to face the world. As a performer, I have to look in the mirror often to put mine on for a show. The more I put my mask on after a lifetime of doing it, the less I wanted to. I found myself wearing less makeup, if any, during the day. To be brave enough to remove the protective mask and let yourself be seen as you *really* are can be so freeing from the pressure of needing to be something you're not. Also terrifying. And I'm not just talking about makeup, but also the wall we hide behind daily for safety.

I don't really like to look at myself in the mirror.

Meisner acting technique of externalization or Stanislavsky technique of internalization? I've always chosen the latter to express myself. To me, it's what's inside that shines out. To my chagrin, Meisner comes out for safety often.

Tina Turner has said she takes the makeup mirror time to transform her energy into relaxation and transfer it into her show energy. Dolly Parton has said she won't leave the house without a lot of makeup — and plastic surgery. European women pride themselves on their hard-earned wrinkles called life experience. The question comes up with American performers all the time about whether to stick a needle in your third eye and Botox it. I read in a magazine article that actors are ruining their tool (called their face) from doing its job properly by trying to keep it youthful.

The Theatrical Mask came up in a circular conversation with a few people around the country and from France, so I thought it was worth exploring.

Alone for the first time in my life, I was trying to really look in the mirror honestly. What did I see, without the makeup and safety wall? I'd been forcing myself to look a lot. I saw someone who had to live with herself and her own conscience in order to be okay with being alone.

What was she willing to accept as her highest standards and values? What were her weaknesses to work on? What did she want her life to be like? How could she wake up every morning, look at herself with her wild hair standing straight up, with a heartfelt smile to greet the day? How could she internalize the idea that it's really alright to be who she really was, not need to please everyone and leave her "jazz hands" mask hung by the side of the mirror?

*****

The "It" Factor

I found out that a very good family friend had passed away. She was a talented, intelligent, classy lady who had a long quality life. She had the "It" factor. The news made me start thinking about the impending doom we are all ticking away till death. Better get to "It," I thought. What is "It," I asked myself? Is "It" what I've been assuming "It" should be in this life? Or am I living a life of routine by default?

I hadn't been happy for a while. All the pieces were there to make a happy life: health, doing what I like for a living, great friends, family, a loyal musician community, a home to live in, pets. Looking forward, looking back, I did not want to be on my deathbed regretting my unhappiness or any part of this gift called my life.

A big part of "It" is quality and no holds barred.

Jerry Herman, a prominent Broadway songwriter, talked about his mom using her finest china daily for no reason except because it was today. Pull out the china, wear the ballgown, have that deep talk, take the chance on love, dance the dance, take down the New Orleans paint job,* and let people laugh at the beauty and rawness of you and all your old barge wood with its 10,000 hours. Let them hear you roar or meow your "It."

On this segment of our Shotgun Sunday Series, I commit myself to getting to "It." I hope everyone else does too. Time is a precious commodity.

*When a poor person can only afford to paint the front of a house pretty while the sides are falling apart.

* * * * *

Real Friends

Kristin Fouquet, bestie, writer, photographer, humble human, called me on the phone, as I sat on an empty Waveland, Mississippi, beach alone with a loaned bike by my side, in the hot bright summer sun, the doggies in my friend's cabin a few blocks away.

She asked me in a quiet, serious voice, what she could do to help.

While making tension angels in the sand with my feet, the tide rose on the sandbar I laid on. We joked as we are inclined to do; somehow, she always makes me laugh and tells me the truth. I hate to cry. She had caught me in a deep moment of heart hurt. And I cried. She asked me what she could do to help.

I thought about her question. I said, in my deepest of deep guttural sorrow, "I would like to feel like I have value again. I feel like nothing. Even though it's egotistical, I would like to show value to women who do the mundane chores for their children and men so they feel like they are special."

We spoke about presenting old-school photos of women doing their chores graciously while finding pleasure alone sitting on the washer. The concept of this series of photographs was borne out of Kristin's affection, love, and kindness.

I am going to make some old-school magic with Kristin Fouquet.

* * * * *

Manifesto Checklist for Changing Times

Family checklists are no longer the same,
Time to review a new refrain.
Women holding jobs,

Dads raising kiddos at home,
Game's changing from old rules,
Dishes alternating today,
Whose zone?
Not good or bad,
Just changing news.
Two single dads on my block:
Both youths, one with a 1-year-old,
One with three boys, ages 4, 6, and 8,
Both discipline their children with care.
New forms of family life are adhering,
Time for some mental re-gearing.
Same sex-marriages,
Now nationally acknowledged,
Buzzing silent questions come
From those with traditional values.
Care comes in many forms,
From that, only beauty will follow.
In love's etiquette book,
Checklist chores still remain,
Relationships become unwound
By the mundane.
Make your checklist of daily to-do's,
Silent expectations kill the game.
Reconfigure for your family.
Wish there had been a dummy guide
To explain how to communicate.
Dinner, laundry, dishes, bills, partnering,
United we stand, randomly for years fumbled in the dark.
Here's the gig pay,
Now what's the plan?
Two souls trying to step up their best,
Tired after long days.
Advice to the newly engaged:
Make a list of the chores to share equally,
For the sake of saving love.

* * * * *

I Love to Dream

I love to sleep. The bedroom is my favorite room. A safe haven, away from life's problems. If you are lucky to have a body to swaddle with, **that's it.**

One of the most important things to me is dreaming. Many messages come through the subconscious. Fellini kept a sketchbook by his bedside. All of the characters in his films came from his dream state. I once dreamt I was dancing the can-can with football players dancing on either side of me. Two years later, I was dancing at the Can Can on Bourbon Street to pay for my braces; Tennessee State was playing the Sugar Bowl, and the troupe was hired. I was 15 years old; it was my first solo feature, a kickline with football players on both sides with arms all intertwined. Bam. Remember the dream.

The practicing Buddhist I met in Orizaba, Mexico, told me the highest connected prayer energy is between 3 and 4 a.m. (The lowest is between 3 and 4 p.m.) My dad comes to me in my dreams. So does John Fohl, my guitarist and co-songwriter. They are silently in the shadows watching my actions.

I've experienced pure love a few starry-eyed times. I see longevity in relationships is possible from the couples' anniversaries I've played for. The starlight is still in their eyes. Advice I ask? "Let it go" 50 years... "Respect" 35 years... "Empathy" is my point of view.

Whether the bedroom stays a monastery altar, a haven for star eyes, or a creative zone... It is my favorite room, above and beyond the kitchen and porch...

Love Letter to New Orleans

New Orleans. Last of the cowboy towns, I like to say. Whatever you like, or whoever you are, you are received and accepted in New Orleans. Every city has a persona. New Orleans is a big mama who swaddles you into her sweaty, slow, suffocating hug, never to let you leave the vortex of her swamp. A gift and a curse.

The city has been my everything. Growing up in a traveling caravan of random wanderlusters, adopted family members, and street family band survival musicians, New Orleans mama beckoned with her silent finger to my San Francisco beatnik dad. It brought this baby girl under her permanent spell.

Musicians' tender street training, words of sincere care by service industry characters, a good hot meal in a place like Buster Holmes for little money, humor by the locals to hold on to hope, acceptance by all here that life is perfect as it is in a $300 a month shotgun with a large family, music, and red beans and rice.

The parallel lines of change in this girl's life and change in New Orleans are almost too much to bear. The end of the safety of a home, a child, and a marriage mirrored the end of the city as I knew her.

I was not the only one to feel the crossroads coming in. I reflected on the word "gentrification" a lot. So did many New Orleans musicians (considered royalty), who felt safe to share their feelings with me. That word represented the end of an era, and not for the better. Unless you consider frozen yogurt and pizza replacing fried chicken and liquor better. I don't.

I pictured the city as an aging Scarlett O'Hara, a bit musty in her tattered velvet robe, but loyal and caring, being given a carwash. Sure, she's pristine, dressed in khaki pants and eating kale, and she's still herself, if only a mirage of the powerful, mystical figure she used to be. It breaks my heart.

I saw three generations of musicians not being able to make a living because of quadrupled rents and no increase in the pay in clubs since 1968. I saw those players with so much pride, impotent to do something about the changes. I saw a beige froufrou mentality moving in and disrespecting the culture that had been layered through sweat, pain, joy, and pleasure. Their unconscious behavior and money made me feel like the city I call home and all the people under her umbrella were being pillaged. I love the city with all my heart. That's why I am still in New Orleans.

My love letter to New Orleans includes many years of laughter, traditional jazz songs, lifers who are content to make a basic living at what they do and give you a kind wave and word of love, an old-school way of living that doesn't exist in any other city in the United States. I know. I've been to them all.

I pray that some miracle will happen to pull back the reins and allow big mama to reign over her cowboy town in the swamp for a little longer.

Why do I spend my precious time in New Orleans ticking away to a hole in the grave? Why did I leave New York City to birth my child in New Orleans? Because I love it. If I ever had a home, as a wandering gypsy freak, it's New Orleans. If there was ever any probability of making a real home, it's New Orleans.

So, I say thank you, New Orleans and all of your wards, for the observations and growth.

P.S. Kermit Ruffins for Mayor!

New Orleans Musicians' Rights

Fair pay for musicians' work was discussed at the historic Carver Theater and aired on an international platform on WWOZ radio. After the forum, I biked home with a big chain in hand for protection and $40 to my name. Who needs a gym membership?

I didn't realize until I got to the theater that the panel was being used as a mayoral contest. Each candidate for mayor shared sketches from their own personal histories on how to possibly solve the problems musicians faced — except none of them were musicians. The panel should have included working musicians to represent the collective, who could ask the candidates key questions.

Gathering at the historic venue, the mayoral candidates shared broad-stroke ideas. That was supposed to be the subject coverage for the evening. Instead, they talked about solutions to the Mardi Gras Indians' problems and washed over some possible good ideas for musicians without detailing any specifics.

I wanted to know how to address the problem of being underpaid by every club in town. How could musicians avoid being ticketed by the police while unloading gear? Why were musicians being charged for everything on gigs, including food, which is deducted from their 20 percent of the bar? How could we incorporate basic rights so that musicians don't feel like animals trying to survive while they're sharing musical love with those visiting the city, when it's a key component of the reason people come to New Orleans and spend their money?

As a bandleader, I've hired players who trust me to navigate the waters for gigs and then been paid $8 for the whole band, all because the club didn't take advantage of free radio and press tools to promote the name I've worked so hard to build upon.

I try to be objective. Nothing in the world is ever about one person. I don't need an ego. I need to pay the rent and eat. It would be nice to take my kid to a fancy meal like she's used to on her dad's side.

We're all broke. The ongoing stories circulating among prominent musicians playing gigs with a guarantee of $100 for the whole band are downright depressing and enough to make me want to hang up the dress, run for the hills, and grow some fresh food. 'Cause I was hungry, broke, tired, and disgusted with investing my life in and believing in New Orleans.

A) The rents need to go down.

B) The payroll needs to go up because it's already earmarked in the city's tourism budget.

C) An entertainment industry that's competitive with Los Angeles and New York City needs to happen.

D) Kermit Ruffins for City Council!

The Paper Trail

I was born cash poor and still remain so.

My chosen field is a very difficult road financially unless you hit The Big Time. Until I took on a part-time job in 2022, I made my living strictly from performing. It was honorable in the minds of many, including myself, that I was able to feed and support myself, my family, and my childhood family by hoofing and hustling. To me, taking a "survival" job meant I would be a loser who couldn't make it in music. How could that be when I'd proven multiple times that I was qualified?

Why do so many not consider music a real job? It is. And it requires as much if not more energy and time than a 9 to 5. We don't just sleep all day and party all night. If you asked a musician (and in my case, a band manager) what their work world is like, it goes something like this: Learn, practice, and walk the road. Find out where the gigs are, build and pay for websites, publicists, arrangers, among others, to be non-negotiable in conquering gigs. Most shows are one-off bookings, so the vicious cycle of hunting for work never ends. Think daily about music. Festivals in Europe will bring in a couple months' rent money... if you're lucky.

Money. There isn't much of it going around in our circle, though the clubs and parties we play for often seem to have a lot of it.

I was disturbed when a list of who got paid how much from a festival in New Orleans was found and published online. The male artists got $3,500. I got $1,200. Didn't that guy realize my whole band is made up of men who all play with other bands that were on the roster? They're making more with those other bands, and I had to explain to the guys why they're not making that much with me. Which left them to question if I was taking more than my share.

There have been occasional "ding-ding" moments. The $50,000 Breakers Hotel gig, the BMW and Ferrero Rocher commercials. As thankful as I am that the latter is being picked up and rerun, it is a flat rate fee, which is split in half between my producer and me. That doesn't go very far. Clubs pay a few hundred dollars for a whole band. Some clubs have paid the same since before I was born, according to an elder statesman in New Orleans. Too bad the cost of living hasn't stayed the same.

These are our realities. In the money equation, youth is a commodity. Especially for women, who have a shelf life. A big part of selling music in a man's world is the pretty package that goes with it. When that's gone... look around with your own eyes and do the math.

People don't buy CDs or records any more. The online streaming sources pay pennies. I have a Pandora station and a million hits on Spotify. In 2021 my quarterly royalties from all streaming platforms averaged $48. The outlets for income have dwindled to almost nothing. Then layer on being a contender in the jazz market, which holds approximately a five percent slice of music's international sales pie. It's disheartening to be broke when you work so hard.

Many times, musicians earn barely enough for their monthly bills. And if the car needs repairs, forget it. It's a constant hustle. Beloved rock stars in the eyes of many, musicians like me are scrounging, trying to survive in your faux fancy thrift store clothing. The image is not what it seems at all.

I would not change this life for anything. Music has brought me and so many others so much joy, and that doesn't have a number on it. The people I've met, the places I've seen, the fact that I own something to call mine that can't be taken away. My memories.

My biggest fear is being homeless when I'm old. Being homeless as a child was hard enough. Since my surgery, I'd been living a better life being supported (temporarily) by the system than I ever did working my booty off.

I advocate for everyone in the arts. Imagine a world of beige, flat, one-dimensional linearity that holds no sound, color, ideas, emotions, pain, joy, or thought-provoking art. Spending your life that way in quiet non-sensory silence without that spark of energy coming into your life. I cry for myself and my peers for fear of what lies ahead. The Nothing.

Remember this when you go to clubs and have to pay a cover charge, a minimum drink rule, or are asked to put money in a tip jar.

Letter to the President of William Morris

New Orleans is at a crossroads. Rents are going up, gigs are less available with incoming lesser talents willing to work for 20% of the bar. Average pay is $125 a man, $150 for the bandleader. No one here can make an honest living anymore. Many of the city's royalty players have chosen to speak to me to vent their frustrations. Why they're talking to me, I don't know.

I was raised in a family band on the road, and New Orleans is the only place I've ever called home (thanks to the traditional jazz players who trained six kids to play music properly), so I feel responsible to pay it back.

This city needs a national vehicle. And an organized source to exploit musical material already recorded for a worthy income to TV and film. You know, as I do too, there isn't a single person in the world who doesn't love New Orleans, yet the music that makes the city so special is being thrown away without care by bar owners who don't seem to care.

A three-pronged plan:

A) National music show out of Joy Theater daily.
   Format: Jimmy Fallon meets Austin City Limits. I will define a competitive layout plan when we talk.

B) Licensing company that pitches local quality catalogue music for soundtracks to Hollywood South.

C) A committee to represent New Orleans to compete on a national level. And me, backed by the Wind Beneath Your Wings players and a new sound.

Dolly Parton said, when she was looked down on by her peers for leaving country music and going pop, she wasn't leaving country music, she was taking it with her.

I'd like to have Pharrell Williams produce my next album with top New Orleans players to shine a light that we can make hit singles that aren't just rap. My very top musicians here, who work with Harry Connick, Dr. John, Preservation Hall, Allen Toussaint, are chomping at the bit to create the "New" New Orleans sound. And they are more than qualified to do so.

New Orleans music could be the equivalent to what Muscle Shoals was in its day.

I may sound like a lunatic, but I have nothing to lose here. I see a gap waiting to be filled. And somebody will do it soon if we don't. Can you recommend a business partner who can take care of the details? I am very good at big picture visions. Not as great at charts and grids.

Thank you for taking the time to read this.

I hope you have a little time for you in this life journey you have chosen!

Sincerely,

Ingrid Lucia

New Orleans, LA (2015)

Update: I received a call from the president's assistant asking me to put together a pitch kit.

How It Feels

Why would someone spend their whole life pursuing the difficult career of music? If you knew the euphoric feeling, you wouldn't ask the question.

There is a formula to get there. The understanding of how to build and ride a wave together, bringing the band and the audience to an orgasmic climax, is the goal. That "thing" creates such a powerful feeling of happiness, exhilaration, and religion when it kicks in. You all silently take that ride to a higher place together. It is more powerful than drugs or sex. Those spiritual moments in the band and in yourself are few and far between. You wait and pray for them. You stay as prepared as possible to catch the wave when it begins and not be the one to drop the ball.

The first time it happened was at the Rodeo Bar. My band, The Flying Neutrinos, as a fully rehearsed, well-oiled machine, hit that wave together while we were performing "Mr. Zoot Suit" for the first time. We were on stage, chugging through the song together. The full audience was listening, and then, out of nowhere, each musician became part of one unified sound. A wall, of a train, of a sound, that was bound for glory, taking no prisoners. We all realized it, making disbelieving eye contact, acknowledging the moment, but too afraid to break it. The roof was about to pop, the audience stood up screaming, out of control. We were all together as one, experiencing that magical energy. So high, so electrifying, so light. It was the emotional apex of the high we wish could achieve every moment of the day.

Then there's the deflation from the reality that even though you know the recipe that got the band there, it is never guaranteed. A player could have had a bad day and is disconnected, the vibe is off, the set list is wrong and not resonating with the audience, the fourth wall just doesn't want to come down, no matter how hard the lead singer tries to crack it.

There are many levels in performing. I enjoy all of them. We may be masochists as musicians, but we're not idiots. When and if you ever have a musician in your life as a mate or a friend, you will find that you will likely always come second.

Whenever I call a guy for a gig, regardless of how good the money is, I always get the question: Who is in the band? Then there is the silent calculation on the other end of the line as to whether this player will find the experience worthy of his or her time, talent, and treasure.

I was told long ago by my father that to be able to grow, I should always make sure I was the weakest link in the band. You learn as a bandleader (if you're smart) to connect the combinations of players who have "bromances" with each other. They love each other's playing; they have musical chemistry relating to each other. The drummer and bassist, especially, should be locked in as one. There are a few different bromances in my lineup choices. When those puzzle pieces of players come together, I know it's going to be gold.

Generally, life is just existing unless you're on the bandstand going for that magic muse.

French Quarter Kid

Concrete dust, an afternoon rain,
Walking cracked sidewalks,
Solitary figure, making her way.

Clouds blowing, oak trees sway,
Magnolia scents,
Where poor kids play.
Church bells ring, trumpets play,
High school marching bands,
Pass neighborhood ways.

Tap dancers in the Quarter,
With bottle cap shoes,
Smells of Lucky Dogs,
Beignets, and booze.

In the Square,
Mimes silently stare,
Artists paint portraits,
Where money flows fair.
Musicians compete there,
For the magic spot.

I am me, a child wildly free,
Feeding pigeons,
Dancing in a Mardi Gras gown,
For all to see.
So much joy
Bursting with glee.

Like the river rolls to the sea,
These are memories
That fill my heart
With bittersweet dreams.

So simple the days,
To wave and say Hey,
Ruthie the Duck Lady

Not strange to see
With the tap dancer, Old Smiley.
Buster Holmes
Walks by with a smile,
Offering beans and rice
At a musician's payroll fee.

You can never go home,
As much as you try,
That boat has passed,
Sadly wave goodbye.
Days of innocence,
Long and carefree,
Say goodbye to those moments,
That made me, me.

A new ship is sailing,
The fog rolls in,
You stand on the deck,
Ready to begin.

A new journey.

Jackson Square: Ground Zero

Jackson Square, a historic park in New Orleans' French Quarter, holds a conglomeration of drunks, tourists, musicians, artists, and gypsy fortune tellers. The big-boned Lucky Dog man silently witnesses all the cacophony of an adult wonderland going down the rabbit hole.

In 1984, our family band performed in front of St. Louis Cathedral daily from 11 a.m. to 3 p.m. Me, my brothers, sisters, aunt, sister-in-law, stepmom, and dad all played instruments that made up a full traditional jazz band. Our family ranged in ages from two up to 12.

Jackson Square held a secondary family of characters who would love and charm the pants off you one day and the next day tip over your wheelchair and stab you in your leg with a corkscrew. The Square was and is a training ground for many young players to get their sea legs. Many of them became quite successful, many are still there hustling change. It was one of the few places in New Orleans kids could perform.

My father decided to pay half of our hat to invited street musicians who could teach us the basics. And they did, in a manner that was brusque and somewhat impatient.

James May played trumpet with us every day, and every day he would aggressively stomp out the time out with his feet and yell at Marisa, who was eight, **"Crack the back beat, Sparky**!" He wouldn't let up on her until she got it.

Mustapha came and played the washtub bass and tap danced. He taught Todd how to do basic old-school tap moves.

Certain professional players, like drummer Shannon Powell and trombonist Craig Klein, would stop for a few minutes on their way to their gig at Preservation Hall and teach us some pertinent info, like the art of tailgating the trombone.

There were two other family bands out there on the street: David & Roselyn, and Doreen & Lawrence. We bonded and stuck together in the middle of all the chaos, knowing any day could hold danger, excitement, or utter boredom. Like a second mother, Roselyn took the time to show us documentaries on great jazz and blues singers. She was especially taken with the 1957 concert of Billie Holiday at CBS Studios, when she was at her most stoned. I wondered where she was. She wasn't there in her body.

Daryl Johnson was a grand marshal and tap dancer, sliding so smoothly. He would show up in his tails with a fake dead bird attached to his shoulder and peacefully say goodbye like he was actually leading a jazz funeral. He was a quiet drunk. We would go to his family house with Popeyes chicken and everyone in the family would be screaming at a decibel level of 11. I understood then why he was a quiet drinker. He also taught us how to utilize the perks of private gigs. At a party for a football team, Daryl was at the buffet, stuffing big pieces of salmon in his tuxedo pockets. My dad asked what he was doing. He said he was making up for the low payroll.

"Uncle Sidney" Snow taught us music theory. He was a fun jokester. He played any standard, but he loved gypsy music in particular. He was a prominent R&B sideman for many major recordings with New Orleans artists. Rumor has it he even taught John Lennon a few lessons.

Many musicians could have made The Big Time, but they didn't want to pay the price of being on the road and corporate requirements. They're happy gigging around town, living the lifestyle, getting stoned or drunk. Some recovered. Some are dead from habits.

We never drank or smoked. Watching from a child's sober eye was intriguing.

Jackson Square has a pattern that history and time have not changed much. It awes, nurtures, and horrifies me to see that same narrative after so many years. With so many layers of history, Jackson Square feels like a melancholy place. From past public hangings to port plagues, from whores and hustlers to the cathedral where the most distinguished marriage unions in society still occur, it is a place where displaced characters find a new secondary family that understands and accepts them with all their eccentricities.

The old-school players hold the traditions as they slowly fade away, the newbies come searching for some alternative way to live a more fulfilling life. The truly creative visual artists who don't have gallery deals, but who must create their art or they will die.

That is the world I grew up in.

We lived on a homemade paddle wheel boat next to the Natchez showboat on the Mississippi River. We trooped from the Marigny neighborhood to the Square every day to play music, eventually creating a homestead in the Treme on Governor Nicholls Street across from the Andrews family. We were surrounded by so many musicians ready to share themselves with us, with no etiquette filters.

"Fuck man, ya know what I'm saying?" said the old jazz man to Marisa, who nodded her head, not knowing what he was talking about. I wouldn't be the person I am without all of the colorful experiences that widened my mind through osmosis, thanks to my dad. I'm thankful to those who gave of themselves with no ulterior motives. Just communion and love.

When I die, I decided long ago, I want my ashes to be spread over Jackson Square with a full traditional jazz band of fellow brother players performing (In Her Sweet Little) "Alice Blue Gown" (Joseph McCarthy and Harry Tierney). Maybe in my afterlife I'll float around and witness all the shenanigans with a smile. Because you know, "I'd Rather Be In New Orleans!"

The Art of Writing

When we were little kids growing up on homemade paddle wheel showboats built out of scrap wood that we all as a big family unit collected on the Mississippi River, we each had a 4 x 8 wood box where we slept on the roof of the raft. After a hot day of long Work Group sessions where the kids were made to listen to the dialogues between issue and solution, it was a blessing and a curse to go to bed in our boxes. I hated to be alone.

Through trial and error, my dad mastered the craft of raft design, but he was never an interior decorator. What he did do was make sure we each had one nine-volt battery to go to a cheap plastic lantern so we could read. If we used up our battery voraciously reading *Trixie Belden* mysteries or the required masterpiece, *Voltaire* by Candide, we were out of luck until the pocket change came in for a new one.

I love the smell of fresh-cut wood. It reminds me of my childhood room on the raft. Shadow-lit unpainted wood with nails holding thrift-store tutus and garbage-find ball gowns for a nine-year-old. In light of us being so poor, libraries around the country were my babysitters to read all day, about topics from Hitler to Marilyn Monroe, while my parents worked a new town for signs and saving souls.

Penmanship was a craft worth developing because one's letter is one's word. My grandma's was so elegant. But I emulated my aunt's bold hand from her high school autograph book that she gave me.

I got an F in English in eighth grade, one of the two years I wasn't home-schooled. It was quite confusing, because I was a straight A student, other than flunking drama as well. (Oh, and I failed the 20-minute mile requirement in PE three times.) I was disappointed in myself because I didn't want to let down Mrs. Palmer. She was my soft-spoken home room angel and my English teacher, who took me under her wing and out to see theater in Austin.

When the hour is quiet, I love to write. There's no one to make negative commentary, no one to judge or put you down, no feeling of insecurity that your pitch sucks and your stomach is too big for the right dress. It's a moment when you are truly allowed to be you. For better or worse. I am still trying to understand the role of semicolons...

After the demise of my marriage and the loss of my dad and my brother, I shifted my focus back to reading. David Sedaris' *When You Are Engulfed in Flames* was my first read after a sabbatical from reading and being a whore for distraction from the pain of life.

I reconnected with a best friend: me. Who needs therapy when a good pen put to paper with truth comes out? It's free. It's your word. And it feels great to speak your truth with no "yeah but"s or addendums. It seems every writer I know wants to write the Great American Novel.

* * * * *

Rules of the Writing Game

Punctuation. I pay ongoing attention to making sure that the comma and period are appropriate to my chosen words. I know the exclamation point is supposed to be used only rarely. I tend want to put five of them after a sentence to exclaim those words to the world. (Also, using fancy words just for the sake of it makes me seem absolutely full of myself, ya dig?) I am still intrigued by the semicolon. I rarely use it because I really don't know what it's for. How do you know if you're just making a run-on sentence in a somewhat allowable manner? Quotation marks are a pain in the rear. The quote within a quote has to be triple checked by my eye. Especially where the period should go.

Words. They make or break a person. I choose my words carefully. Once they come out, I can never take them back. Shortening of words is a sacrilege to some great writers. Chop as much fat as possible off so the message cuts through.

Obscenities. I try to avoid using obscenities when there are so many other options with more power. Generally, cursing is low grade. So, unless a person's character comes from a certain slice of life, I prefer not to demean myself by using vulgarities unless absolutely necessary to make a point.

Content. What is worth really sharing? Maybe it's just stories to be told because they are so outlandish and hilarious, or maybe they represent the broader human experience. It would be spectacular to capture the reader without a pinpoint ending.

Capital letters. I've learned they're not needed on every letter, word, sentence, or paragraph. They make it seem like yelling. My ex-manager did that once in an email with serious information that made me feel like I was being scolded. When I angrily called her on appearing mad for no reason, she blasély said she was just being emphatic. She had the em-pha-sis on the wrong sy-la-ble.

Spelling. Spell-check always corrects my correct word to some other word completely. I proofread (usually). "Bei mir bist du schoen" when spell-checked comes out as "My dingleberry Schoenberg." I now take the time to look up the spelling and meaning, as well as the way to say it. Who knew that "sovereign" wasn't pronounced "so-ver-ain"? I didn't, until my mom and sister almost fell down laughing their heads off when I said it.

I've come to realize a person can be enchantingly hypnotized with the right words. I can make their stomach drop and fall right into my lair. Or I could say the wrong ones and it's "off with your head." For example, "You are so entrancing while you dance freely with the wind blowing through your long, lush hair." "You fucking white bitch with red lipstick" is not quite as alluring.

"Baby girl, you make my heart sing. I look in your eyes and I see stars. Your lips taste like sweet cherries. Without the beauty of you, my life would be so much less enthralling. The way you view the world makes me want to live in your kaleidoscope universe forever" sounds much better than "Bitch, get your big fat juicy ass over here. I'm your man. Do your hair and nails and give me a blowjob, and I'll be your motherfucker for life."

The handwritten letter is a dying art form. I write letters of love every so often and always feel better afterwards.

I wrote and recorded a song called "Bouncing in a Bubble." It had a percussive rhythm, like the way Roland Guerin played his electric bass slap solos. I rhymed as much as I could to the rhythmic cadence he played, mostly starting words with B, for that popping sound on the vocal. At the end of a show one time, after performing it, an uber fan came backstage and said to me, "Ingrid, I didn't know you sang in Ebonics!"

To me, the main rule in the writing game is honesty. Seek the truth and it shall free you. Maybe inspire others to do the same. How *dopely* magnificent would that be?

Performer

Some people never figure out what their life mission statement is. I knew at age four while doing cartwheels for the hotel lobby guests what mine was: to make people happy. What could be better in life? I was a big ol' ham wearing thrift store tutus and 100 plastic barrettes in a crooked home-cut bob hairstyle. Always with red glitter polish.

I started with Isadora Duncan style free dance, evolved into ballet training, and then the dream of working with Bob Fosse. I prepared to move to New York City as a young adult, with a solid resume under my belt. My resume consisted of two Mexican circuses, a cameo in a Richard Gere film, and singing and dancing on every street corner around the world. After being laughed at by a panel of judges at Radio City Music Hall auditions while singing "Some of These Days," it quickly became quite apparent that formal training with "shuffle ball change" was needed, as part of a complete reconfiguring.

Build it and they will come.

I started my own band. What qualified me to be a bandleader? Nothing. Except a vision. I wanted to put trad jazz on the map the way rock 'n' roll was. *What gives you the right to work with the greatest musicians in the world?* asked WWOZ. By being the weakest link to learn, treating everyone fairly with payroll, and finding opportunities by walking the street and not taking a bandleader cut.

The greatest joy, outside of proper love-making, is what happens when the fourth wall comes down between the audience and the band, and you are the conduit to bring that god-like moment to fruition. It is an ethereal feeling.

What's next? Make an audience fall down laughing so hard it hurts.

Write the truth. Create one "bible piece" song that makes mailbox money for retirement, hit that high note like a trumpet player would, so clear with pitch and reverberation like a bell, instead of sliding into it like a trombone. Boy, do I love the trombone. Players like Todd and my ex-boyfriend, Grandville, Bonerama's harmonies... the trombone is the sultriest horn instrument, in my opinion.

No one knows what the future holds. But what I do know is, whatever the vehicle, to be a jokester with 10,000 hours put in, if I can make people laugh, or even better, make people cry by moving them, I will have done my job in this life.

My Voice

My dad once said, "You'll never be a singer."

I replied, "Oh yeah? Watch me."

Every voice that is distinct in music is imperfect. Include me in that equation. When I decided to take a chance and divert from choreography and dance, I discovered my voice was shy but pure. I sang with joy and enthusiasm. The audiences I sang for loved that purity.

In the two years following my divorce, my creative well was dry. I was singing like a war horse to pay the bills. Later, my newfound freedom to really sing what I felt made my heart pound with fear. I felt like a mute who wanted to vomit out and purge the emotions that had been brewing. But I was afraid.

I have a love/hate relationship with my voice. I am a good singer, but as of this book's writing, I haven't recorded my best work yet.

There are so many components to being a qualified singer that constantly need attending to:

Tone
Resonance
Air to sound ratio
Volume level of projection
Diction
Pitch
Timing
Phrasing
Themes and variations on melody and lyric
Relationship and space within in band ensemble dynamic
Tempo
Key
Personality
Feeling
Honesty
Posture
Diaphragm control

Mathematical equating of air to length of notes before breathing
Ear training
Eye contact with audience
Breaking down the fourth wall
Choice of material and style of music that suits voice and personality
Language of musical communication to musicians playing without speaking a word
Taking the song in — taking the song out
Counting right tempos
Physical stance
Knowing when to dominate the stage and when to support players while they're soloing
Percussion and/or clapping (or not)
How to dress
How to create a brand with a look
Knowing what gear to use
Professional etiquette on gigs and (pre- and post-)
How to lead
How to relate to musicians
How to relate to fans
How to network
How to negotiate the gig deal
How to get gigs
How to keep gigs
The front person's responsibilities
How to hang with the guys
How to soundcheck
How to be an entertainer as well as a great singer

These are all variables that must be incorporated to make a living as a singer. My favorite singers are not technicians, but they give emotional content. It's easy to break down all the parts and pieces of how much practicing someone has done to get their chops. Move me and I'm yours loyally, forever.

Some days I love what's coming out of my mouth and other days I want to wring my own neck for failing to hit the high "money" note. The important thing is to relax and keep trying to make the zenith, apex, opus of making the listener happy with what I can share with my thousands of hours put in to be a contender.

*****

On the *And One*

Music is funny. Jazz singers get to hear the chord and come in behind the beat. Soul and R&B singers come in precisely on the *one* or the *and one*.

My licensing guy in Nashville asked me to supply a version of "Love Train" (The O'Jays) for a national commercial. I recorded it as a duet with renowned choir director TC Hawkins. TC told me that he didn't want to lose the pounding urban bass beat from the track that seemed to have disappeared on the overdub sessions, and thought that maybe my vocal tracks should be replaced by somebody more qualified for that style. I told him he could kick my butt into place vocally. After literally counting loose change on the floor of the dark, hot storage unit where my few belongings were housed, and hiking it over to his studio on foot, I was determined to stay in the game. TC patiently guided me on how to sing on the *and one*.

> "All of you brothers over in Africa
> Tell all the folks in Egypt, and Israel, too
> Please don't miss this train at the station
> 'Cause if you miss it, I feel sorry, sorry for you"

The Tree of Jazz

The first time I saw the Tree of Jazz poster was backstage during our first headlining show at Ronnie Scott's, the "Blue Note" of London jazz clubs. I was so nervous to perform for high-end chaps.

The thing about Europeans who respect jazz is that they don't applaud or speak at all until they give a standing ovation at the bitter sweaty end. Until then, you're left wondering what you did wrong after you've gotten used to raucous New Orleans audiences.

My band, The Flying Neutrinos, was signed to The Cure's record label. The Cure's management, who booked the tour, allowed us to acquire prominent press and a higher level of opportunity. Throughout many adventures in Europe, from commune gigs in Copenhagen to being bitten on the neck at an African dance club and kicked by a club goer (both in Paris), I reflected on the Tree of Jazz poster. It became a staple piece in my understanding of music.

When I got the call to perform as a headliner at the Edinburgh Jazz Festival, what came back to me was the map of American music depicted on the poster. I know it almost like the back of my hand. A gentleman who owned a major label stated to me, "The world wants to wear blue jeans, play jazz, drink Coke... Japan, Russia, Mexico... The only gift we have, by default, is to be born an American."

The stump of the tree starts in New Orleans. The roots spread out to Texas and Mississippi with blues chords. As the tree trunk grows up the Mississippi River to traditional jazz in Chicago in the 1930s, branches extend to the 1940s Big Band era in New York City to 1950s cool jazz in California. Every root and branch shows the journey of the artists of that era.

There's nothing as potent as a 1-4-5 blues. Expound upon that and make melodies. Lyrics. Arrangements. Instrumental choices. Closing out a very long phone conversation with my heady manager, my conclusion was similar to what I read in Duke Ellington's biography. He would pick his players by their talents. Orchestrate songs with arrangements around those talents, never dictating ideas that were not organic to what they did well.

To me, it's serendipity to have encountered the poster in London in 1996 and called on it to go full circle back to Europe in 2017.

Louis Armstrong

Louis Armstrong is a hero of mine and one of my greatest influences. New Orleans celebrates him the first weekend of every August during Satchmo Fest at the New Orleans Mint. (I was proud to be presented at The Mint for the premiere exhibition of "New Orleans Women in Jazz." Kristin Fouquet photographed me in a ball gown in front of a train at the Press Street Railroad Tracks.)

I've met three people who met Louis Armstrong. Their stories resonated with me.

1. My dad, who was lucky enough to hear him while standing side stage one month before Louis Armstrong passed. My father said he was in awe at how he lit up the stage when he seemed so tired backstage.

2. A guy from Shanachie Records in New York City used to come to our shows all the time. He inherited a storage unit owned by Louis Armstrong's marijuana dealer. The guy used to ship weed to Louis when he was overseas. He brought me a letter Louis Armstrong penciled in 1932 asking this guy to "ship his Arrangements."

3. The Flying Neutrinos used to play six-week runs in Atlantic City at the Showboat Casino. One day a kind old lady came up to me on break. She was friends with Louis Armstrong's wife, Lucille. She brought a letter he wrote her for me to see. She told me that during the parties they threw, he'd ask her, with a hand in her arm, if she was happy and if he could do anything to make her happier.

Here's to celebrating Mr. Louis Armstrong.

Storyville, Teddy Riley, and Cutting Chops

When The Flying Neutrinos Family Band used to play every day in front of Jackson Square, I was the dancer, washtub bass player, and choreographer. Rarely did I sing.

B.B. King's Blues Club used to be Storyville Jazz Hall on Decatur Street. My dad used to take me there as a youth to get my dancing chops cut with the trumpeter Teddy Riley and his band. It was a special time because it was just the two of us walking from the Treme. My dad and I would have serious talks and get a candy bar on the way.

It was rare to have alone time with my dad. I'll never forget doing the splits in front of Teddy Riley's Australian clarinet player, and the guy whispered in between his reed and solo note to get the fuck away from him.

As I performed on the same stage 30 years later, I missed Teddy. He was a tough and kind man. "In My Solitude" and "I Cover the Waterfront" were his consistent go-tos in an evening full of a huge catalogue of music played.

Full circle.

Uncle Lionel

Uncle Lionel
On the other shore,
"We'll Meet Again" once more,
Please tell my dad hello.

Your funeral,
Most powerful experience I've had,
You gave so much love,
Chills up and down my back.

Kind and funny,
Talent, elegance, and grace.
Never a moment you weren't
Dressed to the Ace.

Sitting in together,
Sharing scotch on the streets,
Mardi Gras day,
Preservation Hall gig,
Your whistling nose solo
Took their breath away.

The end of an era,
New Orleans class,
I miss the things you represented
That are almost passed.

March on with your bass drum, lead the way,
We'll all be there to join you
One fine heavenly day.

Red Roses, Ferraris, and Reality

I was asked to perform at Oak Alley Plantation for the unveiling of the new Ferrari model. The client put me through days of covering their bases with their riders, the most complicated paperwork I've ever had to fill out, other than Russian visas. Why couldn't Ferrari follow through on the contractual agreement? We were paid 50 percent in advance, and we were supposed to be paid the balance at the end of the gig. As stated, 50 percent on completion of performance.

Going on day four after the gig, and still no pay or clarity on when it would be finalized. After playing for a most high-falutin gig, with overtime thrown in free by New Orleans' finest musicians, who cared enough to keep going full steam to make sure the client was happy, we were served dinner on a tea-sized plate and then bawled out because the guys took a photo with the sleek premiere edition Ferrari.

The event was magnificent, under oak trees lit with bamboo lanterns. Ferrari had a thousand roses paid for in advance on tables and the finest wine for the corporate Italians who were flown in for the event. Why was the band lowest on the totem pole, as is so often the case, even with a signed contract? We were paid eventually, but not soon enough for me to avoid an eviction notice.

*****

I had to move on November 15, and I didn't know where I was going. I had given the landlady $1,800 toward my $3,000 debt and told her I could pay the rest by the following week. I still had to move. My roommate was broke, so I was covering her. She didn't know where she was going either. She had a young daughter, Delia, a 4.0 student. I was worried for them.

I was juggling monies and trying to decide whether to leave town. Too many out-of-town players were taking over gigs that didn't even pay enough to cover the insane rents. And the lack of any kind of communication with Ava or bridging a gap by my ex was driving me berserk with rage and frustration. I felt like I'd been pillaged, and it was messing up my self-esteem, which was already low. I was trying to fuck my way out of sorrow like a whore, but of course it was not working. Couldn't any of those guys have brought some groceries over at least?

I was stuck in every way. And I guess the biggest shock to my nervous system was that this was where I ended up, when I had only tried to give my all and be the nicest possible person I could be to all walks of life. The people I had cared for in their hour of need hadn't called once to check in.

I felt very, very tired and alone, even though there had been so much kindness from new sources. My ex and his new partner were living their new lives together. She took Ava to school every morning, not me. I felt like my heart had been broken and I couldn't seem to figure out how to mend it. I was still missing my dad too.

Without Music

Without music,
I don't know what I would do.
The silence of life,
Would kill me through and through.
Every morning,
I wake up staring at the ceiling,
Thinking of nothing,
Existentialism is there.

Until that flip of the switch,
On the thrift store radio,
Playing trad jazz on WWOZ,
I wonder, what's the point
Of being me?

Then the notes play familiar songs,
I remember where I belong.
Here.
Then nothing's wrong.

A dance, a singalong,
This solitary figure
Is no longer alone.
It doesn't matter
That no one's called on the phone.

People, I love them,
But they are strange.
They do things I can't explain.

Music is yours,
Always safe, always close.
And so...
When the lonely night closes in,
And you don't have a lover to win,

On the phone
Held closely tight,
Stevie Wonder
Bids you goodnight.

In the solace of life,
What would it be
Without music?
I would die.
Music is the church of sanity.

Stevie Wonder

Growing up in a family band led by a father whose idol was Al Jolson, a rock star in his mind, listening to Elvis was my rebellion. Stevie Wonder came into my life as a young adult exploring music. He made marker moments in my life.

"A Place in the Sun" played in the car while I drove to a weekly gig in New York City from Connecticut to get warmed up.

While living on a reservation in New Mexico with our family band to learn music from a high school music teacher, my father and I chatted about how such a simple phrase as "I Just Called to Say I Love You," could be such a huge hit. Simplicity and honesty was the conclusion.

The Flying Neutrinos were playing at Nell's, a hot spot club on 14th Street in New York City, and there he was in the front row. On the set break Stevie came up to say hello to the band so kindly and asked if he could sit in with us. All the guys in the band lit up with excitement.

While living alone in Gentilly, I was invited by a good friend to hear the concert celebration of *Songs in the Key of Life*, at the New Orleans Arena. I witnessed our hometown hero Matt Rhody get the featured spot of a lifetime on his violin. The audience went crazy with pride.

That album became my bible piece for a few years. "If It's Magic" was my favorite live presentation. "Love's in Need of Love Today" was the ringtone for my wakeup alarm while I toured the world in many fancy but lonely hotel rooms.

Stevie's music makes me try to be a better person because he chooses words of love. With the world such a mess, I think Stevie Wonder should run for president.

P.S. Kermit Ruffins as VP!

Music Warriors

They carry their instruments
Like weapons and shields
Marching into the night
Fighting the good fight
In hopes of winning a soul or two.

As the nightclub party roars,
Note for note, blow by blow
Exuding their precious energies.

Forging through the waves
Of unconscious people,
Stumbling drunken
In the streets.

A glimmer, a wave, a connection,
A moment in musical time,
not to be denied, by anyone alive,
Success.
A small win in the big war.

Glorious, exhausted, inspired,
They march into the future of the unknown,
Dragging their gear behind them into the sunrise,

"They Shoot Horses, Don't They?"
Yes, they do, for the price of $125.

Security

Gentrification. Call Hail Mary. Three gigs.
Fall breezes have started.
It pains me to not have the means.
Worked so hard, as one should.
Took the bus downtown.
$2.50 left to this 10,000-hour clown.
Best dress and box cutter for security's sake.
A smile for all in this lifeboat called swim.

*****

From the Streets

No matter what the gilded dream,
When raised on the streets,
All that's needed is a can of beans.
Get up on the count of nine,
No matter how bruised,
The boxer is fine.
Bam! Pow! Ow!
Get up.
I was raised on the streets.
Singing for my supper.
Elevated to status quo.
Up and down is how it goes.
The streets are where it began.
No one can tell you where it's at.
Only you make the choice,
To speak clearly and sing your voice.
To dance until your "Red Shoes" turn Blue.
Everybody's rules bounce off you.
Purity Cowboy.
The streets will make you a man.

Ten Cents in a Mansion

Ten cents in a mansion,
The bills are always due,
The first of the month comes,
Quicker than you.

Ten cents in a mansion,
A can of beans will do,
Pursuing higher heights in life,
Outside, society's silly rules.

Ten cents in a mansion,
Dig deep to hold grace,
Never be a beggar
In a real friend's face.

Ten cents in a mansion,
Humbled the spirit, sweat, heart,
Asking for a soda water,
Starts conversations about art.
And life.

Ten cents in a mansion,
No other way I want to live.
When you give to others,
Reciprocation of connection is the gift.

So tomorrow,
These ten cents will up the game.
Take that can of beans,
Some tacos to begin again,
Play an old record,
Jump into creating a dream.
Ten cents in a mansion is the political theme.
Keep on trying to destiny.
Poetry in motion.

Ode to my dad's beatnik upbringing in 1950s San Francisco.

A Rainy Sunday

After putting every penny I owned into my vision of a new creative communal home on Burgundy Street in the Marigny, I awoke on a rainy Sunday. There was no Wi-Fi, the screen on the phone had cracked, and after I set up a desk to work near an open window, the laptop got wet.

I said to myself, it's time to start reading again. I took my two dogs to the local dog run and there was a Little Library box. Yes. All paperbacks. I picked a memoir for myself and the history of the Mets for a friend, and I thought, I should pick a third for a Holy Trinity, so I pulled *The Accidental Tourist* and randomly opened it to a page that had two hundred-dollar bills straight up and a twenty that was bent in half over a note on a spiral bind that said, "Dear Jessica, I love you so much and I don't have the words to say it. Love, Kenny C."

Lunch at Buffa's was on me that day.

Again, I walked to the same dog run and came across a book being tossed out among many in a box, *Gone with the Wind*. Scarlett was an idol to me growing up. I read the book three times. While there are splits in beliefs in the story, if you know the writer's backstory, you will be sold on goodness. Margaret Mitchell gave her profits to her Black lover to start the first college for Black doctors.

I chose three books to replace the ones I took. *Gone with the Wind* would hold the pay-it-forward money for a Christmas gift from the Little Library.

I hoped the bum ten feet away would choose literature.

An Hour in the Life

I spent a day hauling boxes and practicing songs, organizing the chaos in the new Burgundy Street home, a flagship mini mansion. I was feeling anxious, like in those dreams of being naked in school, or ill-prepared for a Broadway show as you step under the spotlight not having every word memorized.

I got into it with the guy renting the slave quarters in our shared space, who was drunk and stoned every morning of every day. He was an Elvis impersonator in Las Vegas. I listened and tried to understand his mentality. We sang Sun Sessions songs to bond. He placed a small pile of dog poop on an *Offbeat* magazine and placed it in front of our back door one morning. Unacceptable! *Offbeat* is like our bible.

My roommate and I wrote him a kind note on the finest stationary we had, saying we would like to be good neighbors. He wouldn't accept the note to read and started yelling at me. Barely holding my temper after the unfair violation, barefoot in the yard cleaning up the dog poop, I told him if he was having an issue, that he'd better watch out because I was about to start my period and I had been nothing but kind to him.

He ate Thanksgiving leftovers in my home, he blasted his music, and when he expounded endlessly, I listened kindly. I was so mad when I walked up the stairs into my space. It was the first time I realized how much rage was coursing through my veins because of other violations. My roommate and I took deep breaths, acknowledging that we were better human beings and worked for hours on the new space.

Boxes, chaos, record player set up, Beatles and Donovan records playing, rehearsal room for the next day's first big to-do here. We finally had a living room rehearsal space set up in a quiet zone, candles, mood lighting, and Feng shui'd. Just as we were talking and relaxing, the art piece on the mantel, which says "Be of Love," and which we spent 15 minutes measuring placement on, came crashing down. It landed on the mantel with a bang, eight inches from where we had aligned it straight up, perfectly placed between Uncle Lionel's photograph and the Asian lucky plants. It was more than strange the way it precisely decided where it, or somebody wanted it, to be. Logically, if it had fallen from its height and placement, it would have broken glass on the floor.

Then, I got a message from the owner's son of the Mexican circus I always fondly speak of, as it changed my life... Rolando "Circo Hermanos" Bell. He was always the disciplined one, juggling, cycling, practicing silently and methodically at all hours outside of the tent. He was with Barnum and Bailey in Mobile, Alabama. I had spent years trying to find out what happened to the whole family, and I guess it was time to know.

Dear Ava,

I love you.

I literally almost died spending two days birthing you. Everything I could possibly do to nurture you I did. From nursing you for three years instead of two months. Sleeping on your floor to try and get you into your room. Taking you to all of your friends' birthday parties, buying you your heart's desire the best I could with the means I had as a singer.

To the very day I was told to leave the house I mainly supported, most of our family time together, bringing you water, detaching the electronics that were clamped in your hand and blaring in your ears, lighting up your face and keeping you from going into REM mode, to the final night I was there before being told to leave.

I never yelled at you, never hurt you, only tried my very best to be on my game for you from the morning alarm until after you were asleep.

Did I drink too much?

Yes. I was lonely. Very, very unhappy. And whatever I had hoped for in my marriage, coming from my strange background wanting normalcy, was even stranger to see that normal families don't talk about their day, or ask how the other is, or do anything fun, spontaneous, and special together. I am not able to pretend to communicate with you in texting language such as LOL or TY. I can't do it in an ongoing way. It's false. I care too much about you.

I want to know what you are thinking and feeling and what I can do to help you get where you want to in this life before I'm gone. That takes discussion. Problem solving. Whatever is going on in your head now with regard to your not being ready to talk to me for a couple of minutes, which I find extremely hurtful, is going to be resolved when you actually see that I'm not the monster you've built up in your own little solitary head.

I was never considered in any way in my marriage. Never asked once how I would like something to be — or to collaborate on the plan from the house design to road travel to your schooling options... That's a hard thing to swallow when you are a go-getter.

So, I drank too much.

My life is very, very hard right now getting back up on my feet. Losing everything, from you, to my home, down to my driver's license with an $850 fine because your dad removed the insurance on my car. But I am focused and no longer feeling like a victim. There are many who have come in to talk in a real way. Share. Create. And be kind.

I hope one day when you are ready to step out of your fear cocoon, you will take the five-minute drive or two-minute phone call to see that I'm different because of a unique upbringing. And I think those values that were passed on to me are good and valuable to survive in life. I hope someday to share some of them with you. All my love to you in these confusing times. I truly hope you have someone to talk to about what you are feeling to process. You know my phone number. I will text you my basic updates as I figure out my plans. You are free to connect when you are ready.

Love always and forever,

Your mom

Majestical Man

There once was a majestical man who magically appeared everywhere I was, driving around in his mint green Rolls-Royce. When I was a little girl performing in Jackson Square with the family band, he would always walk by, stop, and listen behind us with a quiet smile. Who was that refined, sharply dressed, pensive man?

Years passed. When I returned home from a ten-year musical journey in New York City, there he was again appearing in my life's impressions, coming to my yearlong gig at The Ritz to listen silently and solitarily without imbibing. At the post office, Dorignac's grocery, fancy car driving on Veterans Boulevard, his house next to my Irish friend's, in the restaurant window at the Central Business District (CBD), he was everywhere I went.

How does one do that?

I spent years reading autobiographies of others who shared stories of his musical genius and successful business strategies.

After Katrina I was asked to perform with this enigma of a man at the Hearst Tower in **New York City** for New Orleans and New York society. On a winter day, at afternoon sound check in the dressing room, only the two of us silently stood and witnessed through floor-to-ceiling windows on the 57th floor the evacuation of a large plane lying flat in the Hudson River.

We played as a duo together for the dichotomy of New Orleans second liners and **New York City** observers too shy to join in. During the first ten months I spent in Gentilly starting a new life, I was strangely situated directly between the recording studio where this majestical man wrote and recorded his catalogue of hits and the funeral parlor where my dad was cremated.

Every day while walking to the Brown Derby, I would pass the studio and wonder what his thought process was to make such great music.

When my friend and renowned bassist Roland Guerin got married, there he was. We spoke about a few common subjects that bonded us. I watched him standing behind the couple sharing their moving marriage vows under the setting Fall sunlight, wondering what he was thinking.

November 10, 2015: I woke up to a phone call with the news of his death. I was hit with a wall of shock. The man who was everywhere would be there no more.

Thank you, Allen Toussaint, for deeply impressing and inspiring this girl.

* * * * *

Orpheum Theater

It was your final show. You were laid out in a majestic coffin and with grand cascading flowers of white. Every bit of international talent and humanity influenced by you was there to celebrate you.

That one humanitarian could write, create, produce change, and touch all walks of life so deeply is what one could only hope for.

Looking at the stage, listening, knowing every player and their backstory of trials with tribulations celebrate you in this roller coaster journey called life, I felt so many emotions.

The last time I was in that space it was a movie theater. When I was eight, my dad took me to a documentary about the Amazonian people. I watched a naked woman birth a baby alone, holding on to a tree and squatting, after which she ripped off the umbilical cord with her teeth, took her child, and walked on.

Full circle to death, saying goodbye to one of the most elegant men I've ever met. At the end of one of the most heart-wrenching experiences I'd ever been through, a large, kind lady next to me handed me a *Now and Later* candy. That said it all.

Ragtime Talks

At the Finale Ragtime Festival produced by Tonya Excho at Southport Hall, I was wearing the full ball gown flapper dress Lavay Smith had given me. I had a long conversation with Mr. Vernel Bagneris outside the club. He remembered my family as street performers. What a gift it was to talk with him quietly and honestly in depth for a long time. I liked sitting with him by the levy as the sun was setting, discussing the original idea for *One Mo' Time*.

Vernel talked about his work on a few major films, including *Ray* and *Bessie*. It was so nice to have a dialogue with someone doing creative work with care. I'd been trying to get on track.

My original dream was to be a choreographer. That's what he was. Listening to his detailed stories made me happy.

When I was eight years old, my father took me to see *One Mo' Time* at the Toulouse Theatre. James Booker was playing piano facing a brick wall in the hallway before show time, but no one at the bar was paying attention. I was a lucky kid! Sitting in the dark theater seat watching a big mama belt out the blues entranced me. I knew that was where I wanted to be.

Circus Lights

Under the tent
On top of the hay
Smell of peanuts
Feeling gay.

Something is about
To be unwound
A world of beauty
Quite renowned.

Tarnished suits
Warrior chests
Full of strength
On their vests.

Elegant women
Twelve years old
Daughters of the owner
In tarnished sequin gold.

In the fog
Surrounding the real world
Lies a striped tent
Where dreams are learned.

What appears to be
Isn't what it seems
Magic lies
Not a dream.

You can be the glowing star
Whether in the ring
Or on the bench afar.

Under the circus lights
Casts a spell
Glowing bulbs,

Sequin shine,
Acts unveil
This life is mine.

Lady Zipperette

The circus known as the Squirrel Nut Zippers arrived with precision and professionalism at the mini mansion on Burgundy Street that my friend and I were renting. It was 2016, the 20-year anniversary of the release of their album *Hot*. The team showed up from Mississippi, Tennessee, Los Angeles, and North Carolina, with an upright piano and drums to convene musically in New Orleans. They took care of business, setting up efficiently.

I took care of their rider... fried chicken and cheap beer from Manchu on Claiborne Avenue. Two nervous wives were with me, wondering where the hell they were.

Jesus, I'm craving a team who says, we are not moving on from this song until it's ready to be moved on from. A hungry appetite musically fulfilled. I have a lot of personal practice to do. This pop band wants their hooks to be precise; what's their problem? Kidding. That's why they are successful.

Seven hours later, with an eight-piece band set up in my acoustically perfect and cozy 14-foot-ceilinged living room space, we all agreed to disagree about what was needed to make a great show. In the middle of the first rehearsal, the landlord, Old School Sterling, showed up. My roommate, who was hosting the players' wives and girlfriends on the long and winding staircase, came and tapped me on the shoulder in the middle of an ongoing song, pointing a finger to the front door. He was there a day early to collect the rent.

Thinking we were being shut down, I explained while walking him to the bottom of the grand staircase (as the band was blowing their full brains out to "Put a Lid on It") that this would only happen once a month. Old School Sterling had sternly pointed his finger at me three weeks earlier when we signed the lease and stated, "YOU are responsible for the rent," sending a shiver down my spine. Now, with a shoulder shrug, he stated, "It's New Orleans." And he walked away.

The next day, I gave Sterling the rent in cash. I thanked him for this new start. He said, everyone deserves second chances.

* * * * *

They were the moments you wait a lifetime for. They were the moments why I perform. They were the moments of musical church.

I set the alarm for 3:15 a.m., which I slept through, after a few full days of long rehearsals, photo shoots, and surprise preview shows. I had five minutes to throw a tour's worth of costumes into a couple of duffel bags as the band packed its Mercedes-Benz Sprinter outside of the Burgundy Street flagship house. We traveled in the band van as a nine-piece band all day to get to our first official show in a vintage theater in downtown Tucson, not knowing what awaited after the band's very long hiatus.

Sound check lasted three hours and was full of care and detail. We had a couple of hours to rest and dress in the hotel. Hundreds of people showed up with so much love and affection. The house was sold-out. The band conferred and shared positive messages and set list changes backstage pre-show. Then, I watched from side stage as a very nervous Jimbo Mathus, the mighty bandleader and the wizard behind the curtain, silently walked out with the band in front of a drunken audience (and his parents), as he received a standing ovation before the band even played a single note.

Whistles, applause, *we love you, we missed you...* It moved my heart to see him humbly walk out under a bright white spotlight in his red suit in fear of not knowing what lay ahead and be received with so much love.

We played a 90-minute set of utter organized cacophony with two encore tunes, followed by an hour of signing autographs and photos in front of the Rialto Theatre while listening to fans from ages nine to 69 talk about how much the Squirrel Nut Zippers meant to them.

That is why we play music.

I fell asleep in a soft bed in a quiet, dark room at 8:25 a.m. at the La Quinta on the outskirts of Tucson.

Load-up for the next town, Tempe, was in three hours. I was tired and happy.

* * * * *

Going on week three of the tour. Every show in every city had been well received. Almost all sellouts in historic old theaters and swanky large clubs. Most memorable were the two shows we played in Asheville, North Carolina, as the band got tighter and more confident.

We played for a couple thousand kids in a morning show for the Leaf Festival. High energy, hi-fives with smiling faces and drawings to show their thanks. The day before, we had closed out the day at the festival in a valley, fall leaves in full glorious display, with hundreds of peace-loving hippies responding in full love.

Being on the road with an expedited tight schedule is its own creature. After a while, all the theaters, hotel rooms, gas stations, and backstage areas start to look the same. At a certain point, we'd gone by the same road signs for cities we'd just played the week before. It was a bit discombobulating, but that band of rambunctious, talented, good people surrendered to the expectations of road life.

It was a good life. The universe had been kind.

I suggested we just don't go home; *let's take this Sprinter after our last gig for this leg of the run in Jacksonville tomorrow, go down to Miami, build two pontoons, load up and float to Cuba.* Oh wait, my father already did that.

* * * * *

Three sellout double-up shows in Minneapolis and Chicago. I loved that gig.

We walked out to cheers before a note was even played and closed out to standing ovations. After all of the work was done, the routine of the band in the van was to decompress with conversational pieces. After silly jokes, what stuck out to me was how intelligent every individual in the band was. There were discussions on physics, literature, music, politics, human nature, architecture, health... We had avid readers on board. Who needed college?

Better watch out, apart from the multitude of musical talent, if you got into a game of chess with this gang, you'd probably lose your shirt. *Detroit, here we come.*

We drove into downtown Los Angeles through the streets and past stately buildings built predominantly in the 1940s. Long past their heyday, plastered with amateur painted signs selling every good possible to customers who weren't there. What stood out to my eyes looking through the van window was the number of homeless people that were on the streets. That's pretty much the only humanity I witnessed. Tents, shopping carts, hundreds of dirty human beings ravaged by life. An apocalyptic view is what it felt like from the safe zoo cage I was in. I wondered how many of those men, women, and children got to be where they were. Were they crazy? Were they drug addicts? Were they unable to function properly in society? Or were a good percentage, like most of us, one paycheck away from being evicted and put on the street?

Intrigued. Scared. Thankful.

Our family spent many years sleeping in train and bus stations. But that was by intention. What I saw in Los Angeles was overwhelming.

We checked into a five-star hotel. As I slept in the impeccably clean bed with the softest pillows I had ever felt, I felt guilty. I don't take for granted a single second of the gifts given. I'll always know what it feels like to be an 11-year-old street urchin who was given $20 at the grocery store at Christmas to buy something nice to eat. *We raid and pillage the dressing rooms to continue to share*, said Robin Hood.

* * * * *

I'd been outdone on that trip. Asheville, North Carolina, for one night. I'd never been there before. Brand-new impressions. A kind, creative, big town where everybody seems to know each other. At least they all knew Henry Westmoreland.

We arrived in New Orleans from San Francisco at 9:30 p.m. I took a bike ride through the French Quarter, checking in with a close friend on a gig in order to let the airplane, van, methodical survival walking ya-yas out. Right after the midnight hour, me and Henry, Mr. Debonair, horn player galore of trumpet, sousaphone, and various saxophones, drove through six states on an all-nighter, watching the sunrise in a truck stop, eating breakfast of biscuits and grits, and acquiring the traditional road trip Mexican blanket. We arrived in Asheville at 1 p.m. Somehow that guy surpassed my trust in the universe. There was no plan intact, only a studio session with sousaphone to overdub parts on a friend's album, and a friend's house to crash in.

I took a long walk through town. I met a cop, who, when I was lost, showed me his badge and gun to verify he wasn't a pervert, then gave me a ride through the historical city. He talked about how low the bad cop ratio was and asked me to please speak up on their behalf. He seemed passionate about it, having been a cop for nine years, taking care to get his information correct and caring about his field. It was awfully nice to get a ride after walking for a couple of miles.

Make me a pallet on your floor was the plan with a girl Henry knew. I was up for adventures. Lying down with a last-minute connection, in a quaint home in the country, two loving dogs between my legs and arms, fresh air and crickets, and a magical display of stars.

It took ten hours to drive for an early morning solo show in New York City. Then it was back for the Squirrel Nut Zippers' Southern regional tour. I was excited and taking chances. It was a little scary. But worth the journey, as always.

Jefferson Parish Prison

"You have to let me on that plane; I'm irreplaceable!" I said to the boarding flight attendant at MSY airport in New Orleans. It was the last leg of the Squirrel Nut Zippers tour in the Northeast.

November 11, 2016: My tribe, my people, were waiting eagerly for the closing of that year's long, exhausting, exhilarating tour that had taken us all over the country and Canada. I was excited.

The airport ticket lady at the plane entrance obviously didn't think that was the case. She would not let me on that plane. In my inebriated state, I got animated.

I would like to lay out in detail why I got that drunk.

After every grueling leg of that national tour, we would come home for three to five days and then go on the next leg of the tour for another 10 days or so. That particular week I got sick, bone marrow sick in bed with the flu. I was not eating or functioning well, but I was still drinking.

A fellow musician called this kind of touring program the "Golden Handcuffs." Do you want it? Yes. Are you willing or able to pay the price for it? That's a different story.

The routine was to drive ten hours a day in the Sprinter, load into the next venue, attend sound check for three hours, eat and get ready, put on a 90-minute show, sign CDs and T-shirts for another hour, load out, go to a fancy hotel for about five hours of sleep, and then get up early and do it all over again.

I'd never been part of a group with such a rigid, rigorous schedule. No one had ever taught me how to pace myself. All-out efforts every time we played, shimmy and shake till your back breaks. I wanted to give it my all. Add day drinking to that.

I was able to accomplish what I needed to do while I was home that (unknowingly) last time. I bought new supplies for the show: a blue sequin gown, an expensive new feather headpiece. There was no costume budget, so all of that came out of my pocket. I made $250 a show.

Jimbo said we were saving up the war chest. Who was I not to be a team player? He wanted to add light blue to the band look, so I paid for my new performance clothes to please him.

I packed up my Louis Vuitton bag, my dress suit bag, my carry-on 1950s "I Love Lucy" leopard bowling bag, riding jodhpurs, a wifebeater shirt with a zip-up hoodie, and a pair of Kenneth Cole leather hunting boots.

I arrived at the airport after having drunk a small bottle of bourbon in the cab on the way there. I was getting agitated that they would not let me on the plane. I knew that there was no sub for me, and I knew that it was a very serious situation.

Why was I drinking? Why *wasn't* I drinking? I had so many problems hanging on my shoulders. The bottom line is drinking was a band-aid, a way to keep it all copacetic.

I remember entering the airport. I remember seeing the violin player in front of me going to the gate. By the time I got to the gate, the bourbon had kicked in; since I'd hardly eaten anything for five days, its effect was magnified. I prayed nobody recognized me. The band on the road had often spent many hours waiting for some of the other players to show up after getting lost in the night, yet they were never fired.

I was protesting the decision to not let me on the plane when a policeman came along. When he pulled out his handcuffs, I got scared. I pushed his shoulder to keep him from putting them on me. In a slow-motion moment, I saw those handcuffs come out at me. He judo threw me on the floor so hard and fast, yanked my arms behind my back, handcuffed me so tight, it felt like he broke my wrists.

This can't be real, I thought. That wasn't even the worst part. The worst part was being put into one of those 1920s wheelchairs that had wood slats on the back and in the elevated leg lifts. He put my bag and headpieces on my lap, put my suit bag behind it, and basically rolled me out of the airport in front of everyone to see.

Apparently, I do not remember the dialogue, but I read it when the police wrote their statement. It stated, I kept yelling, "It's not my fault, it's not my fault. It's all Clyde's fault. It's all Clyde's fault," in a completely panicked tone.

Obviously, there were still so many issues that were swimming in my head with regard to my marriage and about what had happened. I felt everything had been blamed on me. In and out of blurry drunkenness, hangovers, confusion, and cohesiveness, small tidbits of flashes of memories were coming to consciousness.

I was in a police car at night. I didn't know where I was going, and I was very scared. I kept asking the policeman to please take the handcuffs off because I was behind the metal window that separates the prisoner from the cop. He wouldn't listen to me. That's when I started to get frustrated. Nobody would listen to me. For somebody who likes to talk a lot and explain everything, that was maddening.

There are no words to describe the 30 hours of hell I spent in jail. I didn't understand why the band's management wasn't trying to get me out. If I was the bandleader (as I had been), and was familiar with enduring the trials and tribulations of flight factors, I would have made sure that my tribe was intact onboard. I will never understand why I was left in a prison cell when Jimbo knew what had happened and did nothing about it. Except fire me.

It hurts to be discarded. My offerings are much larger than the mistakes I make.

I arrived at the jail in Gretna, of all places. Gretna, the place nobody wants to be (at least the people I talked to). Gretna, kind of the way some people think of Chalmette. It is the end of the road.

I was in jail. I was put in the holding tank. There were about 30 women in one room, with about six bunkbeds without mattresses or blankets. It was freezing.

When the cop was walking me back to lock-up, I saw what looked like a dirty blanket with big holes (that looked like it had been crocheted by a psycho grandma) in a plastic rolling cart. I asked if I could have it. He picked it up, gave it to me, I put it around my shoulders, he asked if I was warmer, I said yes, then he promptly ripped it off me and threw it back in the rolling cart.

They took away my boots and my sweatshirt because both had zippers. I was in a wifebeater, jodhpurs, and socks, looking like a jailbird.

The women were all different types, from their 60s down to their teens. Most of them were Black, a couple were Latina, and there was one White woman who looked like Gloria Steinem. A couple of them kept inviting me to come up on the bed and sleep, but I sat on the cold concrete floor, afraid for my booty.

When I became completely, miserably sober, they started laughing at me and telling me that I was charged with a "10-50" or some number, which meant that I was arrested for intoxication. I don't remember having a hangover. I just remember being scared, cold, and adamant that I had to communicate with the band.

It was late and the band didn't know where I was. At that point I was desperate to get out of there. That was when panic started to set in. I tried to get the officers' attention. I said, "Please, please, I need to get out of here. I will pay you whatever it costs for the bail. I have to be in New York for a show; I'm a half famous singer, and it's very, very important."

They ignored me. I asked again. They ignored me again.

Then I started singing (a cappella) "When You're Smiling" for everybody to hear so that they would understand that it's really true, that I am a half famous singer and I really did have a place I needed to be. No response. I started to get so mad. Inside, my rage was burning.

I took my two fists and pounded like a gorilla in a cage on the two wood slatted walls with both arms in a second line percussive rhythm meets a jungle Congo beat. I sang like a rapper, "You bitch, you bitch, you bitch bitch bitch bitch bitch." Finally, I got their attention.

A bulldog-looking female cop, with two bigger bulldog men on either side of her, came quietly, slowly, and unemotionally over to me. She opened the cage door, without a word, grabbed me so hard by the scuff of my neck and dragged me a couple hundred feet away into solitary confinement. I landed with my face looking at the shitter hole in the middle of the floor. I sat there cross-legged on the cold, damp concrete floor, staring at it, trying to think for several hours, until they decided that it was time for me to go join the rest of the prisoners.

I started to stop being scared. I looked around and saw a conformity of women. They were talking to each other, telling their stories and joking. The oldest one, who was about 65, kept looking out the little cell door window and making wolf calls at the booties of the male cops. "I'm gonna fuck your brains out. You don't wanna know what I'm going to do with you. Get your big juicy ass over here!!" The concrete room blocked all outside sound. Since he couldn't hear what she said, all the other women thought it was hilarious.

She said she hadn't been fucked in seven months. I asked her, "You've been in here for seven months?" She said, "Yes." It was supposed to be a temporary holding tank. I was wondering what all those women were doing here. I started to feel comfortable enough to ask the question.

The majority of them were there because they had defended themselves from boyfriends or husbands who beat them. A couple of them were there for selling drugs. "Gloria Steinem" didn't say a word; she just faced the wall the whole time.

After a few hours, we were moved to a separate room that had concrete benches along all four walls while the jail cell was cleaned in the middle of the night. Don't ask me why, but everybody was just goofy, tired, and silly. Some of the women started singing, some of them started dancing. Suddenly, there was a tribe of women, like banshees having a wild party in the dark, damp, concrete holding tank with no windows. It was hilarious. Then the guard came down and shut down shop and brought us back to the prison cell.

I was so tired, I decided to lie down on the top bunk with no mattress or blanket. A woman gave me her blanket and I passed out.

The policeman woke me up just as I finally started to fall asleep at about 4 in the morning. He walked me out to the front check-in center and went through all of my belongings. I got my first mug shot. I thought, as an entrepreneur, *Great! Here's the opportunity for the new album cover photograph. Just like Frank Sinatra. Just like Johnny Cash.* It would be pretty rock 'n' roll to have a mug shot for an album cover. But it was the worst picture I have ever seen of myself in my life. Ever. Couldn't they have been a little more thoughtful when they photographed that moment for posterity?

Two cops started to go through my bags, which had been packed for the tour. Random items, including one leaf from the Leaf Festival in North Carolina that I had dried and saved in a book, 66 bobby pins in an Altoids box, two condoms, three $20 bills, one five, two singles, six bags of tea, one headpiece. By the time they got to the gowns and all the accessories, they were quite confused. The more odd and unusual items they picked up delicately with their white plastic medical gloves, the more they thought the experience was hilarious. Every single item was notated in a typed list, bagged in a Ziploc, and put it into a big white garbage bag, which was held until I was released.

In that particular jail, I was not allowed a phone call, so there was no way to communicate with the band, my mother, or anybody about where I was. At a certain point I was allowed to use the phone on the wall, but it cost $10 to make a phone call and I didn't have $10. The cops had my money and cards. The system is so messed up.

Finally, in the early morning, they brought us food. The meal consisted of the cheapest cornflakes ever, skim milk that tasted like water, nasty slimy ham, and white bread. All the ladies had bonded at this point and played the trading game. Boxes of cereal for ham, white bread for skim milk. We weren't given any drinks.

There was a toilet that didn't have a door in the cell and it had a water faucet that came barely dripping out of the top back of the toilet. We had to straddle our legs over the toilet and bend our head over to the top of the toilet lid to drink water. It was disgusting. There was shit everywhere. Besides, my thought process was, if I don't drink, I won't pee or poop. Then all would be good in the eyes of all of the prisoners who were possibly looking at my booty.

I kept asking the female cop when I could get out or when I could make a phone call. After a few attempts, she got nasty and she said, "If you ask me again, you're not going anywhere; I'm keeping you here for a longer period of time." All right then, so I shut my trap. Thirty hours later she came to the door, called my name, and said, "Your mother's waiting for you."

My mother? The very last person I would want to have pick me up from jail. At my age, for her to be going through this was shameful and inexcusable.

I was put in a checkout line at the front of the station. I could see light and windows. A skinny prostitute whose hair was crazy (but who was nice enough) stood next to me, looked at my leopard bowling bag, and said, "C'n I have that?" I looked at her, trying to dig deep into my generosity chest and said, "NO!" really loud. How many final straws does one have to accept?

I was standing with a big white garbage bag, no shoes, no sweater, looking like I was on the walk of shame, hungover, tired, deflated loser I was. I walked out the door of the jail into the bright, hot, humid sunshine and into my mom's car.

She had the most distinctive expression of disgust, pity, sorrow, and worry. I had never seen that look on her before. It made me feel so terrible. I slinked with my heavy garbage bag into the car and we went to a down home breakfast place, the kind we used to eat at together when I was a well behaved 12-year-old. While we were sitting there, my mom pulled out her phone to show me a text from Jimbo.

The text basically said that I was fired. I had left them in an 11th hour situation. My doppelgänger up in New York was going to be taking my place. He felt terrible about it, he said, but it was the way it had to be. There it was, in little cryptic letters on my mom's old flip phone. A breath-sucking reality displayed. It was over. They fired me while I was in jail. Never mind that the road manager had found out exactly where I was and could have gotten me on a plane in time to do the show, properly and sober. Nope. That was that.

My stint as the lead singer for the Squirrel Nut Zippers came to a screeching halt in Jefferson Parish Prison, Gretna, Louisiana.

In the months of touring around the whole country, no one had ever said, "We have a problem, Houston." Not one. Not once. There was nothing but camaraderie. I sat next to Jimbo the whole time in the back seat of the Sprinter, shooting the shit about any number of subjects, save for the elephant in the room, my drinking.

It's not as though the rest of the banshee tribe wasn't partying even harder; they just didn't end up in jail and they seemed to be able to perform without appearing drunk or stoned.

When I finally got home to the house on Burgundy Street, I went into my room, with the 14-foot ceilings, big TV, and king size bed. I plopped down, so dead exhausted I could barely stand up. I reached behind the TV to grab the last of the Old Grand-Dad bourbon and swigged what was left of it. That familiar burn of firewater going down my throat, burning away the horrible experience. I turned on the TV, and at that very moment was a commercial for Gretna, with its middle-class green grass gated communities, the narrator cooing, "Gretna, the quaint, charming place to be." Was he serious?

And so began, my old life, again, new.

Sex Dungeon, Personal Belongings, and Extortion

In January 2017, a miracle happened.

I had to move because my friend of 20 years, whom I helped support when she broke her ankle jumping across a train track, had decided, behind my back, to connive her way into taking over the lease and kicking me out of the place I had found for us on Burgundy Street.

My friend Lex's boyfriend was a young, handsome Uptown drug dealer and partners in crime with a sex dungeon owner who looked like a bearded young carny. Apparently, the drug dealer wanted to be a good person and was trying to pay it forward.

He seemed nice enough, so I trusted him to help me move all my stuff out of the Burgundy Street house and onto a flatbed pickup truck, like some scene from *The Grapes of Wrath*. I was moving a few blocks away to a place I found that was owned by a cool gay couple that I had known for a year from walking our dogs. The drug dealer was five hours late on the day of my move, so they decided they weren't going to rent to me after all, even though I communicated to them the whole time why we were running late.

We were standing in front of a house in St. Roch in the evening, on crime zero territory, shut out of a rental with everything I owned, with a crew of nice African American guys who owed the drug dealer and sex dungeon guy favors. We all witnessed two guys with flashlights and a ladder stealing the tiles from the roof of a house across the street.

Storage units were already closed. The sex dungeon guy offered to let me store my things in his $2,000 a month shotgun for $100 a week while I played in Puerto Rico for a month. $400 for four weeks was doable. But after we made that deal, he extorted me for another $2,000 dollars, and after a payment plan agreement for that amount, he shut down communication altogether. Every single thing I owned was there. Baby photographs, writings, a piano that was loaned by a prominent and family friend trumpet player. Book collection. Record collection. Dress collection. Items given to me by my grandma.

I went to the police, but they said it was a civil case. I went to a friend who said they would cover my back and break the guy's legs. That would be bad karma. So, I decided to let it all go.

I went to meet a lady to talk through helping her produce two tracks of her original songs to help her heal from her husband's tragic death. While I was with her, I ran into another new friend who was across the street at Thirteen on Frenchmen Street. That was the last place I had seen and sealed the deal with the sex dungeon guy before going to Puerto Rico. She had a friend from Australia, a writer who was with a nice young man named Zack VanHoven, who said, "You look familiar." He told me his dad owned the house that the dungeon guy was renting, and that he'd been evicted. He took me there with my friend and showed me that my things were there. I had to get it all to storage by the following Friday.

It had been six months of trying to be gracious and not miss materialism. It'd been a good lesson. But those events make me realize there is goodness and, as I already knew, higher forces at work.

* * * * *

What Are the Chances?

Months later, after the moving saga, I had moved to the Seventh Ward of New Orleans once again. I knocked on the neighbor's door to see if it was possible to share and pitch in for Wi-Fi. Who opened it, but a young man with whom I'd had some serious talks about recording and art the year before. It made me happy to see a familiar face.

There are some energies that put a smile on my face with their positivity. He was one. He worked at Petit Amelie in the French Quarter. I would go there because the croissants are so good. It was a pleasant surprise to see he was my new neighbor. He had just turned 24.

He showed me the multilayering Man Ray style art he created that he was packing up to go sell in the Quarter on his bike. I felt reinspired. He had a unique home recording studio that was waiting to be explored vocally and creatively with new ideas. He showed me the cassette machine he had invested in with expensive mics ready to go.

Was it time to become a cassette artist? I was hoping to make a record for the first time after having made 12 CDs. Apparently, you can't copy and burn from that format.

The thing that really blew my mind was that he liked to weed through items that were discarded on the street. He found a bunch of my photographs in the Bywater that were lying in front of the sex dungeon guy's house. He said to me, "I think I know you."

That Bywater house had been renovated. There were no more handcuffs on the wall.

What are the chances, in all of New Orleans, that my friend's friend from Brooklyn had moved into the same house that very month?

The items I re-collected were, most importantly, my baby photos and the dresses I cared about, as well as the few books I treasured out of the whole lot. Sammy Davis Jr.'s book on photography. My sister's final journal in rehab before she died, which is irreplaceable. I guess those items didn't have a disposable or front face value like my record, dress, and book collection.

Dear Jimbo,

It's been a minute. This whole situation still lays heavy on my mind. I don't have the finger to place on all of it yet. There are always three sides to the story, they say. I don't want the gig back. I don't want anything.

I've had lots of reflection time with gigs around the world by the water. I think for me, the most disappointing factor was that you weren't blunt with me and didn't give me a heads up that I was on bat strike number three before leaving and firing me in the clinker. It hurt more than you'll ever know.

Why you left me in jail and fired me while I was sitting in solitary confinement is still an enigma to me. I was trying so hard to get out and get on that plane to make amends. To be told I was irreplaceable, which placed more pressure on me to get on that plane, and then to be replaced by my good friend Tamar, whom you hired in New York City in the 11th hour instead of getting me out of jail, really messed up my head.

I bought the original edition of *Tom Sawyer*. I am going to read it and try to understand your rhetoric. If you had a problem with me, I wish you would have spoken up earlier.

In light of going to jail and having a misdemeanor on my record, I'm now a jailbird. Thank you for the Golden Handcuffs Experience. It led to a lot of epiphanies this year. I do miss you. Conversations in the back of the bus. Deep and real conversations.

That's pretty much it. I hope all is well.

Ingrid

Angola Prison Rodeo

In 2016, I went on a behind-the-scenes tour given by three incredibly gifted artists. The prisoners had to stand behind chain link fences to sell their art at the Angola Prison Rodeo.

Kevin Seward, prisoner in Angola, painted a portrait of me commissioned by my friend Joe Wall on a huge canvas. He'd been there for 40 years — since the age of 20. He made one big mistake because of his boyfriend's advice and killed the guy's grandma for the inheritance. This kind man was due to be released within a year of my visit. Three times he had been denied his freedom without a reason. As of the writing of this book, he was still there.

* * * * *

I was being picked up by my lawyer at 7:30 a.m. to go to court for what is called "disturbing the peace and removal of resisting arrest."

The front page of the *Advocate* stated that Oklahoma had the highest number of female inmates, and that Louisiana was going to lose the number one position.

When a human being is treated worse than a dog, with no food, water, or blanket and wishing you had an orange jumpsuit to pull over your head to stay warm, it's really not okay. Most of the ladies in Jefferson Parish Prison, who ranged in age from 16 to 65, were there because their men beat them and they had reciprocated. Slave labor at 25 cents an hour with a monopoly called a commissary charging three times the cost of a bag of coffee should be illegal.

I had my mug shot. Thumb prints. And a number. Thought about an album to compose. Made the cops laugh at 4 a.m. My bag filled with costumes to make the Squirrel Nut Zippers' last leg of the tour a better show.

Many good people deserve a second chance. I've learned a few backstories from Joe. Let's change this process of treating human beings like they're less than nothing so individual states can make 40-50 thousand dollars a head. Watch the documentaries on the carceral system. And check out activist Geoffrey Canada's on tackling poverty. Wouldn't it be better to start college programs for half the amount of what it costs to incarcerate people?

P.S. Kermit Ruffins for Governor!

A Reading

My friend Miss Cecile Savage invited me to a reading in 2017 at the old-fashioned bookstore on Baronne Street. The topic was French surrealist writers. Mary Ann Caws was the speaker. She is a renowned translator of French literature with a distinct accent. Originally from North Carolina, she later moved to New York City after having spent many a year in France, where she had a relationship with a poetic surrealist. She had a kind, spunky, energetic way of speaking and sharing her messages and the poems she had translated from French to English.

The most moving part to me was how much emotion and care she had for the words that she spoke: with joy, kindness, and tears. I hope, if I live to be her age and have passionate affairs and stories to tell, that I could be as classy as she is.

The bookstore was across the street from the Roosevelt Hotel and it reminded me of the movie *Bell, Book and Candle* with Kim Novak, James Stewart, and a black cat. Turns out the owner, Dave Brinks, was a fan of mine and our kids went to school together.

With Hurricane Nate due to arrive the next day and I hiked to the Rouses in the CBD for water. I stood in the dark parking lot and reflected on all of the hipster changes in New Orleans while watching the stylistic oddities entering the grocery in an area that used to be old school and Louis Armstrong's stomping grounds. I then went into the store to look for Cecile. The checkout lady looked me right in the eye and said, "I know you." I said, "How?" She said, "I was in Jefferson Parish Prison with you and I never forget a face." That experience in jail will never be erased from my memory bank.

As I walked out to the parking lot with Cecile, it amazed me how the universe works. From the idealism and poetry of beauty and possibilities of love, words, and hope, to the reminder of the "wham bam thank you ma'am" reality of the system since that blessing in disguise moment at Jefferson Parish Prison. I realized, after conversations with people I never would have guessed had gone to jail, there lies a fine line between freedom and incarceration. I would like to be an advocate to help the pendulum swing from hopeless to possible.

Peter Pan Hero

While being booked around the world at famous festivals and licensing my songs to prominent endeavors in film and television, I found myself sleeping in a seven-year-old's bedroom in Metairie.

This kiddo, Alex, who is Renee Shaw's son, was so wonderful, the Peter Pan we all need to remember to be. He was born with cerebral palsy, and he had undergone two surgeries to be able to walk.

I was contemplating what I'd done so wrong in my life. After we took our walk with the dogs (Alex on his scooter), he asked me, "Who taught you to be so nice?" That was a question that I had never been asked before in my entire life of psychological interrogation. I answered, "My mom and dad." After I said that, I realized, that brave kid, a little old soul, thought I was worthy enough to sleep in his room, be an honorary Auntie, and share his honesty. The rest of life's mess just seemed minor.

Dear Ava,

There's a prominent island bird in Vieques called coqui. It sings all night long. A whistling constant high pitch that never stops. Then it wakes the wild dogs around 3 a.m. and the roosters at 5:30 a.m. I woke up one morning wondering why there was so much chaos with animals while it was still dark.

I named you after my favorite free spirit, and the most beautiful woman I've ever seen. Her name is Ava Gardner. If you read her autobiography, you will understand what I wanted for you. She was from the South. Dad and I went to her museum together in Smithville, North Carolina. She went to Spain and fought the bulls after making a collection of unique movies. Your name means "Little Bird."

I'm staying in a really vintage 1940s house the island calls "The Birdcage." It's called outdoor living while safely contained by painted white bars. It's odd to be on a swinging bed outside wondering who's driving by at night after being around New Orleans crime. I'm listening now to the coqui sing in its high-toned voice.

Thank you for saying goodnight.

I love you.

Sending you the sounds of Puerto Rico.

Mom

Tourette Syndrome

We were never allowed to curse as children. My father, being a man of literature and higher learning, said, "you can splice and dice someone with carefully chosen words." I found myself having a potty mouth in the aftermath of my divorce. And I didn't like it.

A friend who has the perfect blond Barbie doll family of athletic and intellectual children allows them one curse word a day. The little kid savors it like a banana split. "Fuuuuuuuuuuckkkkkkkk!" It's hilarious.

When I played Puerto Rico for five weeks, I witnessed Christopher Matson's boyfriend have a Tourette-like moment. It was Valentine's Day and he and his boyfriend had been planning an unforgettable experience for their high-end Jungle Room Club guests. But nothing was going as planned. The dress store downtown had fitted me for a dress that I had to be sewn into on the day of the show. And the pre-ordered surf and turf never arrived from San Juan.

I hopped in a car with Christopher's boyfriend, a handsome man from Lafayette, Louisiana. While driving downtown as fast as he could, he was spouting every curse word in the book at top volume. He was almost banging his head on the steering wheel while driving the winding roads with wild horses by the wayside. I was doubled over with hyena laughter. There had been so many years of having profanities in my head but never being allowed to shout them out.

Maybe somebody should start a cursing gym. It feels pretty good to let angst out behind closed doors.

Once, a female singer from my New Orleans Nightingales project received only half of her music chart from the stage manager before our French Quarter Fest gig. Backstage, 20 of us girl singers in Trashy Diva dresses witnessed her, dressed to the nines, march into the port-o-potty, where she cursed so loud and shook the plastic unit back and forth till the heavens fell down. She came out with her hair in complete disarray and a tomato red face, but she felt much better, and we all had a great show.

Maybe it's okay to let frustrations out. In Japan, workers in offices are allowed to do that.

The next time you're feeling edgy, do what my sister does. It's a White girl funk dance where she pretends to take groceries out of the cart and put them on the shelf. She calls it "Putting Groceries on the Shelf."

San Juan Airport

Goodbyes always break my heart.
Always leaving,
Always new starts.
Always departing from people for whom you care.
Allowing one's feelings, to leave you bare.
Always movement,
Always change.
Always heart strings pained.

Airports are the worst,
The look of tears on people's faces,
Saying goodbye makes my heart hurt.
This life that chose me,
Goodbyes are a constant life scene.
A lifetime of movement pursuing the dream.
My dad always said, don't say "Goodbye," only "Ciao."
That way, we will see each other again somehow.

February 2017

Drop 'n' Roll

I had just gotten home from five weeks of peaceful paradise in Vieques playing the "Jungle Room." I was torn about whether to ever come home. I was sad to leave and had procrastinated to the point where my boss's lover told me there was a hostel up the road. It was my mom, daughter, friends, and musical community I love that brought me back. I really missed my tribe in New Orleans.

I was picked up at the airport with the humid cool smells of South filling my being. It felt good to be back. I spent 12 hours and three flights getting home. I threw up three times with anxiety about the unknown future.

The first leg was a small plane over the Caribbean in the rain. Small planes and musicians don't go together — it's a fact. Six people on board and both propellers wouldn't start properly. In the air we began to sway. A little kid said, "Mom, are we going to die today?" Two more flights later I finally made it home to Amy Stewart, a friend I was staying with until I could find my own place.

My boyfriend at the time and I were sitting in the back yard in Gentilly talking about psychology. A car pulled up on the street at about 10:30 p.m. I could see through the open fence 20 feet away, and the people in the car opened fire with their machine guns. A run of shots and then a couple more. I'd never been that close to gunfire before. My heart was pounding. Drop 'n' roll animal instinct kicked in. *Welcome back to carrying mace and keeping a knife under your pillow until you rent the next safe birdcage to hold the fort.*

Sea Legs and Ships

There's nothing as strange as sea legs. The discombobulated feeling as if you are on a ship trying to keep your balance while walking on hard non-moving land. Growing up on the Mississippi River and the Intracoastal Waterway, I never got seasick. Since then, I have had various experiences that have caused the most impotent feeling.

On my honeymoon in Key West, my husband wanted to go on a deep-sea fishing journey in the evening. I had drunk a substantial amount of Wild Turkey 101 and by the time we got out of the harbor, I was holding on to a pole on the floor of the boat in the middle of a crowd of tourists, begging for mercy. I had just played a New Year's Eve gig at The Breakers in Palm Beach. It was the most money I'd ever made. A $50,000 contract. It was Y2K. I was so desperate I begged the captain to turn the boat around and I would return everybody's money to them. No such luck.

While camping out in our little "I Love Lucy" style trailer at the campground, I spent days walking crooked through the senior shuffleboard courts to the bathrooms, miserable. You would think that I would have learned my lesson to take seasickness pills. But no.

In Europe, when my band, The Flying Neutrinos, was signed to Fiction, we were taken on our first tour through Europe. Primrose Hill in London was our home base and our first stop for a few weeks' worth of highly promoted shows.

The next stop was the mainland. A ferry took us to Copenhagen. It was one of the worst storms, the crew said. Like a scene out of *Titanic*, we were housed in the hull of the ship, the absolute worst place to be. The waves were like huge monsters, tossing, turning, slapping the ship senseless. Every single person on full capacity was taking up a spot on the railing puking, every single bathroom stall and sink was full. I couldn't find a place of my own to join the party.

There were showgirls in big Las Vegas feather outfits dancing their choreographed routines, swaying to the left, swaying to the right as a kickline, their dance skill balance being put to its toughest test. I could picture one of them rolling out the door and flying over the side of the ship into the foamy, angry sea.

After a couple of days of no mercy, we departed the ferry. That night we had a show in a little club in Copenhagen and the next night at Christiania. As a band, we swayed our way through the gigs. Walking the streets and amongst the hippie forest of stoned people fucking, the shadows of the trees made for a strange Dali dream come to life.

The third (and I hope final) time I had to learn to use my sea legs was during all of my hospital escapades. After being pricked, poked, prodded, tested to the limits, and knocked out multiple times, I once again had to learn to walk like a newborn giraffe trying to stand for the first time. The innate need to be a survivor, to stand up no matter what the pain level, is astonishing.

I remember the real feeling of having to make a choice in the ICU bed to fight or surrender. The choice was clear and even more so at the thought of my father ready to choke and torture me through eternity for having been so stupid with my choices. I crawled with every inch I could muster out of the bed to the wheelchair in the corner of the room. No one was with me. Being left alone was punishment by my family for my wanting to go home and not straight to rehab. All the nurses were attending to other patients. That was the shortest and most painful wobbly walk ever.

Airports and Planes

Once, when The Flying Neutrinos were en route to Los Angeles from New York, the flight attendant asked for the five-piece band to come to the front of the plane. Up we went... and so did the Ramones. *Haha, isn't that funny?* we said. Two five-piece bands. They didn't think so. Besides, aren't they a quartet? Sillies.

My father always placed insurance on my head due to his premonition that I was going to die in a plane crash. That way, at least he could start a Chinese orphanage, he said, though he would have been devastated.

Being a touring musician is great if you're up for:

Having your head patted down in Chicago,

Having your Norwegian crackers being taken away, but still being left with your mace and flask,

Seeing big high-heeled shoes in stalls facing the wrong way,

Hitting air bumps on the way to Las Vegas so high that your milk and cookies fly up and then land perfectly on your tray,

Taking small puddle jumpers to Vieques where the propellers stop working and a little boy asks his mommy if we're going to die today,

Flying to Moscow in February and being screamed at by male flight attendants who look like CIA agents, that you can have water when THEY tell you that you can have water,

Being jetlagged and sick for two weeks in Berlin during the five-star Pomp Duck and Circumstance run.

You know what they say about musicians and small planes?

Don't do it.

Iceland and Clothes

Dressing properly and warmly has never been a forte of mine. Ever since I was a little girl, my mom had to make me put on a sweater and I would constantly rip it off and run around like a lunatic, free as a bird.

When going on the road, gauging what to pack is always difficult. You just never know if it's going to be hot or cold. Also, with all the layovers in different locations in the world you have to be prepared, as I have come to learn. Thanks to festival producer Bjarne S **Aaserød**, I have been lucky enough to go to Norway and Greece twice back to back. Needless to say, the weather and terrain are extremely different between both countries.

I like to pack the fun things. What did I do to prep for those trips? I went to the Rainbow Shop and bought colorful bikinis, and to the thrift store for vintage summer dresses. A winter coat? Who needs a winter coat in May?

My first trip to Greece and Norway as a solo headliner included a layover in Iceland. Who knew that we would have to depart the plane on the field and make our way to the airport center like haggard Russians in January escaping communism?

Of course I wanted to look cute; I was a singer going abroad. I was in a black 1950s Marilyn Monroe three-quarter-sleeve summer dress and wearing red lipstick. Did I think to pack a sweater or a coat? Of course I didn't. We don't wear coats and sweaters in New Orleans most of the year.

I'll never forget the look on the Norwegian and Icelandic people's faces when they saw me exiting the plane. They were wearing heavy rubber windbreakers, with hoodies, gloves, and boots. All of the exiting passengers looked at me like I was some sort of oddity from another planet. No one smiled, no one said a word, but they made a point to keep their distance from me.

Another time I felt that kind of cold was in Russia in February. The kind of cold that makes you feel like Muhammad Ali punched you in the face in the boxing ring. Then there was the time vocalist Tricia Boutte and I had a drinking contest in a prominent jazz club in Sweden. It was freezing out and all I had on was an after the gig ball gown. All the guys had gone to bed at the hostel already, so at 4 in the morning I crawled across the cobblestone streets, so drunk I couldn't even stand up. But you know what? They say God is good to drunks. I really never got sick... from the weather, that is.

My father was an inventor of sorts. When we were on the road full-time, he invented a sleeping bag outfit. He cut holes in a sleeping bag at the bottom for the feet and in the sides for the arms. He was a traveling sleeping bag all day long and all he had to do at the end of a long day was just lie down with his pillow wherever we were. In an issue of *Vogue* magazine decades later, lo and behold, there were long, lithe models walking down the runway in big white sleeping bag ball gowns made out of down.

Once I went into a little deli in New York's East Village to see if I could pull money out of the bank machine there. I had performed at a wedding the night before. It was snowing. We were broke. I was with my husband and had my baby on my hip. No coat, no practical shoes (I forgot to pack some) and who was standing behind us in line? Jimmy Fallon.

I stepped up to the machine, put my card in, and tried to make money come out, but there just wasn't any in the account. I thought the machine was broken, so I turned around and told Jimmy that. He walked up to the bank machine next and stuck his card in, and out came a whole wad of money. He looked me in the face and said with a smile, "It's not broken!"

Now, my wardrobe is packed with winter items. I long for snow in New Orleans' summer inferno. The only solace I can take with regard to my inability to dress properly when it's cold out is the fact that I get to witness people from cold terrain countries come to New Orleans, sweat, turn red, and practically die from the heat six months out of the year. That's when I turn to them and say, may I recommend some at Walmart wifebeaters from the Shell station up the road?

Dear Mamacita,

Sorry for not writing sooner. My timing is still off-kilter a bit from being jetlagged. So, I set the alarm with enough time to get ready to do my duties for the day after not being able to fall asleep until the morning has risen.

It's cold and grey here in Norway. And supposedly it's going to rain heavily during the prominent festival days where we are parading and playing on an outdoor ferry. Did the lecture and performance at the international children's school yesterday and the opening sold-out expensive night concert. I really enjoyed both. The kids were between 9 and 14, 80 of them. They were cautious at first, but then with some friendly persuasion and New Orleans gifts, they were primal screaming and second lining like wild banshees. It was hilarious and really fun to do. Kids are great. The only Black kid in the four classes gathered was named Ingrid. She tap danced for everyone.

We played in the old town of Frederiksberg last night. It's right in the river and is so old and quaint it feels like being in a little foreign doll house. I don't know where the sold-out audience came from, because there was no one on the cobblestone streets.

I learned: "Hiya allah salmon?" (How are you?). And, after the 79-year-old bandleader Jan Inge took me home and got lost because we didn't have an address: "Vooti Booti ayi" (Do you know where I live?) [phonetic spellings]. Figuring out the important words here... Everyone is so unbelievably nice.

But the bandleader is set in his ways and locked into the set list to the point where he got really mad at me for making an addition — a song requested by an older couple who came a long way, to asking the organ player who lent his organ to sit in on a blues, which was a big hit with the audience. In light of it being my show with my band headlining, and it was a big success, I found myself upset that he was mad at me, and the promoter wanted me to delete the post that included a line saying the piano player was five hours late to rehearsal. Why should I have to wait five hours after the agreed-on time, after getting up early to be there, and be professional when he's still got the gig and not reprimanded for his behavior? Somehow, I always seem to be the problem, and that bothers me a lot.

They made so much money at the show with exorbitant ticket, food, and drink prices while I'm the one reading the audience to make them happy and being underpaid once again. I think I really need to be a booking agent to negotiate details in the future.

The sisters, Karin and Gerd, are hilarious as usual. They drove me around Sarpsborg for a few hours, pointing out all of the key places that made up their childhood, from the farmhouses to the cartoon factory. I'm making them a fish fry on Tuesday with the New Orleans items I brought. We are taking an excursion to Sweden to go shopping Monday because things are cheaper there. Gothenburg, Sweden, where Anders [Osborne] is from, is not too far away. I really like it here.

The first night, the promoter invited a few select friends to a Greek restaurant for dinner, where, after a nice evening up to that point, I was promptly yelled at by a drunk male Norwegian who thinks I'm a Christian Trump supporter because I'm an American. I tried to explain that that wasn't the case at all. I said, *you don't know me, I've been baptized three times in my life and I do not support Trump.* It was upsetting to be judged that way and verbally attacked. I wish Trump wasn't our president. I can't even look at him in the news anymore.

Ava reached out for your number yesterday. She seemed good in her texts. I'm sorry to be missing Jazz Fest.

Thanks for reading. That's my update so far. I hope things are going well for you and your hip is behaving itself. I wish I had the money for you to be here too. I know you would love it.

Well, there's a microphone and coin collection to sell! We need to figure out how to get on the money train. If other people can do it, we can too. You deserve to have a running car and a vacation. You are too smart and hardworking to not have that.

Apart from having zits like a 14-year-old on my third eye, my health is actually good. I'm not stuffed up or throwing up at all. Maybe I'm just allergic to New Orleans? I dunno. Okay, I'm going to get up now.

Karin and Gerd are wonderful, but Karin keeps trying to make me eat weird stuff every morning. Yesterday it was pate, fish eggs, and pickles with garlic butter on really heavy grain toast. It was good, but I wasn't ready to eat that the second I woke up. I guess this time is allotted to figure out why I'm unhappy and how to fix it.

Been trying to surrender to silence and learning how to be alone. Getting better at it. I love you lots and lots.

Your Pippi Longstocking,

Ingrid

P.S. No one here really believes my name is Ingrid, and I have to endlessly explain how you named me after your favorite actress, and then they smile.

Xoxoxo

*****

I'm sorry to hear about your bandaged hand. Please let me know what the reports say. As my friend Renee Shaw says, there are no mistakes, everything happens for a reason, and there are blessings in disguise. Maybe you need to not paint signs for a moment?

This trip has been an affair of so many impressions. First and foremost, how unbelievably kind, funny, smart, and bonded the Norwegians are as a community.

Today was the day of the laborers, celebrated apparently everywhere in the world except our country. Bands were playing and people came out wearing the deep red, cream, and dark blues of the flag.

I may not be making any money really, but everyone has brought me into their homes to share their traditions and ideas. We sat on the balcony of a dignified older couple who served traditional waffles, cream, and berry sauce, while overlooking the river, which is called a fjord. We went to Sweden specially to take a picture of Ingrid Bergman's coastal hometown because I told the ladies who you named me after. They were adamant that we had to take the longer journey to take a picture for you. Norway has very high taxes, so most of the people go to Sweden to shop for groceries because it is much, much cheaper.

I met some amazing ladies here doing great things with their lives. There's one in particular named Ann Kristin who has such a lust for life and has made me laugh so hard. She is a teacher and was lucky through her work to meet the Royals. She and her husband live in kind of a pink dollhouse. She gave me so many unique clothes 'cause she's a clothes horse and really should be a stylist. Her husband loves her so much, he wakes up to a literal wall of *très* fancy clothes in their small bedroom.

It's very quiet here. Most Norwegians don't like background music. I honestly could not understand what they are saying at the dinner table. They talk in commanding guttural tones and everyone tries to outtalk the other to have the last word. But nobody seems to be concerned who has the final word.

I brought New Orleans supplies and cooked a fish fry for a big crew who have been a part of the team that helped make Bjarne's festival come to fruition by being there at beck and call.

Oh, by the way, Norwegians have good appetites. And somehow still can keep their vocal cadence going. I love how spontaneously they sing and laugh. I wish we had more of that in the states.

Anyhoo — Gotta pack now. We leave for Greece at 11:30. I really wish you could be here. If I had the money, I would make it so. You would really love this country. And Greece! I come home with presents.

I love you and miss you and home.

Xoxoxo!!!!

Norway

Sarpsborg Sunday

It was such a crisp spring Sunday in Sarpsborg, Norway. Every flower thought it owned the day. I was lying in the yard in the sunshine writing, thinking, and relaxing. It is the most relaxing and cheapest hobby ever. No matter where you go, there's always a tree, a bird singing, and impressions to be had.

I'd been learning a lot there. I had a promoter and bandleader who were outspoken in a no-frills manner. It was disarming, as my manner is much different. But I was raised with the same direct approach. Baptism by fire was the example my dad set.

I had some sort of a Fellini dream while I was there. A ferry ride gig on a scenic river with happy people communing, there was a second line through old town village, where the Mardi Gras beads given to me by singer Banu Gibson and Sinead Rudden lit up every kid's face as they watched something they had never seen before. I got pulled over by security at the airport because of the beads, but the guy behind me had a suitcase full of bagels.

I always thought I had creative ideas to put into play to make people happy. Bjarne S Aaserød, the festival producer, outdid my wildest ideas with a team that believed in his dream and saw it through in detail, from the bandleader to the tribe of interesting people I got to meet.

I love how chaos and order can coexist. Everyone I met in Sarpsborg was an open book for discussion. From a teacher sharing her methods and discussing real issues, to a world service peacemaker discussing why she would rather be with a woman than a man, to a couple married for 26 years, to the funniest lady I ever met, Ann Kristin, who kept giving me all her clothes and enjoying every moment of her life in her perfect pink dollhouse house.

I was in awe. And I felt so lucky to be there singing to all of the open-minded intelligentsia who had no problem singing along at full volume on the way home to a song on the radio. Lessons come firsthand for me in life, never in the classroom. And I'd been learning a lot about how to be a better person with some order to my chaos.

After Sarpsborg we went to Greece. Paris reached out. I was tempted. But at the end of the day I felt I must pack up the tchotchkes and a little profit and come home to make New Orleans a better place with what I learned.

* * * * *

Norwegian Blue Eyes

Every Norwegian I met has blue eyes. My dad did too. So does my sister. I'm the only one in my family with green eyes. My mom's eyes are light brown. It was sad to say goodbye to that memorable experience. I didn't understand a word the Norwegians said. But they all had smiling blue eyes and ended the cadence of their speech with a laugh.

I learned so much. About history, politics, etiquette, traditions. I guess the gift is to experience pure kindness, and it almost puts our New Orleans community to shame. And that's saying a lot.

There's an unwritten agreement to share the family meal table, talk, and sing songs of the homeland daily.

* * * * *

Midnight in Norway

It's hard to fall asleep when it's still light at midnight. My alarm was set for 4:45 a.m. to fly home to New Orleans.

I was hosted by wonderful people with whom I had meaningful conversations. (It seems Europeans don't like accolades, so few names are mentioned.) While quietly lying there, unable to fall asleep, I looked around at the room I was in. Quality, great book choices, woodwork made with detailed care. The bed and linens were set up with love and softness.

My bandleader and his honey made an extra special effort to take me on a driving tour around Oslo, including by the Kon-Tiki Museum, even though they were so tired after two weeks in the Greece gig zone. Nothing material could possibly replace the gift of sharing history.

I looked at a raft designed by Thor Heyerdahl. My dad had created his rafts around the concept of building sustainable designs that were inspired by Heyerdahl. All of us kids had to gather wood and stuff bilges because of his dream.

Thank you, Jan Inge and Mona.

Dear Ava,

I love you.

The past is the past. Now is the now. And people do change; even moms are only human.

I decided to give you all the space you need and not bother you because you asked me to. When you are ready, we can start slow. I cried for four years, heartbroken because I missed you so much.

I'm staying with my 79-year-old bandleader and his wife here in Oslo. They are amazing and hosted me two years ago as well. We have had really long talks. He was an alcoholic. He's not anymore.

Drinking or taking any substance is putting a band-aid on a problem instead of fixing it. I've been going to counseling.

You will be 18 shortly. I have shown a few close friends over here your photo. You are old enough to hear my truth. I can't promise to be a saint, though that would be ideal. But I can promise you and show you that I am trying to be the best person I can be in this life.

There's a reason I have a fan base and good friends. They see I am trying to share goodness in the world. Let's start small doing something you would like and feel safe with? I'm home late tomorrow night. And I will need some rest for a couple of days after working hard these three weeks over here, but after that, I'm free to connect if you like, even if it's just for a real talk on the phone. It's 4:30 a.m. here, so I have to go back to bed for a few hours before going to the airport.

On a funny note, in the future, remind me not to keep packing too much stuff, every muscle hurts from carrying all of it and security keeps pulling me over to take the dumbest stuff called Norwegian crackers, a butter knife, and sunblock!

I love you so much. I don't want to be the one to cause you any pain.

All my love for you.

Mom

Norway to Greece

The 2017 Kardamili International Jazz Festival in Greece had an incredible roster of international talent thanks to Bjarne's love of jazz. I started the week feeling like that moment in *The Jerk* where it seemed like I'd been there for five years. But it had only been a week. The concert was sold out, and the villagers had looks of awe on their faces. I was trying to give my all with the very best band from Norway.

On a break, I had a moment to go into the oldest church I've ever been in. I had been feeling lifeless, tossing around in survival mode, so I decided to go to church since sound check was running way late a few feet away. I walked into a majestical space with two people in it: a glamorous lady dressed in black who looked like she was from a Fellini movie and a man who looked like he was in charge.

The three of us heard a haunting voice singing a cappella and witnessed a ritual of incense burning. The Father's ritual was hypnotic. He came in, faced the simple cross, meditated, and began trance-like singing. The incense was up and running thanks to the precision of the caretaker banging the church bells precisely at 6 o'clock. Why couldn't our sound men hire him? I was inspired by the Father's intensely precise pitching of the incense metal burner at the paintings of the saints. He looked me in the eye directly as he sprayed the black incense and something white mixed together. *Does that girl need a saving or is she just sneezing in my face?* Both. I wondered what he was thinking. *I am a good girl, Father.* He sang in low tonalities. I didn't understand a word. His low droning voice was enough to leave me moved.

I bought a series of artifacts from the religious store a block away after sitting in the sunshine pre-show, hanging with our Norwegian festival gang and band. Europeans love to sit at outdoor tables and commune in random silence with clipped random dialogue for hours. They all kept their act together while drinking. I'm not used to sitting in a chair for so long. Everyone was so content there.

Later, in my hotel room, I lit the incense from the church store and almost set my finger on fire trying to replicate the smell that created that breath release.

I got to be a part of a traditional Greek wedding when the whole town of Kardamili shut down. They all turned up to show respect for love and tradition to the oldest church in town.

I spent quality time with Tricia Boutte, who was also on the festival roster. During the festival she was wearing a spectacular, large, heavy silver Greek-style cross on her chest. I admired it and asked her where she got it. She told me that she asked for it and the person gave it to her. "Ask," she said. "The worst they can do is say no."

My old neighbor's church grandma in Gentilly calls it ABC: *Ask for it, Believe in it, Claim it.* I didn't want to go home to face the reality of having no home. But I did go home, because the music I was raised with and trained in is my home. The players I call family cannot be replaced by an island paradise. With that advice and my own experiences, I bravely reached out to a few trusted sources when I got home, to ask if they would help my new album come to fruition. They said yes. That faith from them brought back my fire, self-esteem, and creativity.

Then it came out all of a sudden like a silent volcano erupting. After roaming like a lost child without direction, I was back on track. Thank you, Tricia.

*****

Gypsy Basket Weavers

In Greece, there are gypsies that weave baskets all day by the sea. They have two trucks. One is an old Mercedes-Benz Sprinter (like the one I traveled in with the Squirrel Nut Zippers!). They park in a quiet alcove right below the old church. They are a family of sorts. The kids and women hawk the homemade baskets by the downtown plaza. The men sit outside the trucks weaving all day. I learned they don't call themselves gypsies, which is considered offensive. They call themselves *Romanes*.

We traveled with a gypsy tribe in Mexico when I was a little girl. The head of the tribe was sick and bedridden. The large family who lived in a wood caravan sat around him and ate communal meals together. What I most remember was that the gypsies used their hair as napkins. Savor the flavor for later, I guess.

There was something intriguing about their quiet camp-out, productive mode by the water. I was walking home, going by them, wondering if maybe they could adopt me.

Dear Mamacita,

We had the best concert last night in Kardamili, Greece. Me and Tricia Boutte together with a really great full back-up band playing their very best. Most of them are Norwegians. The bandleader, Jan Inge, is 79 and plays trombone. He is a great person in every way, and we have honest conversations about every subject. It's really beautiful here, and I can see how much joy these Europeans feel who have come here for the festival. I'm trying to do my very best because the producer also has festivals in Croatia and the Canary Islands.

I really don't know why, but somehow, they think I'm a really great artist. What? I'm happy here.

The front door to the bed and breakfast is left open and it's an unwritten agreement to show respect. There are five rooms. Most of the people here are elder statesmen Norwegians, including our piano player and the two sisters. It's a nice little family.

I'm really happy that your test results are healthy and good. That means a whole lot to me because you have been on my mind these last few days.

I have found some really nice gifts for you. Somewhat looking forward to the long hot summer. I have things I want to accomplish and I miss you, Allie, Ava, and yes, my boyfriend.

I love you.

My last show here is Friday. And then it's back to the hamster wheel. Xoxoxo

Me

An Aesop's Fable Come True

Selina is her name. She came from European wealth. To understand the quiet rules of what wealth represents after playing so many millionaires' parties over the years: Nouveau Riche lacks class; Old School understands etiquette. She displayed it in every part of her bone marrow. Yet she decided to be a free spirit, releasing herself from the constraints of her upbringing.

On my final day in Kardamili, Selina took me to her haven. We made the drive to the top of the mountain. When we reached the peak, with three doggies and a little picnic basket of Dutch cheese, Grappa, crackers from Norway, and solitude. We sat and talked by a natural creek, and drank out of a waterfall dripping out of a mountain.

Every spring flower and herb was blossoming. The majesty of the moment was a quiet monastery sitting on the highest peak. Walking back to the car with the dogs, we climbed the oldest rock steps to a solitary silent church that had been there long before, with overgrown grass and spring flowers attaching themselves to a higher energy.

Really?

The currencies I value are honesty and loyalty. What really pains me is that one of three people I trusted to come into my home while I was in Greece stole one of the last material items I own; i.e., the large flatscreen TV that my ex allowed me to keep. I feel sorrow that some feel the need to steal to survive.

The security footage was about to be reviewed. I really hoped it wasn't the person I suspected. If that person had asked me to give them the TV, I would have. The way I was raised, you don't steal, ask for welfare, or depend on others. In an hour of need, sometimes it's cringe territory, but you don't steal from your friends, neighbors, or community. We have each other's backs. I was mad and disappointed as hell. But I forgave and wished the person the best.

In Greece, there isn't a single homeless person on the streets, there is no crime, and people are nice to each other. Why can't every human being have a place to sleep and food to eat? My ex-roommate from last year is on the streets now with her four-year-old daughter. I tried to take care of them in my space while I was gone. I didn't really have any money either.

Katrina ruined our culture and home with rents that were no longer affordable. But that's another story. At that moment, it was about observing and forgiving what one is forced to do for survival.

Irma Thomas

On Ava's 16th birthday, my mom and I met her at Angelo Brocato's ice cream parlor. She started to open up and come around after two years of us being estranged.

After the visit, I watched the rainfall out of the security gate into a pretty summer pre-light sunrise in the Seventh Ward. I was awake all night, thinking, listening to music, figuring out the next moves, and eating my way through the TV series about Celia Cruz.

I wanted to write an update about my kiddo, but at that time I didn't know her anymore. What came about in my thoughts was how much Irma Thomas' music played such a huge part in the soundtrack of my life with Ava.

The first part of that soundtrack was playing in the hospital room while I was birthing Ava, which took two days. Clyde played "Take a Look" (at this girl). In 2001 I returned home from New York City to New Orleans to make a family and a record. It took a lot to suck the emotional breath out of my husband, a Connecticut Yankee boy. When I was very pregnant going home with him after a gig, WWOZ played "Yours Until Tomorrow." He was so moved he had to buy Irma's *Down at Muscle Shoals* album. Gerald French almost fell off of his drum seat in rehearsal mode thinking I could possibly outdo her version. He was right. (I love it when Gerald laughs at me like that.) "Sunday Morning Coming Down" garnered the same results.

When my marriage was falling apart, Irma and I started to become friends because of her husband's cocky kindness. He said he knew about girl singers like me because he was married to one! The next night, he brought Irma to my show. We bonded. She said she had grown up in a gypsy family too.

Voodoo Fest, an annual music festival that takes place in City Park around Halloween, asked for my project, The New Orleans Nightingales, to be a part of the experience. The budget allowed for a female guest who had a bigger name than the rest of the 17 singers in the project. I chose Irma. I took the fat contract by hand to their house in New Orleans East. Her husband greeted me at the door in his underwear. What happened to the dapper gangster golfer look?

Irma allowed me to pick three songs from her catalogue. What a privilege. I chose "Take a Look" (at this Girl), "Yours Until Tomorrow," and "You Can

Have My Husband But Please Don't Take My Man." I chose them for my husband and daughter. (Little did I know divorce lay imminently ahead.) The show was a huge success across the board.

As I was wandering the world on gigs in cheap and fancy motels, very lonely, "Make Me a Pallet on Your Floor" became a daily listen. I called Irma one day to ask for her advice when I was having a really hard time. Knowing she had been through so much professionally over her life's creative journeys, I left her a message without defining the details.

She called me back and said one word before I opened my mouth to say hello: "Menopause." We then had a deep lengthy discussion on many life subjects. There are very few people who are part of my life soundtrack who I hold in the highest regard, esteem, and appreciation.

On my daughter's rainy Sweet 16th, I played Irma's music, thankful for her influence in my life.

Billie Holiday

Vincent Roppolo was the first person to tell me I sounded like Billie Holiday.

She's been following me around my whole life. Like a dark, silent phantom. My claim to fame is sounding like her, a bittersweet gift. Two singers who phrase like Louis Armstrong and don't have large voices. Two Aries girls. I never liked the comparison; it would be nice to have my own distinct voice. She scared me with her sad and unconstrained behavior.

I reflected on New Orleans jazz vocalist Sharon Martin's mesmerizing performance of *Lady Day at Emerson's Bar and Grill* at the Pontchartrain Landing on France Road. That venue was my church go-to in my lowest hours while living in Gentilly after losing everything. I met the owner, who built his dream compound there. *Lady Day* was the first production there. The band was stellar.

Sharon has four sisters. Pre-show they locked themselves in a dressing room bathroom stall, fashionably dressed and laughing their heads off over a topic they were kind enough not to share. It made me really miss my own sisters, and it also cracked me up. What mature grown women ever do that? It moved my heart.

The first time I ever heard Billie was on a cassette tape I listened to outside of the bus our family band lived in at a campground in Provincetown. Then a young teen, I distinctly remember thinking what a sorrowful voice she had and wondering who could possibly ever be so unhappy in life.

I moved to New York City, hopeful for The Big Time. While street busking on Astor Place as a young adult with my family, I met jazz singer Madeleine Peyroux on a street corner. She was busking too. She was taught to sing Billie Holiday standards by our beloved friend Danny Fitzgerald, who passed away in 2017. Madeleine is still a friend with whom I have many commonalities.

Why is Billie Holiday always in my life? I made a point to not listen to her music. If I could choose to sound like someone, it would be spunky Patsy Cline.

Clyde used to photograph my album covers. At a certain point he told me he wouldn't do them anymore because he knew the "real" me too well. While playing at the Ritz-Carlton, on break one night, I looked at the gargantuan black and white photograph of Billie Holiday. She had a scar on her neck. She seemed authentic. I cold-called Herman Leonard, who had photographed her. He shot my *Almost Blue* album, and we became good friends.

The years went by, I was barely making a living at music, and I finally decided to read Billie Holiday's autobiography to try and understand her a little better, since she had "allowed" me to have a basic claim to fame through her. I got to learn about a unique person whom I respect highly. After reading her story, I realized we had a lot in common. Her mom's name was Sadie, which was a serious option for my child's name. She had a boxer, my first choice of dog, she loved bourbon, she went to jail, she was an open book in her writing. *Go away lady, you're scaring me.* I don't want to end up a sad mess, broke at the end of it all. So many people loved her. Why couldn't someone who was so beloved be happy?

I was asked by my manager to put together a tribute show with Billie Holiday's material in order to book dates in Europe, because that's what the bookers wanted. I asked myself, after trying to run away from her ghostly shadow that's attached herself to me for some unknown reason, how to do justice to her and what she'd given the world.

She offered her heart on a silver platter with love, trust, and vulnerability, only to have it stomped on. That would be enough to make any sensitive soul a heroin addict.

So, Billie, in tribute to you, I'm gonna sing all your B-sides in a major key. You're not going to drag me into the minor key blues with you.

Edinburgh Jazz Festival Headliner

"Do you want to play the 2017 Edinburgh Jazz Festival as a headliner?" my manager of six months, Boris Chlumsky, asked.

"Of course, I do!" I said.

"It pays $1,300 plus expenses," he said.

The pay to be a headliner seemed awfully low. But I was at the bottom of my resources at that point in my newly single independent life. So, I agreed. The contract included two featured solo shows backed by the David L. Harris Quartet, and performing two featured songs in trumpeter James Williams' big band.

Boris's priority was to secure some of the top up and coming players to ensure he landed this gig. But he miscalculated the mentality of New Orleans players. There isn't one scrambling musician in the city of New Orleans who is going to give 15 percent of what they've already booked to a manager who has not acquired additional work for them. They are different creatures who are used to hustling in the asphalt jungle. They'll shove your head down a toilet bowl if they feel they're being screwed.

Boris was an intelligent, young, well-to-do, Jewish New Yorker of good breeding. He could put a website together in an hour and organize a whole tribe of New Orleans musicians for a major big band experience in Scotland. From all the time I spent in New York City, I learned that a lot of New Yorkers are very heady and practical. We had a lot of deep conversations during our occasional evening walks. I understood his mentality. Some of his ideas were great. In general, his mindset was to come to New Orleans and, as he said verbatim, "Save the Black Man."

What went down on that trip to Scotland was a total nightmare. There was no itinerary, no per diem, no rehearsal, no inclusion with the "bros."

Boris sold the headliner deal as me singing a Billie Holiday tribute show. I'd tried for years to get away from the Billie Holiday comparisons, but fair enough. So, I decided that a set list of her B-sides would be a unique way to pay tribute to her after all the years of opportunities coming through for me.

Boris also asked me to sing two songs with a huge New Orleans big band featuring many of my peers. One of the songs was "Summertime" by George

Gershwin. The other was "It's All Right With Me" by Cole Porter. There are many versions of that song. It was never made clear that I was expected to learn the Ella Fitzgerald version. He just told me to learn the song. I learned the Doris Day version, which has completely different phrasing and did not fit in the compact vocal spaces left by the charging horn section.

Moreover, there was no rehearsal that included time for me to work it out, even though the guys in the big band had rehearsals before Europe and during sound checks. In Scotland, I was given all of ten minutes to run those two songs. Boris attended to his "Saving the Black Man" tribe and left me to attend to myself.

I did have one rehearsal with trombonist David L. Harris Quartet's rhythm section at home, before I left for Scotland. David was not there. We ran through two sets' worth of Billie Holiday material that was foreign to me. Two hours was not nearly enough time to do it justice. This rehearsal was only for my two solo shows, not the big band songs.

International jet lag can truly mess me up, especially on "in and out" gigs. Add to that daily cocktails and lack of any knowledge of where food is coming from. I was no saint when it came to alcohol. I had to pace my drinking to exist and maintain my professionalism. But most of the guys were also partying, drinking, and smoking pot on that banshee excursion. Scotland was foggy, wet, and cold, and as usual, I didn't think to pack a coat, as it was July.

I arrived in Scotland alone. Boris flew with all the guys. Once we were all there, he completely ignored me, the only girl in the gang. When I arrived at the airport in Scotland, a host picked me up. She was a sweetheart. I got a little backstory from her about the city and country. I was dropped at the boutique hotel and I checked myself in.

That evening, when I arrived at the theatre, Boris proceeded to scream at me in the dressing room in front of everyone, ridiculing me in front of people I work with from home, for showing up wet in my daywear ten minutes before showtime. I had no guide and had gotten lost. A young Indian man I met walked me to the theater in the pouring rain.

Just before the big band set, Boris told me that I couldn't perform with the band because I had learned the wrong version of the song. The bandmates were nice and sympathetic, especially David L. Harris, who took the time to have a real conversation with me.

I was mad at Boris for not doing his job, for prioritizing the "bros" he was trying to save, and for throwing me under the bus. Every time I saw that little dictator, who was supposed to be my manager, he was yelling at me, or he was so agitated he couldn't even be patient enough to give me pertinent information. I was made to feel like I was a bad girl when I was supposed to be one of the stars. I wasn't even given my per diem until the end of the third day. Each location we were supposed go to as a whole unit had me trying to find my own way because I wasn't included in group transport. *Who the fuck is he to do this to me and treat all the other guys like they're kings?* I knew I wasn't crazy, because another featured female on the headliner was treated the same way by that pompous man. He made me feel so worthless.

Despite being hungry and angsty for a bottle, I tried to be a good sport. In my free time, I walked around the downtown area. I spent a good amount of time in St Giles' Cathedral and meandered around, window shopping. By that time, I had started to sip away.

On balance, I had two great solo shows (with standing ovations) with David's band and one flop show where I was ousted from the big band. Two out of three wasn't bad.

I was set to fly home alone. Boris refused to give me the $1,300 that, as stated in the contract, I would receive upon completion of my work in the festival. I pulled an all-nighter in my room. The "assigned" car never showed up. I called everyone, from the promoter to the nice lady who drove me to the hotel, as well as Boris himself. I paid for a cab with the last of the money I had, but I still missed the flight. Boris deducted $400 from my pay because he had to buy me another plane ticket. The return ticket he had arranged left me in Chicago after an overnight layover in Dublin. I ate crackers for dinner and reached out to a friend to borrow money to get from Chicago to New Orleans. Boris also deducted $300 for the two songs he wouldn't let me sing. Instead of the promised $1,300, I received $600, two months after the festival.

I had been living at Boris's apartment in the Marigny in New Orleans before the trip. He had two security cameras attached to the front and back doors at his house in New Orleans and could clearly see me drinking his bar dry, no matter how hard I tried to crawl on the floor under the camera radar to get to the booze. Granted, he didn't realize I had every intention of replacing them when I got home with my $1,300. Granted, I had snuck my little Frenchie into his house. It was survival.

Everything in his apartment was top of the line, including his $3,000 bed and big screen computer. The liquor that tasted like cherry cough syrup cost $300. I could have told him he was wasting his money (as I drank the whole bottle).

In Scotland, Boris had asked for his key back, even though all my things were still in his house. When he returned to New Orleans, he called me to come and get my stuff. I got to his place, where everything I owned, including a huge yellow ball gown and new MacBook Pro, had been thrown into a big pile on his porch with no one watching it.

As the Scotland story turned into a telephone game among New Orleans musicians, my name got frowned upon even more than it already was after the Squirrel Nut Zippers debacle. *Ingrid in Edinburgh...* eyeball roll. There's that dubious face from a player who was on the gig who had absolutely no clue what that guy had put me through.

Rumor had it Boris gave up on trying to "Save the Black Man" and went back to New York City, but not before several unfortunate reverberating actions befell him at the hands of some of the musicians he had screwed over. Karmic payback.

I truly hope to have another opportunity to go to the Edinburgh Jazz Festival and get it straight 100 percent.

Dear Mamacita,

I got your email. Thank you for the update. The choices one makes with their life are so complex. Been doing a lot of thinking lately. Okay, the last few years. The blessing and curse of traveling for 24 hours to get somewhere is being alone in your own head with no distractions. At the airport I asked myself what I want. I'm tired of being unhappy.

Real fun. Life is supposed to be fun. I think so many get into covering up the pain with medications. I always admire you because you immerse yourself without self-medicating.

Edinburgh is truly one of the most unique cities I've ever been to. It's very gothic architecturally. The people are really nice. I had a full house for the show yesterday afternoon. I'm pretty tired, to be honest. The whole jetlag factor takes more than a few days to get used to.

The guys look the same. Makes me feel a little better knowing it's not only me. I have one more show this evening. Then it's pickup at 5 a.m. for the airport. Ouch.

I wish there was a little more time to explore. Went to the most magnificent cathedral I've ever entered, called St Giles. Lit a candle for Dad.

I'm not sure I can keep up with this travel routine. It's too tiring for the short hauls and lack of money I'm coming home with. It has been a gift to see the world through these eyes for a flash of a moment called two and three days. There is so much vitality and variety here in Europe compared to New Orleans.

Just looking at the flight schedules on the airport board and knowing you could be in Paris, London, Berlin, Copenhagen, Rome, on a short flight is pretty exciting.

Not sure what's next. Figuring it out while tumbling through beauty.

I love and miss you.

You inspire me to do better.

Me

Dear Ava,

I'm trying to get my pay from the Scotland festival now so I can rent a place. They are being difficult.

Staying with a friend of a friend in a really nice fancy house apartment on Orchid, which is near the CC's [Coffee House] on Esplanade. The rents are so expensive these days here and musicians' payroll isn't. It's all good. Living in a shed was a nice experience, but it's much nicer to be in air conditioning in August. I was asked to leave because I got too close to every family member, and they were having problems and trying to figure out their stuff without me in their way. I just need to find my own home and figure out how to pay for it.

The Holy Trinity of messages that circulate the last two years...

[Fiddler and vocalist] Amanda Shaw's mom said, there are no mistakes. Everything happens for a reason. And she's right.

Things are a little hard right now, but who gets to go to Mexico, Puerto Rico, Greece, Norway, and Scotland back-to-back to do what they love to do?

I have some high-end investors who are helping me put a business plan together to make mailbox money out of Los Angeles, Nashville, and New York City.

It's a hot New Orleans August and people are hot and grumpy.

That's it.

I'm proud of you.

You are welcome to borrow the laptop if you're stuck. I could actually use your expertise in merging the phone and laptop and backing up all the tracks and writing I've been putting down. Maybe we could get together soon at CC's?

Goodnight, monkey.

Love, Mom

From White Flight Land to the Bayou

As soon as you cross that parish line from Orleans to Jefferson, all bets are off. I was in Harahan, still waiting two months for my payroll after headlining the Edinburgh Jazz Festival. Hugh O'Donnell, the young man and sorta boyfriend I was staying with, was a good person, but he didn't love me. I was merely a faux housewife in his home. Okay, his attic. I'm pretty good at folding clothes. But when the rafters are low, you have to just laugh when you whack your head multiple times every day.

In 2017, the year of the solar eclipse, I was about to go and live in a musician friend's shed on the Bayou St. John. Transplant wannabes were spending, according to my mom, $1,800 a month to live in that part of New Orleans. I was getting ready to be a nanny to the wildest little firecrackers I had ever met called Trouble #1 and Trouble #2, three and four years old. Two banshees on the loose in their large overgrown yard. They liked me and I liked them. Their musician dad has been a good friend for many a moon. Their mom was a paralegal from out of state. She was living in a fourth-generation Creole cottage with a hoarder musician and two wild kids and having trouble acclimating to the idiosyncrasy of his Southern mentality.

My life was already a chaotic nuthouse; what was I doing going into the fire? I went because, regardless of the lack of air conditioning, I'd be close to my mom, my kid, City Park (across the street), the center of town, and my gigs.

Suburbia had been kind in its own prejudiced manner. I signed off from the suburban attic in Harahan and started up yodeling the blues at Sidney's Saloon in St. Bernard while reclining for the month of August in the shed on the Bayou.

*****

Ingrid Garcia

Sometimes, I merely feel like I'm a pawn being pushed around by the gods for a joke. And somehow, they plop me in the strangest locations on the chess board of life to take two steps forward and one and a half steps back.

In good old Harahan, I was in one of the few last old-school "white flight" neighborhoods. I have heard a proud justification by a few different people around me how "niggers" aren't allowed to be around these parts. It makes me physically sick to hear that word. The town had a Nazi-like police team driving around keeping an eye. An old guy across the street started to go off about his hate and used all kinds of words, after he went out of his way to give my friend and me a ride when we got stuck in the rain. I asked him why he didn't like Black people. My friend said it was time to leave the conversation.

Hugh told his neighbor about a firecracker jazz singer named "Ingrid Garcia," because even as my friend of six months, he still didn't know my last name. Turned out I was staying three doors down from one of my good friends, who used to be my accountant.

I walked to the gas station and there was an old man with his slicked hair in his air-conditioned F-150 pickup offering a ride. He connected me to a friend, a second chance to be friendly. I asked him where he was going. He said he was hunting down the mail lady, said she was driving 40 miles an hour and passed the stop sign. Besides, she's Black and even more reason to get "the bitch" out of his neighborhood. Strike two. He dropped me off and then said if I needed anything, he and his wife were across the street.

In a whole year in Gentilly, a predominantly Black neighborhood, I had never, ever heard anybody call a White person a "cracker." That got on my nerves. I felt like telling him I was pregnant with a Black man's baby.

The Mayor of St. Bernard Avenue

There was a kid named Israel. They called him the Mayor of St. Bernard Avenue, which is in the Seventh Ward. He was the kindest, most innocent, protective little ten-year-old I had ever met.

The couple I was subletting a room from was an all-organic family with a two-year-old baby girl. They kept their back door open for Israel, that being my bedroom door. He knocked on it way too early. Every day. He was my new little buddy. He seemed to think I was his new best friend.

The thing I really admired about Israel was his discipline. He showed up every day with a positive attitude ready to play drums, share his dance, and have breakfast together. I wished he was a grownup. He had taken on the "big man" role. He carried all my grocery bags for me because he said that's what real men do. I wish all grown men did.

That little guy, one of six kids who were being raised by their grandma, had an unusually positive spirit. I met his mom and apparently all she did was hit him. I met his grandma and all she did was worry. Somehow, I thought, *this special young man is going to do great things, because he's wise and street smart and has his eyes on the prize.*

While we were walking, we diverted on the side street (because there had been shootings on Saint Bernard), and he told me of his dream to go to Miami and swim with the dolphins.

I loved that kid. I was going to try to be a big sister and help him get where he wanted to go in his life. He put a smile on my face with his enthusiasm for life. His bowling needed some work. *It's not a baseball field, Mister.* Gifts come in strange forms. I guess I had a little bodyguard. He told me he wanted to be a policeman when he grew up. And he said he would never throw me in jail for being drunk at the airport gate.

I met him when he was giving away ice cream (bought with money from his own pocket) to the kids playing in front of the school across the street. He became their leader. I helped him begin his YouTube career with a video about positivity.

Fabulous Flora

New Orleans has spectacular gardenias, magnolias, and jasmine growing luxuriously, lazily in front of shotguns, even in the poorest neighborhoods.

I walked into the Seventh Ward home of the married couple hosting me. I wasn't feeling well. The aroma and look of the glorious bouquets she got from a nearby wedding on her way home from a hard day's work at the Waldorf School took my breath away.

I remember the days of playing extravagant dot-com parties in New York City when the florist got paid more than the band. The gold was to go home at the end of the night with many bouquets to share.

My mom taught art at Hahnville High School for a year. She loves art so much and won scholarships to go to college for it. She had to be a disciplinarian to kids who had no interest in art and only made fun of her efforts. She called me, crying, often wanting to quit because she couldn't make headway to share her love and wisdom with them. It's not her way to be mean. I sent her a huge bouquet of roses when she completed the year. She said it was her first gifted bouquet. In 17 years, my dad never once gave her flowers.

Jasmine reminds me of London. Cheap plastic flowers on plastic tables remind me of Mexico. Flowers in hair remind me of vintage Vargas ladies from the past. Births, weddings, and funerals seem to be required to send them.

The happiest smile I couldn't negate was on a strapping Irish handyman with a gorgeous bouquet of flowers he'd plucked from the neighborhood yards. He was standing at the front door of my ghetto apartment in the Marigny, dressed to the nines on a perfect backlit sunny day to go to Easter Sunday church in Treme.

Maybe giving flowers isn't a luxury. Making someone feel happy and thought about is quite paramount.

Bicycle Thieves

I always try to control my anger. I have Martin Luther King and Malcolm X to thank for lessons learned.

I guess I'd hit a wall. I'd been without my driver's license; because of the large lien placed on it, I'd been bicycling and taking the bus for two years. (Blessings in disguise; I got to meet my community up close for $1.25.)

My second bike in a month was clipped and stolen within ten minutes in front of the church thrift store where I was buying baby clothes and books for my host Liz's two-year-old. I was talking to a melancholy woman who was coming out of her marriage about what my dad always stated about approaches to life. *You come from a place of either love or war.* I was telling her his concept and how maybe there's a way to win life's game and do both.

I spent a gig's full pay buying and researching the proper lock system from the guy who had the bike shop on Frenchmen Street. After the theft, I walked two miles home through the ghettos in a massive sweat with bags and a clipped kryptonite chain and lock that weighed over ten pounds; it was war, my friends. That bike, as well as the last one, held personal meaning.

Dear Amanda,

It's really nice to hear from you, my new friend. Thank you for the words. I think I just hit a wall in every single way and am feeling really, really depressed at the moment. I'm sure it will go away with reflection and digging deep to believe that people are good and that my invested choice in life hasn't been a huge mistake, as I sit here on the Westbank in a friend's bedroom without a single dollar, literally, to show for my work.

I think maybe I need to get some counseling, because the situation with Ava's dad and his parents, with the rejection by the business I chose to be a part of, the rejection by people I gave to over the years in their hour of need, then with a cringe in mine, said no to a place to stay, has made me wonder, what's the point of being a nice person in life?

I keep trying my best, but it doesn't seem to be good enough or appreciated by the ones I really care for. The guy who started to make me feel alive again, with his beauty and thoughtfulness and care, drove off into the night last night and left me standing at a gas station in a neighborhood where I didn't have a clue where I was. He got mad because I gave a corn dog that he paid for to a homeless family asking for help. He drove off in his pickup truck with my bag, which had everything in it. Dropped it off to the person I'm staying with, told the guy I was out of my mind, and left me behind. I feel like an absolute nothing at the moment.

I think I need to go and be around some family and friends right now. The friend I'm staying with asked me to marry him two days ago out of the blue and I don't feel comfortable here now. I have a place to stay for two weeks in the Seventh Ward starting tomorrow. Oddly enough, it's an ex-lover of my friend who dumped me last night; she lives in the house of Ava's Waldorf School guidance counselor, who was my favorite person there. Her name is Liz.

In the time period since I lost everything and went through so much chaos and ghetto survival, she had a baby who is almost two now. I spent time with her family in the backyard yesterday. Normal people doing healthy normal things. This little girl loves me. I think it will be healthy to be around that kid and family energy for a little while and not people who have strange thoughts, actions, and ulterior motives. I don't understand why people are scared to be open and kind and just be able to get along and if not be happy, at least be content.

Allen Toussaint's daughter, Alison, posted on the anniversary of his one-year death, his belief quotes. Number one was (not verbatim): "Show me who you hang out with and I'll tell you who you are."

But, as I sit here in a low moment, having lost pretty much everything, I want to kick myself in the pants for the choices I've made in trusting everybody. There have been many wonderful moments these last two years, with many good people and experiences, but they have all been a dance of chaos. I need to figure out how to be sustainable and build a home of my own with a tribe I trust. My nervous system is utterly gone after being on the receiving end of insane actions by those I thought I could trust.

Thank you for listening. How are you doing? I gave you my goods. I'd love to hear yours.

Love,

Ingrid

Asphalt Jungle

Muggy summer drag,
Natives are restlessly mad.

Tensions rising
Locked inside
Isolation
Currents high.

Nitpick mundane,
Too much time,
Equals pain
Insane.

Left to devices
All alone,
Wilderness
Of the mind roams.

Lord of the jungle
Who will claim
The crown
For a day?

Musical chairs,
Get tossed,
Bullies claim
To be boss.

Testosterone sweat
Gentlemen's ideals
Put to the test
No rest.
Clawing, scratching, hungry
Animal need
Survival of the fittest
Is key.

Christmas will come,
All will rejoice.
Fresh air, kind living
Make summer's roast...
A faraway dream.

Miss Sarah's Domain

One room for rent. Private door exiting to Esplanade Avenue. Inverted yard. Broken gate at ground zero for crime in New Orleans. Claiborne Bridge. Quaint characters. Flat rate of $500 per month with Wi-Fi.

The price that I paid was much more exorbitant. Rules and regulations by Miss Sarah, the landlady. No, you may not speak in your normal exuberant tone. Silence. No, you may not enter the kitchen quietly at a musician's morning of 4 a.m. to make Earl Grey tea (*without someone hovering over you telling you how to do something you already know you're not good at. Who cares what temperature the water boils at as long as the tea tastes good?*)

But the solace to be allowed to be yourself should be permitted when you are running around trying your best to please. I swear, I wanted to pump music up so loud and dance like nobody's business. Containment has never been a PowerPoint for me. Why should it be? It made me feel like I couldn't breathe.

My dad always said, never let anyone tie your hands, or else you're done for. I say, with a lot of thought, never let anyone take away your exuberance. My new mantra was to ignore negativity like a Pollyanna and say, "Oh No You Didn't."

I lived in a room in a small prefab Montgomery Ward house with an uptight waiter from Trinidad, a trombone busker, and my landlady, Miss Sarah, who was 70 and in a wheelchair. There wasn't a more intelligent or optimistic person than Sarah. She was from San Francisco and had studied every school of philosophy and technique to be learned in any trade. She couldn't move her legs and was utterly dependent on Miss Rose, who came three times a day to take care of business.

Miss Sarah and Miss Rose were in a codependent relationship. Witnessing the love and hate like a marriage between them, I'd found myself being a third party to fill the holes and gaps; being the one to buy diet root beer and M&M's after Rose left, being the one to watch *Saturday Night Live*, converse with and tuck Miss Sarah into bed, making sure her legs didn't fall off the edge.

Miss Rose told me to just pay the rent and not be a party to Miss Sarah's needs. I couldn't do that. When Miss Rose wasn't there, she didn't have anyone else. How would I feel in her position? Miss Rose was a tough cookie with a heart of gold. She carried a gun with her. She played cards and spoke her mind. When the agency dropped her, and she realized the case worker didn't have another agency set up to take care of Miss Sarah, she got one up and running and got herself assigned to continue caring for her. It awes me how many forms love comes in. Miss Sarah and Miss Rose squabbled incessantly. At the end of the day, Miss Rose tried to be there for Miss Sarah no matter what hour of the night.

I observed how much struggle some go through to just exist from day to day.

* * * * *

Miss Sarah called on me to raid the orange tree I had told her about down the street in a stranger's enclosed yard. The freeze was going to kill all those big juicy oranges anyway, she said. People down here get shot for that stuff, I thought. But Mr. BMW didn't pluck the fruit or cover it up. And Miss Sarah loved oranges.

So she, in her wheelchair, me, dressed classy in thrift store British tweeds with the one pair of pants I own in case I ended up in jail again, and Allie, dressed in her jailbird striped sweater, hauled it over there with three canvas totes. We made a perfect criminal team. We wrote a note explaining what we were doing, and I foolishly put my cell number, in case he wanted fresh juice in exchange for our thievery.

(Have you ever climbed over a huge metal gate with fleur de lis pokes on the top side? One mistake and you'll never have sex again.)

Thank you, waste management industry, for your solid cans to land on. Pluck, pluck, shake, shake, jump, jump, and then the neighbor came out. *Freeze.* I pretended to be a branch. Pluck, pluck, pluck, the juiciest lemons and oranges. There were little satsumas plucked in for lagniappe (a little something extra).

After configuring how to climb over the gate again with the heavy bag of citrus, I felt both guilty and high about the adventure. I don't believe in stealing, but if you're going to steal, it's better to Robin Hood it. We had a juicing party thereafter where four people got a good solid shot of vitamin C to divert all the sneezing going on in that house.

Afterwards, a friend who lived in Israel for a year suggested that we should be like Johnny Appleseed and plant citrus trees around the city for anyone to enjoy. Then we could climb trees for the fun of it.

None of the kids growing up in our family were allowed to have purchased presents. As a child, it was hard for me to understand watching everyone celebrate the forbidden word associated with Christ's birthday: commercialism. As a family, we attended midnight mass with respect for Jesus.

In *A Tree Grows in Brooklyn*, a sister and brother weather the indignity of having a Christmas tree flung at them to win a contest and proudly walk away with the prize. That was my brother and sisters and me: collecting thrown-out Christmas trees in the Marigny a few days after Christmas and dragging them home to be decorated with homemade popcorn and paper rings.

Even though she was physically suffering and frustrated as hell with the system, Miss Sarah diligently followed the rules and regulations that led to no solutions for her health. We all tumble tumultuously through stories and realities without a clear compass.

I was lucky to be surrounded by so much positivity from so many who were struggling in their silent configuring refrain. There's a code I have noticed called the "Yes." As I strive to be that Yes person, through trials and tribulations, what Christmas means to me doesn't happen on one day. The "Yes" code is every day. Eye contact, offering, and a kind word every single second of the day to everyone. What can I do to be of service each day?

* * * * *

One evening, a policeman came in response to Miss Sarah's phone call. Officer Blount deserves thanks. He listened discerningly. He asked the proper questions as a neutral third party while Miss Sarah, who I had attended to for four months (with no compensation for my services), ripped me to shreds.

I was two weeks behind in my rent. Officer Blount evaluated the situation under the kitchen light after I opened the latched gate.

There is a reason, as my mother stated, why my landlady is alone. Her daughter and her few friends and family don't call and don't show face. I tried my best to take up the slack in every single way. As she and I explained both sides of the story, he was able to see the truth.

From my perspective, I had been used — and abused — by her in a calculated manner. Despite claiming to be blind, she was able to access information about me that required reading. She found out the phone number of my ex-husband and exposed every piece of information to him that I had shared with her only to have me shut down after I had given her so much.

What does one do when an elderly woman with a disability attacks you physically and provokes you to the point of rage? She called the cops on me. Twice. There were three separate witnesses affirming her wrong-headed behavior. Even so, the police determined that I was in the right.

My friend Curtis, a civil rights activist leader who was recovering from three types of cancer, called it well. He stated, "She does not want to help herself." She stuck with her power crutch, playing the victim.

I was done.

Everyone from here to there that I have given my heart and soul to and asked absolutely nothing in return can stuff it. I was ashamed of myself for having a yelling match. I was ashamed of myself for allowing a woman in a wheelchair to put me in that frame of mind. I was ashamed of myself for not being in a better place in life after having worked so very hard.

As I wrote in a song yet to be completed, "I'm not the person I used to be, I'm not the person I am going to be, but I am the person I am now."

* * * * *

Miss Sarah had caught my heart, even though living with her was a roller coaster. She called me often after I moved out. She asked me one night to come over and change her diaper, which I did. It cost me almost $20 in an Uber. Grandville, my boyfriend at the time, asked me why I'd do something like that. I answered, "Because she asked me and I can." I realized not only did I connect with her, but I also feared that I would end up like her. She passed away shortly after that last incident. I went to the hospital to see her. We laughed and talked. I said goodbye with a hug and that was the end of our story.

The Temptress Hotel

There's a place in Treme
Where trouble goes to play.
Pandora's box is open
For the addict's faith.
You can rent by the hour,
You can rent by the day,
You can rent by the week,
Maybe never go away.

The woman that owns it
Is a cowboy type,
She keeps a gun by her bedside
She'll shoot you in the night.

It's a fluorescent lit oasis
Amongst ground zero crime,
Prostitutes and drug addicts
Go there to make the dime.
Luring tourists into their snare,
The 5 o'clock news stating
Another innocent ended up dead there.

Why they're still open,
I really don't know,
It's a scary location
One would never want to go.
Except when having hit
The bottom of the bale,
The only option from there,
Is to end up in jail.

The Temptress Hotel
Wakes at midnight,

The freak show begins,
Small stark rooms
Hold stories within.

The down on their luck,
Living laissez-faire,
If you have habits that need tending,
That's the place for you, *mon cher.*

I've known musicians
To abode there,
Head to toe sleeping,
After selling their wares.

Those are the innocents,
The drunk, pot-smoking kind.
Lucky for a roof and bed,
TV and security of mind.
The doors there lock. Sometimes.

The only place left on the totem pole
Is the Claiborne Street Bridge,
Where the homeless troll,
At the end of the road
Where the crazies go.

If you're thinking of going
To the Temptress Hotel,
Think twice, before you choose
The home where lost souls dwell.

It's been there
Since before I was a child,
Next to Congo Square
Where drum rhythms bang wild.
The Temptress Hotel
Sits quiet in the shadows
Of a neighborhood street,
A quaint little sign
Gives the appearance it's sweet.

Like a black widow waiting for prey
To fall into her sticky web,
Check-in is easy,
Check-out might be dead.

College Try at a Dating Ad

Hi, my name is Ingrid Lucia.

My interests are Charlie Chaplin movies, or anything black and white.

I especially like black.

Four-fifths of my wardrobe are in that elegant color tone.

I love love.

Lust is an option.

Literature and books are predominant in my make-up, but a pure quote by Steinbeck or Shakespeare can do the job.

Deal-makers and -breakers:

You must have sex with eye contact every night.

You may not curse at me.

How do you feel about menageries that include monkeys?

Cleaning resume not needed, but a helpful hand is a must.

Doesn't matter about your past, only your present frame of mind and your sperm count.

Overall, I'm a pretty easygoing girl (if you don't mind "Oklahoma" being sung every morning).

I know there's somebody out there for me to love.

I'm one of a kind.

I can promise, as a girl singer with a catalogue, to leave you pennies in my will.

Shout out "504!"

Black and Mild

He's mellow,
Rough and refined,
A slow burn
Who takes his time.

He's sweet smelling
When he smokes that brew,
Pensive and thoughtful
A tall man too.

He's Black and Mild
I love this man,
He acts in ways
I don't understand.

He's Black and Mild
His personality extends
All dichotomies,
That make up men.

But I love him,
He's the slow burning flame,
That keeps this butterfly
Coming back again... and again.

Body and Soul

"I'm in love with you." No one had ever said those words to me before Grandville. No one had ever bought me a $40 bag of chocolates with their hard-earned street gig money. I saw the honesty and vulnerability in his eyes. His divorce backstory was the same as mine. We were part of the same musical tribe in New Orleans. I had hired him off and on for 14 years. We moved in together. Two musicians in one room. I hadn't laughed so hard in a long, long time.

He seemed reluctant to open his heart. So was I.

Doing the love dance is exhausting. But we were committed at that moment. For the first time in my life, I was not going to be pragmatic in my relationship choices. It was magical to witness close to my face those doe eyes that loved so deeply they showed fear and hope. Oh my God. What was I getting myself into?

I believe in the idea of unconditional love. I write songs of love. I sing songs written of love. But when the cacophony comes along for the very first time in your life, it brings with it a roller coaster of emotions. Love is a non-negotiable emotion. To me, it is the ultimate attainment. He said I was going to kill him. I felt the same. The love game. It's too bad there are control brakes that come with it, out of fear of the heart being vulnerable and possibly wounded.

I was being exclusive with somebody after a 16-year marriage. The odd thing was that he wouldn't stop playing Jack Teagarden's "Body and Soul." It was my dad's favorite song from the John Garfield movie of the same name about a boxer. It was hard to have my dad's memory in my face all night long.

How many times does one have to repeat the same track to become a master? I guess it could have been a lot worse, listening to some other genre of music that wasn't consistent with my catalogue of work and listening choice.

I thought about putting Vicente Fernandez on repeat a couple hundred times to see if Spanish would permeate Grandville's nervous system in his sleep.

Beaten with a Broom

I made a pact with myself to do better. Cleaned the house like I had OCD. Took Allie for a nice walk. Sat under the shade of an oak tree thinking about music and life. Went to a meeting with one of my good friends at Bob and Jane's classic French Quarter home to discuss the lineup for season two of Parlor Parties. That is an idea I came up with, not to pat myself on the back. I felt a lot of pride that two wonderful ladies, Jane and Tonya, were taking charge and making action happen.

Later, I went to dinner at Muriel's with a visiting family and had a serious discussion about God and religion with them. These kinds of discussions are rare for table talk.

Our new neighbor, a big woman whose husband kept walking up and down the breezeway doing something suspicious, had the worst attitude. I asked in the afternoon if we could just be nice neighbors and she ignored me. That night, as Grandville and I were listening to gospel music and I was dancing, she started pounding on the wall. I pounded back. She pounded again. That's when I decided to knock on her door and try to talk to her. She charged at me full speed with the end of her jagged metal broom and tried to shove it down my throat.

The next day the pounding started again. I went outside and she took the same broom and started beating me on my backside with the sweeper end of it. I called the police. One White cop started the process and took the situation seriously. Then two Black cops showed up and took the situation seriously.

The landlord, who lived a few feet away, knocked on my door and started yelling at me. Next thing, the cops were hanging out with the couple who sells drugs and smokes pot all day. They were all laughing together while I was waiting inside as I was told to do. How was that possible? It's not okay to be beaten by a broom two days in a row by anyone, much less a rude bitch.

I wished I had the money to go live somewhere nice with green grass and trees and nice people. I wished I could make that happen for so many. In the meantime, the rent was due. And the property was due to be inspected by the Louisiana Road Home program, but the landlord had not been doing his job maintaining the studio apartment at all. The place was falling apart. The stove was broken, the door was broken, the windows were cracked, the AC didn't work, and there were hundreds of cockroaches and bedbugs having a party daily.

Everything was falling apart. I felt beaten up. Oh, because I was – literally – and the cops and two landlords watching thought it was funny. The landlord told me I was lucky I was White or I would be in jail, just for dancing to gospel music on a Saturday night.

Behind the Red Picket Gate

BANG BANG BANG

"Open the door!"

"Who is it?" I said.

"It's the S.W.A.T. team."

After paying our rent on time all year with proof of receipt, we were told that the landlord was sending a vacate notice. Why? Because it was the holidays and we couldn't provide the W-2s for his Section 8 paperwork, as they don't come in until January.

BANG BANG BANG

"It's the S.W.A.T. team and we're going to break down the door."

After cramming music work until 4 a.m. with the alarm set for 10 a.m. to go to practice, at 8 a.m. I opened the door to a squad of about 15 bulldogs with bulletproof vests and machine guns aimed at us. Scary.

"What apartment are you?"

"B."

"Who else is in here right now?"

"My boyfriend, who plays trombone." He showed his face with his hands in the air.

"Have you seen this woman?"

They showed us a photograph of a woman who resembled Diana Ross at the beginning of *Mahogany*. Nice makeup, classy looking. She looked like our neighbor from six months ago, I thought, when she was healthier and not on crack.

Bang, bang, bang, on the next door. I wished I had a photograph of the couple who lives there. He sold pot, she beat me with a broom. They looked completely terrified. Karmic payback is irreplaceable.

Bang, bang, bang, on the landlord's door. I could only imagine.

I tried to get my heart to stop beating so fast right as I spoke with my mother. She said, after all the months of the front door being broken and stuck shut, at least the S.W.A.T. team will have solved the problem by knocking it down. On top of that, she joked with Grandville about how the trombone should have scared them away. They both love crime shows. And apparently even trombone players could be drug dealers affiliated with a mob boss.

The lady they were looking for was nice enough. The only problem I had with her was that she hadn't returned our dustpan.

Ingrid's Book of Etiquette

Etiquette: noun

et·i·quette | \'e-ti-kət

Definition: the conduct or procedure required by good breeding or prescribed by authority to be observed in social or official life

Growing up the way I did, I was always living in other people's spaces. When my dad allowed me to stay in Mexico with a family at the age of 11, he said one thing: "Always give more than you take and you will always be welcome." I've learned there are expiration dates on a welcome.

Oak Alley Plantation shared a rule about the stately guest room: When the wood-carved pineapple at the foot of the four-poster bed suddenly disappears, it's time to depart, and the hosts don't have to say a word.

I've learned a lot from living in so many wonderful people's homes around the world. For the sake of sharing what I've learned, giving a good laugh, and also trying to get back to the simple things that make a person feel special, here goes...

What not to do:

Drink a bottle of your host's Chateau Neuf-du-Pape without replacing it.

Bring your dirty Frenchie into their $2,000 bed made with white 600 count Egyptian linens.

Borrow their expensive underwear while they are on vacation.

Bring a Mexican fisherman home to make love to with a bottle of tequila while your mother is sleeping one floor below you in the cabana. (Why was she so mad?)

Give all your money away to homeless people and get evicted three times.

Wear your favorite perfume without permission in someone else's space. (You may get yelled at by your ex-father-in-law. But hey, in my case, at least he finally spoke.)

Don't disrespect anyone's rules and regulations that make their home a home.

Good etiquette is always making the other person feel at ease. How does one do that while living with them in their home? There are so many dichotomies that make up an individual and their routine of habits.

What to do:

Always show respect for yourself and the people that have to look at you every day. Lunch in your beard and pants below the booty showing Walmart undies are not recommended for a good first impression. Thrift store dresses and polyester suits are (when ironed).

When you look in the mirror, do you like what you see? Sometimes I don't. Once in a while I do. Like my dad used to say, get that crap off your eyes, you have perfect skin. Be an open book and make eye contact.

When you walk out the door, always make sure you have your keys, a snack, bus fare home, and your sanity (don't forget your home address no matter where you are or you could end up under the Claiborne Street Bridge). Remember clean undies (in case you're hit by a bus), something to read, and a notepad to jot down your random thoughts through the day, and most important, the perfect shade of red-blue lipstick.

Whether the rain is pouring or the sun is shining, always remember to keep your Ps and Qs intact.

Converse with everyone from the street urchin to the millionaire. You never know what form Jesus will be living in and where your epiphany is going to come from.

My dad always said, behave like somebody is always watching you. So, dance like crazy to loud music when you are in your office gig. Steal that roll of toilet paper from a fancy hotel to give away to those who need it, and remember to pick your nose only when you are alone. Know the FBI will be witnessing you though your smartphone.

Seriously, I have spent so much time witnessing bad etiquette. Especially by those who have money, who know where the eighth spoon in the silver placement setting goes but don't really know how to simply be kind.

If the world were my oyster, and could be a better place, here's what I would say:

Always be kind. Always. I've been ashamed of myself for the way I've behaved when others have provoked me and won because I went there.

Always open the door, make eye contact, and share a story with a stranger, even if they are dirty and missing a tooth. It could be you.

Always be generous. There is an excess of food, space, and blankets. I know what it feels like to be homeless.

Always know that whatever you give comes back multifold. Currency isn't a dirty piece of paper.

At the end of the day, always treat people like you would like to be treated, even if you are a palmetto bug.

We all deserve to be here. Empathy is my favorite word. Etiquette is the vehicle to get there.

Upstanding Citizens of New Orleans

Royal Discussions

It was a gloomy rainy day. I was at McDonald's, and I was dealing with a lot of personal problems and not in a good mood.

Eight elderly African Americans were having a shouting match over England's royal lineage. One was the leader and well versed. The others don't understand why the "fuck" the old lady with the big hat was the Queen when her husband was still alive. He tried to explain that the lack of a son in the royal family is why a woman becomes Queen. "Somebody needs to strap on the pants." Most of the guys were outraged that Philip was not the king and man of the house.

Then, there was an elderly woman explaining who's who and what's what and how every man should respect the Queen. They were laughing their heads off understanding the impotent position the men in the royal family were placed into while the Queen on the chess board got to navigate the waters. "That old bitch with the big hat?" Never negate your Queen. The King is only allowed one move on the board.

Who's laughing now? Well, they changed my mood.

* * * * *

Corner Grocery Conversation

While I was waiting at a crowded little store checkout, there was a lady behind me on her phone really, really loud: "Bitch, that bitch from Dallas, yeah bitch, that fat bitch, she got married and now she's skinny. Bitch, I don't know where that bitch's husband is now. I know right Bitch...!"

I was reading David Sedaris' book *Theft by Finding* and had just read how a woman walking in front of him said "fuck" at least 11 times in a one-block walk and how he wanted to follow her to see how many "fuck"s she would say, but his groceries were too heavy.

The two millennials in the back of the store noted she said "bitch" 20 times.

My dad wouldn't let us curse.

"Therefore, henceforth that voluptuous grand dame bequeathed her squire to another bitch."

* * * * *

Grandma, Git the Shotgun

I liked our neighbors on Franklin Avenue. Everyone was usually nice and quiet.

However, while watching the news one night, we heard major fighting across the street at the pot dealer's house. The whole household was out in front of the house. The grandma was on the steps with a shotgun backed by one young man and fronted by another, with major fighting between two of them.

"Grandma" yelled and yelled while the guys' testosterone was raging. Then she shot the shotgun in the air. Next thing we knew the two guys were scrapping on the ground for their guns when six police cars showed up. Then all was quiet.

Todd was visiting from New York for one day. He got quite an eyeful.

Is it time for a white picket fence yet?

* * * * *

Two Goats in the Road

One of my very first pets was a nanny goat that we found almost drowning in the Mississippi River when we lived on a homemade raft (I was six). I loved that goat so much. I named her Mary Jane. She started to eat the whole wood boat. My dad gave her away to a restaurant in the French Quarter and told me her job was to eat all the garbage there. Right.

I went to the corner store, breathed in fresh air with time to think, sat on the front porch for the first time feeling awkward because it's a throughway avenue, and there I was, on display to drug addicts and beggars.

Just as I was thinking of the sequence of songs recorded and an order for my new album, two goats, one black, one white, walked across the street. They almost got hit by a car. I walked over to the neutral ground where they stood under an oak tree.

Well, that bonded pair of quirky goats ran off into the night together, diverting traffic and public buses. But not before they gave me a *baaaaaaaaaa*.

"Isn't It Pretty to Think So?"

Halloween 2017. I was completely in love and it was terrifying. To be so vulnerable to someone is a delicate place. But with a whole lot of thought, my conclusion with a pounding heart was yes, Grandville.

Oh my goodness, I can honestly say, no one knows what each day will bring, but we must keep our eyes open to lasso the moment. One day it was survival mode on an incremental hamster wheel, the next day held the rhythm section tracks with my dream players to make album #13. I'd been funded by three benefactors who believed in me: Clay Conrad, Marshall Wood, and Jonathan Olsen.

Somehow, by being persistent, Grandville and I signed a lease for a home across the street from the bedbug-infested dump we had been living in on Franklin Avenue. We were going to build our own self-contained compound that included live music, baked goods, and a creative haven. *Ya ready to have a home-cooked meal twice a month with an intimate concert?*

I was (and still am) a one-woman corporation. I'd been juggling so many booking dates for our family band since I was ten years old. If the numbers added up, I'd be a thousandaire. Hemingway's line, "Isn't it pretty to think so?" applies.

The game isn't over until it's over. I'm not qualified to do anything else. Unless you'd like slow typing. This thing called music is it. Besides, unless my alter ego becomes a librarian or a burlesque dancer (or a mix of both), I've paid my dues to sing to you intimately. One song, Nashville says, is all it takes. If not, playing music to make people happy is all that matters to me.

I was so excited to start that new rebirth, I couldn't get the smile off my face.

New album.
Parlor concerts.
Jazz Fest.
European summer festivals.
Game on.

A Day in the Life

The view out the window from our new two-story home on Franklin Avenue, the daily to-do. Same characters, same narrative, including moi.

The one-legged man in a wheelchair and with a crutch asking the same question in front of McDonald's, if he can have a dollar for a hamburger, not remembering I was the one who found the wheelchair he was sitting in. He got ahold of a gun and held up the McDonald's drive-thru. The neighbors chastised me for having enabled him. Otherwise, he would have been a one-legged pirate who couldn't hold a gun and his crutches at the same time.

The dreamer youth painting their mission statements on abandoned buildings with creative graffiti murals, showing how ethereal the world can be while used needles, cheap vodka bottles, condoms, and fried chicken bones lie below the daily drying paint.

Across the street lay an array of kind neighbors, some who sold pot, others who owned Airbnbs, while the Baptist church wailed the word in song, breaking down the walls and stating the truth of the almighty three times a week. At night the Domino's Pizza sign flashed through my window, interspersed with the red and blue lights of police cars and ambulances. One never knew whether to look out the window out of curiosity.

A neighbor who was on his way home was hit on his bike in front of our house by a Domino's driver going the wrong way. And Domino's was closed. Turns out, Morris Bart (a personal injury attorney) got him $400,000 as I saw him again on TV one day.

Another neighbor, a gay costume designer, was awfully nice for a whole year when we lived across the street in the dumpy apartment. But when his ulterior motives to move in where we were residing were squashed (because after a credit check by the landlord, they found that he had tried to blow up a FEMA building), he wasn't so nice. It kind of made me question whether to trust mankind.

I was trying incrementally to keep building my utopia and believe the world was a good place even while I was carrying mace in my hand. I woke up every day staring at the ceiling, trying to think. I wondered where I fit into the big picture.

One night after a gig, I wanted to walk to the corner store to shake off tension, get some fresh air, and buy some soda water and lemon. My roommate advised against it. I stayed home instead and a little while later two big gunshots went off right nearby.

I do love all of the characters in the St. Roch neighborhood (a subdistrict of the Bywater). They come from all walks of life and overall want peace. They make eye contact, ask "How you be?" and acknowledge that you exist, whether homeless, local old school, or nouveau bohemian. Those who don't acknowledge others aren't from around these parts.

Viva Las Vegas

The eighth anniversary of my dad's death was in 2019. It was hard to believe. I still saw his thoughtful dreamy sky-blue eyes in my mind so clearly. His mannerisms and stories.

How did I end up with such a great gig in Las Vegas on that day of all days? It was thanks to Nick Parrotta.

My father loved Las Vegas. When I was a child, he had a gambling problem. Our caravan would roll in as the sun was setting. He would find the coupon booklets for free steak dinners and circus shows and give them to the women and the kids. Then he took off into the night with all the money. While we were watching the trapeze acts at Circus Circus Casino fly across the slot machines, he was trying to hit The Big Time. He never did. Many a time, the next morning we would drive (broke) to Lake Mead and wash our clothes with a swim in the muddy red water and be on our way.

I was lying in the grassy yard of my promoter's 1950 Rat Pack style home, staring at the light blue skies, the shade of my dad's eyes, listening to the birds chirping in the peaceful silence and sunshine. I sure did miss him so much.

Being in Vegas after being on guard in the dirty streets and ghettos of New Orleans was surreal. I do believe there are no mistakes. If that's true, I took it as a sign that he was up there and watching me.

I bet 21 on 21 for you, Dad; if anything ever comes of it, we can give it to that family you adopted in Cuba.

White Girl

I feel like I don't have a right to speak on this subject, but I am highly curious as to how the blue-eyed, White man-devil came into complete power, when Jesus dwelled in a land of dark-skinned people.

A nice old lady at the bus stop asked if I was Creole as she pointed at my skin, hair, and eyes. I wish. I'm Russian and Irish. My mother told me to take an ancestry test because she swears there's Romanian and English in my blood, which would mean I am a mutt. The truth of the matter is at that time I was jaundiced from cirrhosis.

One of my first boyfriends in New York City was a Black bassist. He did (and still does) quite well playing with many jazz legends. We were in love. After his rock star gigs with fans idolizing him and world tours and limousines, he would stand around the corner while I hailed a cab to Brooklyn. They wouldn't pick him up.

I've been teased about White people stuff. Some of it is true, I guess. I put pretzels on meatloaf to be creative, and I like grilled cheese sandwiches and French toast. I've heard that only White girls let their dog sleep in bed with them, have flat booties, would get into tanks to swim with sharks, run toward danger in the woods in a horror movie, and ski. I got called a Snow Bunny once, which sounded sexy and cold.

The worst no-no as a White girl is knocking on someone's door in a ghetto to resolve a problem face to face. That can lead to a broom beating or a drop 'n' roll.

When I was in Mexico, the Latinos had words for me as a White girl: *galleta*, *bolilla*, *guerita*. I guess what bothers me the most is the guardedness that sometimes comes from those who think I am trying to get one over on them because I'm White. It's simply not true.

White girls get dirty feet fast. Well, mine do. White girls like the windows open when it's breezy while letting in the flies, wasps, termites, and ants. So what, we're all creatures of God and maybe they need a bite and a break too.

* * * * *

My first French kiss ever was with a Black girl when I was nine. I hadn't thought about it until I started writing this book.

The usual routine for our family when I was young before the band started and between raft living was to drive the school bus to the park or drop the kids there or at the library for the day while the group painted signs. It was a sunny, hot day. A girl my age and I were the only ones in the park. We had the best time until the slide got too hot and the skin on our legs started burning and sticking to it. We played on the monkey bars until our fingers got so puffy and sore, we knew popping blisters were to ensue. Looking for cans of Coke and Tab was short-lived. A black Maybelline pencil got used for makeup and then it melted.

We were best little buddies for the day, laughing, running, tripping, singing, cartwheeling. We ended up hiding behind a big shade tree and decided to practice French kissing. It was the strangest feeling, both of us trying to figure out where our tongues were supposed to go in the other's mouth. She tasted like cherry blow-pop and we were both so sweaty and dirty and hot. We both agreed it wasn't all it was built up to be.

After a long while, our moms finally arrived to take us home, never knowing what had happened. We had the best day of fun and learned something new. Kissing that long was actually kind of boring and awkward and made us really thirsty for a cold root beer. We said goodbye and that was that. I got in the bus and we drove to the next town.

Blurred Lines

Creativity in the 1950s was dominated by Jews, African Americans, women, and the gay community, who were the ousted underdogs. During a conversation I had with Jerry Leiber and Mike Stoller, I got firsthand information.

I'm the first to give my musical services away for free out of love. When I was a female bandleader at the Showboat Casino in Atlantic City, I found out I was obligated to sign minority status paperwork because it was required by the state. I asked for an additional $2,000 a week for the band, and I got it. It paid for our first recording, *I'd Rather Be in New Orleans*.

No one wants to be placed in that position. It's degrading and humiliating, and it made me feel like a lesser human being. But in that case, I was able to leverage it to my advantage.

Choice Words

I've been told that certain members of the musical community hate me and have "choice" words for me. With persistently asking why, it was stated I write "novels" on Facebook. We live in a country with the principle of freedom of speech. If you don't like it, flip the page or scroll. Maybe the "novels" need some feedback. I'll take that gladly. I can't improve without positive critique.

Once you tell people to shut their trap, burn their masterpieces, and censor them because you don't agree with their point of view, you've become like Nazi Germany, destroying great art and literature. The list of banned books includes *Lolita*, about a nymphomaniac, Anais Nin's *Erotica*, *Junkie* by Burroughs, as well as books by Langston Hughes, Tennessee Williams, Maya Angelou. Should they all be removed because their point of view doesn't fall in line with yours? There is a book-length poem from the 1920s called "The Wild Party." It is one of the bawdiest presentations of characters that could be taken for slotting everyone into a stereotype. But it's truly great.

I'm not going to shut my trap or slangify my words and diction to accommodate people's short attention spans — that is a disease of technology. Read any *New York Times* article. Challenge your brain with questions and debate dialogue on a subject until it hurts.

While I have been accepted (within reason, especially as a young girl) and allowed to advance in an antiquated mindset of the boy's club, it has been an honor. I've seen the way many women in New Orleans are spoken about. It upsets me.

There is a code of honor in New Orleans: Zip your lips on the truths that become telephone game gossip (even if you weren't there to bear witness). Just mind your own business and keep your trap shut until you're behind closed doors, then the telephone game starts.

A lot of musicians are not held accountable, and that seems to slide. Showing up late for gigs, not caring or being willing to take the time to rehearse to make it perfect, because it's all about the paper trail hustle. I've been on the brunt end of it and it's a no-win situation. Rumor spread that I slept with a father and son of a prominent name lineage in music. It's absolutely not true.

Yet because of other people's cattiness I've lost a very dear lifelong friendship with the father without a chance to state my truth.

"Choice" words can be dangerous and devastating.

A lot of New Orleans musicians' unprofessional behaviors have kept them from session work in Nashville, I was told. While it's impressive and desirable to watch a free spirit do what they want, as I know, some are undependable.

As much as I have made "novels" of every subject, I've never once broken the code of honor and divulged the gluttonous behavior that goes on both on the road and in town. Everyone had too much time on their hands during Covid. I couldn't wait to get back to playing music instead of listening to a bunch of repetitive gossip about you know who or this and that.

Dear Jessica,

I thank you for your brutal honesty and clarity. With deep reflection based on your statement (*in regard to my drinking*), I needed a few days to gauge my own real thoughts. My first thought was, who cares, what is there to live for? I've pretty much done it all. My second thought was: it would be a disservice to go out this way; my third thought was how unbelievably depressed I've been for so very long. My fourth thought was tracking when that depression started and why. My fifth thought was what I would really like to do now in this life.

In detail: I lost my joy after the whole band label dream team fell apart, coming back to New Orleans, doing shit gigs for food money and bills solely because someone (ahem) was too good to get off his butt playing video games ten hours a day, trying to live a normal life, not asking for much except a walk around the block with Ava and the dogs but being denied that small request while working my ass off when he wasn't. You know the story – it's old news.

Then I was in survival mode through every ghetto and being used by the [Squirrel Nut] Zippers for four years and still standing after being robbed of everything. The whole drinking thing came into play with a two-prong factor. It's the social world I work in called nightclubs. Then it became a passive pity party, because it would have been a bad look to go out on my own adventures and enjoy life and then be accused of cheating every time I walked out the door. Then it became a band-aid for wounds that never healed of loss, neglect, frustration, lack of a thank you, or any respect after trying my very best for so many years, from relationships to record labels to bandmates.

My self-esteem was already low from the way we were raised, so it takes very little to squash me into a submissive position. With reflection on your words, with being surrounded by Black churchgoing women giving tough love wisdom, pointedly telling the word to my boyfriend while I receive information about God, to acknowledging I am destroying my body through my own actions, my conclusive statement is this: I want to live. I want to redirect playing shitty gigs and being on a hamster wheel of survival that never ends. I would like to find a sustainable way here – because I love this home, city, and neighborhood, to be able to write my story, finish my album, get some counseling, pull way back the reins on daily drinking, which I already have, wake up each day to have something to be excited about to create and dig into mentally.

My counselor of ten years died last month. I need to find a new mentor. I really don't give a damn about drinking; I'm just trying to not have an aneurysm or a heart attack. There's no way in hell I'm going to rehab after the "One Flew Over the Cuckoo's Nest" experience in the emergency room. As soon as my new paperwork for health care comes in, there are prescriptions waiting for me to take. It's already in motion.

At this point in time, as you stated, that Dad stated, only YOU know your truth, I know, I am still standing on my two goddamn feet and paying my own damn bills with my brain and wits in an honest way. Anyone from afar who would like to come and inquire in person is welcome to do so. Otherwise, my stance now is: I don't care if you are family or friends, if you don't care to really have the dialogue, I don't need the secret behind-the-back whispers.

I look in the mirror each day. Intensely. I know it's time to straighten up better. And I will do so in my own way.

Know that I love you. And I am so excited for your new up and coming little peanut. I would love to see you while you are here. But if you don't feel up to it, that's fine too. Thank you for your honesty. Don't forget to take breathing classes and eat protein.

All my love,

Yo sista

P.S. On a humorous note, I don't go out anymore. My boyfriend and I trade subjects from documentaries about male warriors to female warriors to politics to true historical movies to the funniest and strangest segments on the African kingdom animals around the watering hole.

I'm content.

* * * * *

Why did my sister Jessica (who's a smartie) jokingly ask, "What's on your side A / side B playlist that represents it all at the end of your life?" We both agree (in unison): "Is That All There Is?" by Peggy Lee is side A. I confused her by saying "The Clown" by Mingus is side B. "I thought you were more Pollyanna than that." Buwahhhhhhhh, maybe inside this existential heart, I'm not.

The Turning Point

We were living it up in a dilapidated mini mansion in St. Roch next to the large brick Baptist church on Franklin Avenue where Music Street starts. We were three drunks who could barely pay the rent: myself, Grandville, and one roommate, with multiple jolly drunks coming and going.

The front living room with perfectly shellacked wood floors held one shabby couch that was there when we moved in, an enormous empty fish tank with nothing in it, and a little 1970s "grandma" glass table. There were built-in bookshelves; living in a house that had them was a dream of mine. All they held were a few books I had found in the healing center on St. Claude Avenue. They sat there without being read.

I was too distracted by the nothing, buzzed all day and all night.

The house had old Southern charm. There was a long, winding staircase leading to the street, on which a few drunken friends had tumbled to the bottom, breaking some body part on the way. The most memorable of those incidents involved a petite friend who cracked her head open, leaving a bleeding halo around her head where she was passed out on the concrete.

Blood stains are almost impossible to remove.

My bedroom had a king size bed on the floor, too many ball gowns (without gigs for me to wear them to), all my journals in a corner of the walk-in closet, and my little Allie. My roommates and I all seemed to exist in a suspended state of pursuing our dreams but not really getting anywhere. How can anyone aspire to anything when the buzz disappears and they're left with a hangover, counting pennies and nickels from the floor for their next bottle of Skol from Hanks corner grocery store?

Those days seemed to be just an existence, nothing more. A gig or two here or there, a few laughs, a lot of journaling and writing, a lot of sorrow, a lot of running away from something I couldn't really run away from – me.

The three of us perpetuated the drinking with our camaraderie. All of our socializing was based around the bottle. It was the watering hole. The irony of our status quo in that house was that it originally belonged to the church where religious people lived and helped the community with the senior center below.

We were being blasphemous. Three times a week the church pounded music so loud it seemed about to break down the brick walls with salvation.

That street corner had the most unusual combination of subjects. Religion to the left, drunks and druggies in the neutral ground across the street, a throwaway of oddities coming and going. It seemed to me, apart from the people who were affiliated with the church, that most of that area was full of losers, including me.

* * * * *

One morning, I woke up with heart palpitations. I felt like I was having a heart attack. I went into our opulent 1930s bathroom with white tiles and built-in woodwork, looked at myself in the mirror at my yellow eyes, got a bottle of aspirin, and took a few, thinking of the time that my grandma used to take an aspirin every day for her heart.

The next day, my leg blew up like a balloon. I could barely walk. It was extremely embarrassing to appear this way in front of my boyfriend. So, I just stayed in bed and covered up my leg. Even through his drunken eyes, Grandville could see something wasn't right. Later that day I had a major seizure. No warning, no heads up, no classical orchestra playing a lead-in to the dramatic moment in the film; just him standing there yelling at the top of his lungs with such severity that I was shocked out of it.

He was on the phone calling 911. That was it. He forced me to go to the emergency room. I took my last little bottle of vodka in a ginger ale bottle with me. And that began the longest two-year journey of my life: ICU, rehab, IOP, Covid isolation.

He Saved Me

In my hour of need, he saved me. I never acknowledged that while others got the credit from my mouth publicly. If he had not shaken me out of my seizure and forced me to go to the emergency room, I wouldn't be alive.

He's a shy, quiet, behind-the-scenes guy. He doesn't like to be out on Front Street. In retrospect, I should have made the executive decision to give him his due in the public eye. So many blamed him for our days of wine and roses. It wasn't all him. I chose to drink. We drank together.

He stopped drinking for a year and got himself together. I continued drinking, and he warned me along the way, even when he was drinking as I puked up blood daily. For almost four years he was my lighthouse. A haven to come home to. Someone who made me laugh, pushed my brain to think, my art to grow, and a person who, when in my deepest days of loneliness, accepted me for me, broken and all. He was broken too. We took care of each other to make sure the porcelain dolls we were didn't get that final blow to shatter into smithereens forever into eternity.

I loved him deeply. Not only for being there in my lowest hour, but for being the unique person that he is. Through thick and thin, sober and drunk, he was always there in the shadows making sure I was okay. It was his way.

As I acknowledged him watching me perform live online quietly from afar, never saying a word, or every time I thought of him, he called. Every time I talked to a fellow musician, they asked how he was. Every time I dreamed of him, he was there.

I tried my very best to save him when he fell off. He was more of a wild horse to tame than I was when it came to rehab.

I woke up thinking about the people I hurt unconsciously. I would like to say, "Thank you, Grandville, for saving my life. I wouldn't be here today if it wasn't for you. The rest that followed could not have happened if it wasn't for your quick thinking and bossy way of being. I'm sorry. You never received that credit in all the hours of being judged as the problem by so many."

Happy To Be on This Journey

It was one of those late winter, early spring, golden light sunshine days in New Orleans. It had been a long couple of months.

On December 20, 2019, I went into the ICU for ten days, and on January 17, 2020, I went to rehab for a month in a rural area outside of Nashville. I was in good health (except for my liver) and had done a lot of work on my mind, body, and spirit thanks to a tight-knit circle of family, friends, musical peers, and an incredibly gifted team of professionals, from the Musicians' Clinic saints to MusicCares to Cumberland Heights to Imagine Discovery.

The psychological tools I learned are incredibly powerful in understanding how the mind, body, and spirit work. I feel humbled, lonely, and kind of lost back in the real world making changes. I'm lucky to be alive and know so much beauty is in the world.

On that day, I was waiting for the bus in Uptown New Orleans after an intense counseling session in front of one of the old-school "grandpa" bars. I sat on one of the high stools outside and listened to two middle-aged guys talk while the birds chirped and the private school kids walked by. The guys were talking 'bout the good old days of shotgun houses, aunties, gas heaters, neighborhood antics, receding hairlines, judgmental wives, being too old to do floors or blow up mattresses anymore, drying clothes on ovens, and remembering the marker spots that made New Orleans special.

One of the things I love about New Orleanians is that they don't mind their own business, so the next thing I knew, the grandma waiting for the bus was telling them where they could buy the old gas heaters... the kind one of the guys had just said kills you in your sleep, as he is a firefighter.

Taking buses is a great way to meet people. So, I hopped on to go home (well, at that time, somebody else's home), and there was a lady standing forever at the front ticket machine. I asked five seats back if she was short and the whole bus looked at me. I realized I was talking to a short person, asking if she needed extra change. Can't win them all. But I can keep trying.

Transitions

While I was in rehab, I became a writing fool to save my sanity. I would write about anything and everything. I even wrote a tell-all journal called: *Ingrid Lucia, 60 Days in a Country Rehab*. One really thinks about mortality when they are a 35 on the MELD Score and 29 days away from dying. So, with fear and trepidation at that time, I asked myself deep questions about what I really wanted with my life. That vision board was created, and lo and behold it had come to fruition. It wasn't quite the *Vogue* magazine photographs I had cut out and pasted, but in essence the parts were all there.

We were called the White Girl Rehab Brigade when we were shipped offsite to NA and AA meetings in churches in Nashville's poor, predominantly Black neighborhoods. All the girls with their black spandex running pants, ponytails, fancy sports jackets, and expensive tennis shoes listened to the plights of the African American community who only had that church, their inner strength, two bus rides, and meetings for salvation.

And they told their stories with a vengeance and with humor. One of them had to do with this guy and his johnson that was so unbelievably funny the whole circle pretty much fell off their chairs.

On the flip side, there were also a bunch of spoiled brats who were served steak and five-star buffets, clean bedding from maids and Haagen-Dazs ice cream bars from Christian bookstores. And they bitched and moaned about jogging rights and the food causing farts.

Meanwhile, in Grandville's asphalt jungle rehab experience, one could hear the front desk screaming for Laquisha. The only privileges were smoking on the hot roof of the building in the ghetto.

My wish was to have a little country home with air to breathe, a continuation of the relationship I was in, maybe to the next level, my kid, animals, healthy food, and the financial space to write the story, make the album, and write the song to make the world cry.

Who knew it would take a pandemic to bring financial space? Who knew all of the rioting, racism, and protesting would be happening while I was in an interracial relationship? Who knew the most frustrating writer's block would come about in my sobriety?

The Grammys approved money to help. I was sure they'd had enough of my name after paying $40,000 for rehab, a month's rent, and a check to use in the near future. The next time they hear "Ingrid Lucia," it had better be affiliated with success.

I had a talk with my doctor. The reality that I alone screwed up my body and would have to be on medicine for the rest of my life made me so sad. The realization that it's time to get to "It" is imminent.

There was nowhere to go. And besides, where else would I want to live except New Orleans? Where else would meter maids get loaded at Kermit Ruffins' place and in uniform vent their work frustrations by jumping on all the parked cars and twerking so hard the cars were shaking, all on a video for the world to see?

I began to go down the rabbit hole of the mind. As it twirled deeper and deeper through the millions of impressions, from having my hair washed with strawberry shampoo in the Mississippi River at age four, to being screamed at by my father, to millions of hours of walking the road to learn a craft, to the randomness of a life led by intentionality for The Big Time.

My father played rhythm on a fishnet mannequin leg while singing "Darktown Strutters Ball" through a bullhorn to the public.

There isn't anything you can't do, Anna Mae. Go collect wood from the Mississippi River, children, so we can build a showboat. We're going to float down the river to China and start an orphanage for children less fortunate than yourself. Now, read Voltaire like a good girl, drill practice on time, beat, melody, rhythm, and harmony before we dance freely for the people in front of Jackson Square. Your daddy's gonna randomly take you right to the top, my little Judy Garland. Hi Ho, Hi Ho, we're off to follow the yellow brick road, Norma Jean. One day you will be Marilyn Monroe. The Big Time is right around the corner.

Bitchin' Birthday

March 30, 2020. Happy birthday to me!

Some women are real bitches. And they get what they want that way. I was raised to not complain. It's too easy and doesn't accomplish anything. Maybe it's good to get it out sometimes.

I messed up either my rib, liver, or both falling on a table in storage trying to reach a shoe, and the pain was getting worse by the day to where I couldn't function or sleep. My neighbors smoked a lot of marijuana, which, when it wafted my way, was the only time I felt the tension go out of my shoulders. Yoga, meditation, good mindset... all work within reason.

My dog had fleas that I couldn't seem to get rid of no matter what I did, bought, or used. Poor thing was miserable, and we were both up all night. There was $28 in my PayPal account and that was it. I was up for trying alternative ways to make an honest living, but in compromised health I was limited to outdoor options at that time. It's never too late to learn how to use a pressure washer.

Imagine Recovery, the IOP where I went Uptown, found morphine in my required urine tests because I had eaten a poppy seed bagel. My next test was clean, but they wanted me to hike it over there twice a week with no car. I was finding it extremely frustrating to try and get back up on my feet as an independent person. I knew there were so many blessings shining on me that I couldn't complain one iota, and I felt the deepest gratitude, which made me mad at myself that I couldn't have that switch on 24 hours a day.

I just wanted to throw a hissy fit in the new old house, which was previously inhabited by drug dealers. I was lucky to have it, but it didn't have electricity or water, it had some blood stains on the wall, and it needed a lot of TLC and deep cleaning as well as a bed and a couch. I was trying to do what I could to start a home because rent sustainability was questionable. I had nothing but a broom and incense to work without water. I wanted to do some sort of exorcism dance and get back to feeling like myself. But the house had a lot of windows without curtains and I didn't want to scare my new neighbors.

I said my prayers at night and was really trying to understand why if God is so good, he would impose the plague of Covid on the world.

Did I feel better bitching and getting it off my chest? No. I felt like a jerk.

Porch Watching

Once in a while, people pass by you. Pistol-whipped pot-bellied husband with a K-Mart American Flag T-shirt and neon yellow Nikes following like an obedient oversized puppy behind a ponytailed skinny senior in her neon pink spandex leggings getting every bit out of her workout by exaggeratedly swinging her arms.

Moped man driving back and forth ten miles an hour methodically, not going from point A to point B. Four times by in five minutes? I wanted to shout, *ghetto to the left, lakefront to the right.* But I didn't.

Old-school grandpa in pork pie hat tipped back, pressed ironed slacks circa 1966, followed by his overweight granddaughter slacking behind with her phone in her hands and her buds in her ears, lost to the world. What was she listening to?

Masked man with Rouses grocery bag and grey throw rug determined to get home in the high noon sun. Neighbors across the street drive off with a happy wave and movie star blond hair blowing in the wind driving a Lexus.

A masked woman drove up to a neighbor yelling loudly six times that she had an Aretha Franklin CD for Elvira. Which one, I wondered. "A Rose in Spanish Harlem" would have been nice to hear right then. Leiber and Stoller wrote that song. I miss them. They gave me a song from their catalogue to sing, about a maid with a broom (which wasn't what I was really hoping for).

The postman went by wearing a chili pepper mask made by the neighbor around the corner. He had smiling eyes.

I wondered when the subscription for *Vogue* I ordered (that I put in my dog's name) was going to arrive. Sure, we used to be poor and the $12 bill was never paid. Wait, "used to"? We had just eaten chili dogs for lunch.

Then there was the gentleman pot dealer on the corner with the low rider pickup from Mississippi and who lived with his "grandmother" who, it turns out, was his older wife who supported him while he smoked, drank, and waved when passing by a hundred times a day asking if I was married. I said, I had a boyfriend. He said, we can share. I was thinking his "grandma" could probably kick my ass in a second. *Jerry Springer, here we come.*

Porch hanging. It's the good life. Sitting in a bean bag reading the newest *Readers Digest*. Is this what retired people do? It's hard work, people watching.

Mr. Hudson

(My Covid Puppy)

He jumps like a sprite
Out the door with delight
To greet each brand-new day.

New to explore,
What was old hours before
God, I love his mind.

He's so full of joy,
He greets every new knock at the door,
His kindness drops down to the dew.

Inspired with a smile am I
As I watch sleepy-eyed,
A lesson I wish I knew.

He owns his own prance,
Goofy way
And stance.
He's so happy to be here today.

He'll kiss you till you drown,
Lick your legs up and down,
And gaze in your eyes with wide adore.

He is a big little man
Who tries to understand
How to please.

If everyone could learn
From this wise canine fur,
We would be winners at life's game.

An Unusual Massage

I had to get out of the house. Trapped by Covid, I'd had too many days of loneliness, ruminating, becoming OCD over the placement of every item to overcome the lack of control in my life.

I was trying to do right and stay away from people. I had one day left on the temporary license on the lemon of a car I'd bought. I went downtown to the French Quarter, trying to stay away from ground zero aka Jackson Square, where 95 percent of people were maskless.

It was windy and cold. The sun was disappearing and the French Market vendors selling their wares were packing up for the day. Meandering around, I saw most of the businesses were closed. The lack of life at the end of Decatur Street was a sad sight. So many memories.

I heard the sound of a highly trained musician playing classical music on his expensive keyboard with weighted keys. It was deeply satisfying to hear music streaming through the streets. Precision, emotion, dynamics. The composition he was playing was one of the floral, major key, kind of melancholy pieces, like a part of *La Bohème* before the ending when its loud passion kicks in. Alright. I got a grande size hot chocolate from the corner coffee shop, got change for a nice tip, and enjoyed that moment. Every door was wide open in the French Quarter coffee shop. Not only was the music coming in, but so was the intense cold blowing wind. It reminded me of two cold weeks I'd spent in Paris.

Chug chocolate, burn throat, leave tip, enter Asian massage salon. My mother had gifted me a massage. I'd been in physical pain for so long I wasn't sleeping well. There was one customer there and two older Asian masseurs. When my turn came up, he pointed at my stomach and said, *baby?* I said, sick. I sat in the chair face down and he began to work. Deeply kneading every knot representing hurt, sorrow, suffering, and then gently rolling them out. The pain and the pleasure.

It had been such a hard five years, peaking with the last one. Every deep breath removed toxins. Strong hands dug into the neck, knocked on the head, yanked at the arms, searched, removed the lumps, marking the physical memory map of the nerves, muscles, and sinews. Then he got to the heart.

Right below the shoulder blades. The delicate spot desperately holding a cover for the most vulnerable part of the body.

I started to cry silently into the chair, all of the struggles and losses coming out. Sorrow over the ending of my recent relationship, sorrow going all the way back to my dad. And then the massage guy's phone rang with Asian wood chime sounds. He had the caller on speaker phone and she was obviously not a happy bunny. She was yelling at him loudly in a cutting dialect that stiffened my whole body and opened my ears. It was obviously his wife and some travesty had happened, but it couldn't be that bad because he was trying to pacify her with his tone while massaging my back with one hand. This went on for about three minutes before she hung up on him. He continued working on my back, but his intensity had been interrupted. Didn't she realize the man was bringing home the grocery money? The phone rang again, but he didn't pick it up. The healing spell had been broken. He completed the massage with karate chops on my bum-bum.

As I paid and thanked him, I asked if that was his wife. He nodded yes. I said, it sounds like she needs a massage. The two elderly men in the empty massage parlor laughed their heads off. I went home back to the Covid twilight zone, got into bed, and promptly fell into the first deep, long sleep I'd had in months.

"It's a Boy"

I don't like to lie. And I wouldn't want anyone to lie to me.

I walked into Five Happiness Chinese Restaurant to get a bowl of wonton soup. The host seated me in the booth next to two high-class elder socialites who held themselves cut and cloth with complete class. Before I even sat down in the booth next to them, they said, "Congratulations." I've lost count of how many times someone has said that to me.

I decided the last time, after telling the truth and seeing the look of pity on strangers' faces, I would just make it as simple as possible, so I said, "Thank you." Well, it didn't turn out that way. They wanted to know what I was having. I said, "It's a boy." They said, "When are you due?" "Next month." "How much will he weigh?" "I don't know." The whole conversation continued through dinner.

Like me, the socialites, Judy and Marilyn, were also named after movie stars. "You're a singer? Sing something for us." I sang "Somewhere Over the Rainbow" as the whole restaurant stopped eating and listened. Judy and Marilyn were 81 and 83, married 33 and 52 years, respectively. "Dahrling, it's a shame women outlive men. It would be so lovely to have a companion." I thought, *I'd like to matchmake, and the 84-year-old trumpet player who's been my friend for a long time told me he is lonely too.* It's the least I could do for lying. So I told both of them about Charlie Miller.

They talked about their trip on the Queen Mary and dinner parties of 16, their children, reminiscing about places that "ain't dere no more."

After their dinner they sat at my booth and kept asking when the baby was due. Was I going to get married? *Don't forget, the man is responsible for at least half.*

I enjoyed those fun-spirited ladies so much. There's a certain spitfire spunkiness to that generation I love. I gave them my number; Judy looked at it and said it looked like "fuck" spelled backwards. "I was married 33 years, that's the last time I was fucked," she said, as she kept telling me to eat because the baby needed hot food. Then they started talking about who had a bigger place and the taxes on their homes, competing about who paid more. I almost choked when I heard the numbers. Beyoncé wanted to buy a house in their neighborhood for 19 million, they said, but the broker wanted 20. Beyoncé in Old Metairie? What?

The hot cha-cha was dressed all in black in something like a couture Vivienne Westwood, and the more reserved lady was dressed like Coco Chanel. The cha-cha loved Bach, modern art, and Abstract Expressionism, by the way. Long story short, my mom, Charlie, and I were invited to their house for dinner. I hoped it would be soon or I'd have to explain how I could leave such a young baby at home with a babysitter.

What should I name him? I wondered. Grandville Junior?

Always Late, Early

I'm usually on the minute, but always rushing to an appointment time. How did I go to my hospital procedure appointment a day early? The three ladies at the front desk check-in were so nice, overly nice, actually. I looked around to see if all of the positivity from those normally tough cookies was being directed at me.

On my last doctor's visit I had told one of the ladies about the two socialites from Metairie who thought I was pregnant. She egged me on to tell the story to her two coworkers. So I told it to them like I was from Metairie, in a Southern version of a Valley Girl voice.

They thought the whole story was so hilarious and that my interpretation of the accent was right on par, they were doubling over in their office chairs covering their mouths and holding their stomachs. Who knew carrying around 20 pounds of fluid with people thinking you're pregnant could be so oddly funny? I had to laugh too. That totally changed my mood and made me so happy to be able to make somebody laugh without even trying.

The couple of days leading up to that day had been rough with relationship decision-making and coming to a painful conclusion based on what I heard from my own ears and witnessed with my own eyes. I was feeling kind of down. I don't know why some relationships have to be so complicated. I'm not one to be talking, I guess. We have to figure out these things. Why do we make ourselves miserable?

Food for Thought

There is a disease going on with young women today who are exquisite as they are. They are doing terrible things to themselves, from Botox to implants, trying to live up to some imaginary standard that is unrealistic and sometimes causing death or permanent deformity. I had a conversation about this with my daughter, who has been fortunate to be graced with stunning beauty.

If men don't stop having a double standard, this problem of women not feeling good enough will continue to the demise of physical and mental health of women. Too fat, too skinny, too old, too Black, too White, too much bull in a game no one will ever win.

An ex-boyfriend said his next bang would be a Coke-bottle-shaped 25-year-old. Okay grandpa, good luck with that. The only last laugh I can think of is that you men think women who have gone through all that pain and torture to look like that are going to put up with your piggish behavior. Hell no. You want all that, you're going to have a high maintenance "B" to deal with. Isn't it time to accept women as they are?

The night before our wedding, my ex-husband asked me quite seriously for two things. He didn't want me to get fat or wake up to me in curlers. When I got pregnant for the second time, he said he didn't want it, because he wasn't attracted to me. At a size ten I was too fat in his fashion photographer's eyes. So, I had an abortion. I consoled myself with the reality that we were rebuilding after Katrina and living in one room was not ideal.

As a glorious big Black mama Uber driver once said, "Girl, don't let it get to you, fat, skinny, ugly, pretty, my daddy said we've got one thing they all want." I asked what that was, she said, "Wet pussy, girl!"

Food for thought: Ladies, it's time to tighten the reins and whip your man into shape. Teach them how to dress, show them how to use toilet paper properly, maybe look into hairline receding and erection surgeries, stomach liposuction definitely, how to cut their toenails and fingernails, ear and nose hair, back waxing, definitely a lesson in moisturizing, especially feet, and smelling good, eyelid wrinkle Botox, cheek and butt implants. While we're at it, don't forget about table manners, posture and etiquette classes, and the art of diction. Then come back and see us and then, only then, we will see if they pass the test to come in the front door. Right, ladies?

* * * * *

A few hours after that conversation with my daughter, I was called by Brianna Owens, who handled my social media. She said the booking agent was hitting a wall with some local clubs. They thought I was in great voice, but they didn't want to hire me because of the way I looked. I was very shocked and hurt. These are clubs I'd developed relationships with and had given my best for little financial return over the years.

After sleeping on it and still feeling disturbed, I realized this: There are so many local artists who have recovered from their issues and were welcomed back with wide open arms. They looked like they had been dragged through the mud. Drug addiction, pock marks, missing teeth, broken skin capillaries, skinny as a stick, and all dressed poorly. The difference? They are men.

I wanted to remove myself from the equation in that story. My feelings were hurt, and I'd already moved on to better things. You don't want me, you don't get me.

Namaste, Newbie

I woke up feeling like absolute *puro cargar*. My usual tendency to get back in bed after letting the dog out was displaced by the thought that I should make a cup of tea and sit outside on the porch.

It was so peaceful out with the leaves, birds, and church bells. I never really appreciated all of that as much as I should. I told myself I was going to sit there through the whole cup of tea and not get up and be distracted.

I absolutely suck at meditating. The second I try to feel peace I find myself thinking about burning incense or crossing my legs. Forcing myself to sit and really just let go with my legs spread, even if I look like a dead grandma on the porch in my pajamas, is very hard to do.

While I forced myself to sit there and drink that tea in a pretty cup made in Turkey I got at Marshalls, I closed my eyes so I could feel every part of my body. I felt like I'd been poisoned, so my body said, *more water*. I felt around my body some more, I thought, *my ovaries hurt and I'm horny as hell*. That's an inappropriate thought while meditating. Is it sacrilegious to acknowledge real feelings and thoughts? Then I realized that I had no rituals, traditions, or culture to call my own.

As an adult I have incorporated pieces of what I have learned from other cultures throughout my life. I've observed that Americans tend to create their own rituals and traditions rather than adopting and carrying on those of their ancestors. In *Travels with Charley*, Steinbeck said Americans are nomadic people traveling to Western lands seeking opportunity. Going as far away as possible away from the tribe of our forefathers. It was brought to mind when I had three cold Sprites at a sushi restaurant with my Russian friend from London, Anyalita. So American! Talk about ritual! I should've had a tea in honor of where I was.

She told me about her life in Russia and in London. Her grandmother, who was still in Russia, would not share her secret recipe for tea. She told her, *this is mine; you go find your own*. That made me realize that all of the traditions that are carried on and passed down by our forefathers are extremely important in order to keep a culture alive.

That is why New Orleans is such a treasure in this country. I would say it is the only city that insists on holding on to its culture like a protective baby blanket. Nobody may rip it away with homogenization. Younger Americans don't seem to have their own cultural fabric. It's special to show people how to make their own. And that is something I am ready to do: Make a patchwork quilt of rituals and traditions that create a sane haven of solace in my life.

There are reasons for cultural traditions. They make sense. Beans on Monday 'cause it's laundry day and you have to cook something like you don't have to stir (or 'cause you're broke from partying). Fish on Friday, po-boys for the working man who had no money. The irony is that every great food from every great culture comes from the poor man. How can they be so expensive now?

By the time I was halfway through my cup of tea, I started to get up because I couldn't be still anymore, and I really wanted my phone. I thought of my daughter, I thought of everybody that I bitch and moan about because they can't live without their phone, and I realized I was one of them.

Come on, Ingrid, you can sit here for another ten minutes and listen to the birds fighting with each other. You can watch your dog almost fall over the side of the porch. You can look at the little blooms growing on that plant that you thought was dead. You can notice that you need a pedicure. And you can suddenly realize you don't feel like shit anymore; everything is relaxed, you're breathing deeply and apart from a little pinching in your shoulder blade area, you actually feel happy to be alive and ready to greet the day.

Is this what the Sufi people have been talking about for all these years? The wise ones' number one ritual of finding peace is through meditation. Peace is lying dormant within us like a lotus in a hot mess of chaos, waking up every morning and tumbling out of bed to the left, to the right, straight ahead while inside lies a peaceful little haven.

Holy crap, I get it!

Listen

We are all ingrained with psychic skills. As kids we played the psychic guessing game. Think of a color, and the first impression that comes into the opponent's brain is almost always correct in its answer. Pick a number, flower, etc. Growing that muscle for the larger life picture. I played it with my kid.

My dad loved the desert. Under a full, blue-lit moon and the constellations, he would take me as a five-year-old outside the camp and ask me to point out where the turquoise was buried. I would point and was never wrong as he dug it up with a shovel.

It's easy to get distracted by complications and lose that intuitive skill set. It was coming back. The dreams that hold answers. The *deja vus*. The clarity of what moves to make. It's kind of scary to know it's all there in your brain, but also reassuring to know the answers lie psychically within.

You are thinking of the color... green?

Lady Charmaine

She slipped a note under the door of my room that said, *Meet me in the lobby, we're going for a walk.* I got dressed quickly and met her in the lobby. We were both on the same bill in New Zealand for the Waiheke Island Jazz Festival in 2000. That was the first time a musical colleague had ever given me that commanding order. We walked at a brisk pace; she asked me questions about myself and told me about herself and things that she had done in her life. She took me under her wing and gave me pieces of advice about how to be received fondly in foreign countries: *Always learn a few lines of the language to show that you are trying to extend an olive branch.* Which I never forgot.

We sat side stage together in a little tent waiting for our turn to perform on the big stage. I remember how grand she appeared to me. Her posture, her braids, the multiple bangles on each arm. Her bag of accoutrement percussion instruments. She was great at putting herself in the right mindset pre-show.

I've always found myself completely distracted when in the chaos of players warming up their horns, breaking in their new reeds, bro joking. She didn't let any of that affect her. I went out to the front of the house to watch her set with the jazz festival creator, David Paquette. There was a little girl about nine years old standing next to him and she was entranced by Charmaine Neville. When she impersonated Louis Armstrong that little girl's mouth dropped wide open, and she said, "Oh my God, what was that?" I had to laugh my head off. I'm sure she had never seen a woman do an interpretation of the king of jazz.

Over the years, in New Orleans, Lady Charmaine was always gracious enough to let me sit in on her weekly set at Snug Harbor, the premier jazz club in town. Not many female singers are confident enough to bring another female on stage. When she performed, she dominated the whole stage, making it loud and clear exactly what she wanted from each player, with her percussion instrument directing the way.

I got to know more of her backstory. Over the years she overcame many difficulties and still stayed positive and even more so year after year. Here was a person making conscious choices to better the world by taking others under her wing and teaching them and guiding them with what she had learned.

Her strong personality indicated she wasn't going to put up with any crap. I admired that about her because I was a pushover and seemed to have no boundaries or willingness to put my foot down with anybody.

Before rehab and when almost nobody in the community wanted to have much to do with me, Charmaine called and reached out to make sure I was okay, and to show her support. She even offered money to help me get a storage unit when I went to rehab. When I got out, she had me over for tea. We had a great visit sharing stories about music, musicians, and men. She gently gave me tips to help remove the yellow from my eyes and skin and how to cleanse my system with a tonic of healthy items.

March 31 is her birthday, one day after mine. She is a fellow Aries, and I adore her. Over the years she has given me and others the wise type of care, that of a real friend.

Going the Distance

At five months with no drinking, the most important tools for me were (and still are): boundaries, expectations, and knowing it's okay to just be me. Maybe striving for the best version of myself that I can be, a daily chore.

Five months isn't that long when you think of some superheroes, such as Mary Cowan, one of the head counselors at Cumberland Heights. I called her "Miss Sunshine." She had 28 years of sobriety at that point and she still calls me weekly.

Being sober really isn't that hard. There have only been three times that I was tempted. Once pre-gig in a mansion there was a glass of untouched wine in the bathroom. The end of a tradition, having a drink while doing makeup. One glass would have been too expensive a price to pay after all the boot camp hours logged in to get my head on straight.

Another time I was waiting for over two hours in the freezing cold for the bus at St. Claude and Franklin across the street from the nice house we had just gotten evicted from. Good old Hanks across the street. The thought was there and then passed, and a funk song I wrote on the spot called "Waiting on the Bus" and Tourette syndrome ensued.

The third time was while watching a Woody Allen movie and a 1940s doll was dressed up, sitting at the table with a pint of bourbon and a little glass. It made me a little sad to give up that comfort of feeling the firewater go down my throat and all the cobwebs in my brain wash away into pinpoint clarity.

The prize outweighs the risk. My health and life. My daughter's and mother's heart and trust again. Redeveloping my reputation as a performer. Intimacy, front face honesty, acknowledgement of one's feelings are "getting back on the bike" type exercises that are scary. But they were slowly happening. Seeing the world through sober eyes is both hilarious and horrifying. As the phrase goes, *Did I just saw what I saw?* Human nature is its own show.

On TV, I watched grandmas in the windows of nursing homes displaying cardboard signs saying, "Need More Wine." Mothers admitting to Lester Holt that they were drinking to stay sane while cooped up with homeschooling their kids during Covid. Old bums on the bus trying to scam a dollar for a beer... Good on them, I say. Having a buzz is fun.

I'm glad I'm not hiding liquor anymore or walking around in a dazed dream of day drinking. Add the money saved and you have a vacation on your hands.

On a funny note, a very good friend who comes back home often to visit would always bring me a bottle of the nicest, most expensive version of bourbon he could find as a gift. At Christmas, he told me, he outdid himself and ordered a big bottle on which the makers actually printed "Ingrid" in old-school wax. Another good friend told him I was in the ICU. He asked me, "What am I going to do with this now?" I said to save it for when we are grandmas and grandpas; who will care about our livers at 101? My grandma had two margaritas the night before she died at 98 1/2. That's still a ways to go for me.

To celebrate, I had an ice cream cone for breakfast.

Raymond Weber Jr.

Another day, another funeral for a good friend of mine. Raymond was a very talented and unique drummer. He played with me many times. He had just made 25. He was thoughtful, unconditional in his friendship, adored by many, smart, funny, talented, and handsome. The full package, but never to live a full life with so many things waiting around the bend for him. He was the only one in my loneliest hours who would call to wish me a Merry Christmas with no ulterior motives. We always had real conversations when he would give me a ride home after a gig. He had a special light.

His memorial was held on a perfect Fall day with the birds singing. Maybe a going-away gift? It made me even sadder. I will always miss him.

See you down the line, Raymond Weber Jr.

The Soundtrack of Your Life

What can I give of any value? Nothing, because I have (almost) nothing to give. Just a song and a thrift store dress or a trinket from around the world. That's what I do to reciprocate for all of the generosity I've received unconditionally from so many over many years.

Whether it be a meal, a dress, a trip to play abroad, an investment into my music, a thoughtful reach out to share their lives with me, it has all been worth more value than a dirty piece of paper in the bank. Music is my value to give back. It's all I have to give.

I have learned that it is not the only prism in my kaleidoscope. "I sing because I'm happy, I sing because I'm free... his eye is on the sparrow and I know he's watching me." ("His Eye Is On the Sparrow," C. Martin and C. Gabriel, 1905)

This life is a massive gift of a diamond that is still being chiseled into cut, clarity, and carat of a gem. It's not an easy road to attempt to be that perfect diamond. I don't think it's possible. In imperfection lies perfection.

I watched *The Hollywood Reporter* songwriters' roundtable talk about their processes, ideas, thoughts, growth, and realizations. After all of the hits, flops, attempts to write hits that flopped, then writing a true statement from the heart and it becoming a wild card hit, the participants agreed that the most rewarding part was not the money or accolades, but to be part of the soundtrack of someone's life. They were right. The humbling gift to make an emotional mark in their chapters of life. A marriage, a passing, a lonely moment.

I have received those moments from music throughout my life from others. When I listen again, it brings me screaming back to those frozen moments in time, making them technicolor again.

It is my intention to give that gift to others.

"Without a song,
the day would never end.
Without a song,
the road would never have been.
When things go wrong,

a man ain't got a friend
Without a song."

("Without a Song," music by V. Youmans, lyrics by B. Rose and E. Eliscu, 1929)

Summer in New Orleans

The hot sun burns white heat below,
If you dare to make a pilgrimage,
Only gear is slow.

Sun pounding on umbrellas,
Streets empty with the blues,
Sounds of sirens speed by.
Watch the evening news.

Day after day,
Night after night,
Time has no markers,
'Cept Saturday night.

Drinking, laughing, loving,
Dressed to the nines,
Cavorting with no rules.
Lady Sunday
Reveals not a sign.

Air units blow
As high they can go,
Roaring out noises of abuse with use,
Expecting any moment,
For the rattling to explode.

Surrender.
You can't win this fight.
So you become
A creature of night.
Closed doors and curtains
Make the mind start to roam.
What are people doing
All day inside their home?

Routines get lost,
Seeing people feels like a dream.
Lost in the wilderness
Of your mind, so it seems.
Or have you just gone crazy?

Porch sitting,
As day turns to night,
Every little critter
Wants to take a bite.
The cool air beckons them,
Moving right on in,
Mice and palmetto bugs
Invite all of their kin.

You're sleeplessly tossing,
In restless pain,
They're having a party so loud,
It's cray-cray.
How did the brand-new loaf of bread
Just go away?

Fighting the currents,
You go upstream,
Get dressed up pretty,
Go out for routine.

The currents of summer,
Drag you sweaty,
Back to your door,
You are absolutely
Not in charge of the score.

Metal bannisters burn the skin.
Don't touch anything,
Just hurry back in.

Oh. Right.
What precedes that is a hot car
With a broken air unit.
Red alert, red alert.
I'm just a girl.
What do I put in, Mr. Auto Zone,
To make this thing twirl?

Shoes off, bra off,
On couch with a thump,
You got two things done,
Enough for the day.
Yay, you won... sort of.

Ice cream,
Ice with lemonade,
Chugalug the whole bunch.
You've got the golden wand,
Iceland shows
Are what's for lunch.

New Orleans,
The land of dreams,
Hurricanes form in the Gulf.
In the cone of uncertainty,
It seems.
Canned beans,
Stay or go?
It's gonna be a 4,
Time to join the contraflow.

Shadows walk streets in the night,
Your spine prickles,
Sensing someone behind you,
Fight or flight?
Mace or wasp spray won't do,
When a perpetrator with a Covid mask
Is aiming a gun at you.

Brass bands sweat in the streets,
Melodic notes play,
For destination weddings.
Suckered by a dream,
The couple had no clue
About summer's reality.

Magnolia hair flowers wilt.
Armpit sweat in the satin wedding dress,
Photographer sends the bill.
What a doggone mess.

STELLA!!!
Yes Stanley? She hisses.
All her bridesmaids,
have turned into bitches.
Second lining,
On cobblestone streets,
In Louboutin heels,
Toothy smiles,
Hide blistered feet.

Church bells on the hour ring.
God Is Good,
Have a blessed day,
From the lips
Of the innocent sweet.

Sweat, stink,
Who cares what anyone thinks.
Wifebeater t-shirts
Stained and wet,
Walmart with tight shorts and bra bank cash.
Lottery ticket? You bet!

Why, why, why
Every summer do we stay?
Third world countries
Don't have vacation pay.

Raise minimum wage, ya heard?
Unemployment is ending soon.
How to pay the rent,
Creates feelings
Of impending doom.

Accept your lobotomized mind,
Do as little as possible,
Remember to stay kind.
Kings wave, eye contact, how are you?
Listen to street gossip,
Have you heard who's through?

Have you heard who won't be re-elected?
How 'bout that musician making a fool,
Not quite from society rejected.
Keep him around,
He's good for a story or two.

So tell me, tell me, tell me,
What is his latest news?
Needing new ways,
To keep oneself amused.
As the hurricane turns,
It's getting dramatic,
Stay tuned for season two,
It's going to be erratic.

Tragedies occur,
Unexpected deaths
Beget the innocent,
Hearts broken
Are all that's left.
United we stand as a tribe,
To see the family through.
No one is alone in this utopia,
Silently watching,
To gently know,
The right thing to do.

Afternoon thunderstorms
Start to circle round,
Cool water flooding streets
Will soon come pouring down.
Cars float down streets,
Just like Venice town.
Take your pick of the rain or heat,
There's plenty going around.
Daily rotating roulette table,
Offers rainbows as a treat,
When the two collide,
Up on heaven's street.

A second line
Pops up from nowhere,
Like an oasis dream,
Suddenly there are hundreds,
Dancing in the street.

Did I just see what I saw?

A bum
Jumps out of a dumpster,
Grand marshalling
To the beat.
Hankies shaking,
Youngbloods baking.
Beer cans ringing,
Grandmas singing,
Umbrellas swaying,
Brass bands playing,
Everyone dancing
Down glory road.
Where did they come from?
Where did they go?

Did I just see what I saw?
I really don't know.

New Orleans,
The land of dreams,
Where the siren lives and plays,
She loves company,
Enchanting you,
In every single way.
When she beckons,
Call the next of kin,
You really must stay,
She says,
With a hypnotizing smile,
Do please come in.

Dahling,
As she puts her arm through yours,
It's teatime.
How about a splash of gin?
It's going to be a long hot summer,
Did you bring your suit for a swim?

Cone of Uncertainty

Like school dodgeball, duck and let your playmates on either side take one for the team. You feel bad, but it wasn't you getting stung. A Catch-22 of guilt. You can even see the weatherman with his hand manually trying to push a Category 3 hurricane on the map to the west.

Our poor neighbors in Lake Charles. They got hit twice back to back: Laura and Delta. Who evacuates to New Orleans? Our local neighbors in need, of course. The city of New Orleans hosted them graciously in the fancy hotels on Canal Street, where they sat outside on lawn chairs in pajamas and curlers, smoking while shooting the breeze. The few tourists walking by were utterly confused.

Meanwhile, the mayor furloughed police and fire department staff. It was advised by a few to get a Glock to protect the home while the country fell apart. I didn't even know what one looked like. I got lucky once to be a dead shot and killed a puck on the first aim way up in the sky in the cotton fields of Mississippi.

Some New Orleans hot cha-cha had a pink thing in her pants. I asked if it was mace. She said no, it's an Ncc 7 gun. All I knew was what a Beretta 25 is... Don't they stick it in their garter in Western movies?

I didn't blame people for getting scared and desperate. Who can live on $107 of unemployment a week with gentrified rents? The economy was booming? There wasn't one open venue to play music in. Even if there was, there weren't any people to play for. How were we supposed to make a living?

I went into the studio to re-record a vocal for Ferrero Rocher. The head of the New York ad agency wanted more Billie, more Billie... more Billie! He wants more BILLIE! The producer, pianist David Torkanowsky, said I did a great job sounding like Billie on heroin doing a Christmas jingle... but then he said, let's do it again.

All of the tension over that year finally popped. David asked me to state the words to the bridge I wrote, but not a word or melody note appeared in the chalkboard of my mind. I started laughing so hard I almost fell off the couch. He rolled his eyes. I laughed harder. He'd already said working with me was like working with Helen Keller. Hahaha... I couldn't stop laughing. Lost brain cells, he said, hahaha... everything seemed so funny. ICU, rehab, containment, hahaha, Covid isolation, hahaha... I hadn't laughed that hard since I can't remember when.

I told him, *I promise I'll be on my A game next time we get together,* he said, *What year is this?*

Seriously, I hoped Billie would come through for me on that demo. It would mean a roof, food, and space to create. I wonder why she never made a Christmas album. Did she even like chocolate or do a commercial jingle?

I walked for a long time meandering and thinking while Hurricane Delta's winds blew away the summer heat. There were more homeless people, closed stores for rent, empty streets with construction, and that cursed Hard Rock building was still standing like an ominous ghost figure. Tourists were taking pictures of it and I wanted to let them have it for being so thoughtless.

How were we all going to get out of this one?

I went into the African store run by Indians and bought sage, Egyptian musk, and sticks to burn all the bad *juju* away. I refrained from the desire to buy a colorful African halter jumpsuit and gypsy hoops, walk myself to the Greyhound station nearby, and get on a bus to the cornfields of Iowa.

Three to five years to recover the city's economy was predicted. We were already poor before that.

Here are the words in the bridge to the first Christmas song I ever wrote:

Hearts without a care,
No sorrow or despair,
It's Christmastime again
With hope we're meeting.
Gold dust fills the floors,
So open up the doors,
Watch the angels fly,
Dropping dreamlets from the sky.
It's Christmastime again, my love.

c. 2020

Hurricane Zeta

Someone up there must have been having a good laugh. We were all quite familiar with Covid, the economy, the election, protests, and riots. Add two big ol' storms in the Gulf.

In October 2020, New Orleans was a port party city that had been second lining without masks and breaking the rules daily. Who had money to evacuate anyway? And it was too hot to camp out. Besides, Grandville and I didn't even own a car. Somehow, I flipped over the metal dog gate in the dark and had a bruised left leg with a changing canvas of purple, blue, and yellow murals daily. I never did fall down as a drunk. We battened down the hatches with some beans and water and Jolly Ranchers.

I got a call to be interviewed on WGNO-TV about hurricane preparedness. If they had asked me before Katrina, I would have told them my actual routine was to blow up the inflatable dinghy, attach dog leashes to the side, and pack an emergency bag supply. But this time, we just locked down like we'd been doing for the last five months. And 3-1-1 hadn't been much help when it came to the big sinkhole in front of the house, so good luck to us in an emergency.

We'd all become nocturnal creatures. Sweat, write, create, and behave like one of those eccentric characters out of a Tennessee Williams play. *Dahling, don't make me come out of the shadows.*

Who knew that a woman of the same name as that terrible hurricane would replace me in the life of the man I loved?

Make a Wish

If I could make a wish
On a dandelion and blow,
I'd blow the monster back to sea,
Where it would die alone.
Instead of it being a dictator,
Taking with it,
All in its path,
Leaving brokenhearted,
With the aftermath.

A wild card no one can tame,
The beast is angry,
Mother Nature wants to shame.
Disrespect
To her sacred land,
Why do we deserve to live,
Off her kind hand?

We are the barnacles,
Attached to the whale,
The vulture who eats,
Leftover remains.
We are the takers,
The ones to blame.

Nature is pure
With her fresh air,
We smoke pollutants out,
Like the devil may care.
Nature gives
Rainbows of greens,
Every one's custom made,
Why do we rip it apart,
With corn syrup schemes.
Can you blame her?
She's tried

Like a beaten woman,
Calm nurturing mamas,
Been put to the test.
Vomiting out toxins,
With hurricane ways,
Survival of the fittest means,
We all must make change.

An offering of thankfulness,
For all the love she gives.
Time to do right,
Because against her wrath,
Mortals will never win.

Fairy Godmother

Sometimes I wish I didn't feel or think so much. It actually hurts me when I see other people hurting. They used to give lobotomies to depressed people at the turn of the century. Maybe someone can invent a short-term lobotomy pill. During Covid, I found myself more depressed every day.

How many times can one do the same thing every day or go through the motions of pretending they are a singer or entertainer when they have no one to entertain? I knew I should be practicing scales, but the thought of standing up and doing so on a cheap keyboard felt too exhausting. I could barely get up in the morning, yet someone up there thought it was hilarious for me, an eternal night person, to wake up at 6:30 a.m. when there was a whole day of nothing ahead.

I love people. Me, myself, and I get along pretty well until the question of whether to even attempt hair, makeup, and outfit vs bedhead and pajamas for the day comes to a head. What color lipstick to wear. *Who are you fooling? You're not going anywhere. You don't even have a car and the bus drivers are getting doggone grumpy, if they even show up on time, that is. And if you make it to the grocery store, your lips will be covered anyway.*

I found it very difficult to not have strange thoughts, between the BLM protests and Covid. I felt like I needed to explain why I'm a good person despite being White. *Your people*, someone said disparagingly... *My* people didn't do anything to *your* people. My mom's grandparents were Russian Romanian Jewish peasants who came to Ellis Island at the turn of the century trying to escape persecution and mistreatment. My father's side probably suffered through the potato famine.

I even found myself telling "White girl jokes" that were told about me and my likes while I was in an interracial relationship. I guess some of them were funny and some weren't, but maybe if I made myself the butt of the joke, I wouldn't be judged for my skin color. "White Fucking Bitch, holding supremacy with my flat White booty who likes French toast and having her dog sleep in bed to cuddle with." I guess most of it is true except the bitch and supremacy parts.

I don't know what else to say. I'm a good person. *You're lucky you're White*, I kept being told by multiple people. *Are you kidding me?* Do you know the number of clubs in New Orleans and festivals in Europe that won't hire me because, as I was told point-blank, *you're not Black?*

And Covid... I found it disillusioning that bringing music back was in phase three, yet close quarters, drinking, and tattoos were allowed in phase two. I kept thinking, will we ever get to phase three if two doesn't work because everyone is getting drunk and doing whatever they want from touching, hugging, kissing, and who knows what else after being in isolation? I also wondered, what about when the unemployment money was to run out at the end of July? Then what?

Oh, there was a turbine that broke and couldn't be fixed for the heavy hurricane season that year. That's why the city flooded after a small rain.

It takes two months in advance to book clubs — clubs that we worried might never reopen. It takes six months to book festivals abroad. In June 2020, I felt scared. For everyone.

I knew from the texts and postings so many were feeling the same way. I didn't know what to say except *Want to take a walk?* But nobody answered their phones.

I threw up blood one morning. It happened a lot when I was drinking, but not since being sober. This time blood kept coming out of my nose. It truly was the perfect shade of red. Why can't the lipstick companies get it right?

I always wanted to be skinny, but I had a little Ethiopian baby stomach. I was thinking the only thing I owned in this world was my recording catalogue and I wondered who I should to leave it to. Who could extrapolate money out of it to do good things?

What was I thinking wasting money on a storage unit? I came across notepads from 2000, when all the dreams in the world were possible. Checklists on how to accomplish them. And I did. It made me sad that innocence felt gone for so many. Every item I was buying then had to do with survival tactics. Boots for all seasons — Siberia or the rainforest, check. Battery-powered travel amp and mic, check. Swiss Army knife and mace, check. Three performing dresses, one pair of phenomenal heels, a journal, and book, check. Money for a train or cheap car, check. Who needs undergarments? They only have to be washed anyway.

What was wrong with me? Was I planning on a Fellini movie meets hunger games, death, or going on rent strike if need be? Either way, I didn't see a quick happy ending coming if that mess stayed in full gear for much longer.

Who was in charge? It didn't feel like anyone had a solid plan of action. It was all vague. When was the mission statement going to peak and the issue resolved in regard to the riots and peaceful protests? Who was going to step forward and say, "I hear you"? Where was the intent to make peace and amends? When was the severity of the virus going to be taken seriously? If we can go into space, why can't we find someone who can fix a turbine? Where were the problem solvers?

I wanted a fairy godmother who was also a muse to give me a shot of enthusiasm and a kick in the pants!

Gay Brothers

I watched *Uncle Frank*. I was very moved.

Any action causes a reaction. Reflecting, I realized that long-term and short-term friends from the gay community have always had my back covered beyond the call of duty.

I wouldn't be a singer if Vincent Roppolo hadn't plucked me off the streets for his production of *A Midsummer Night's Dream*. He took all the time in the world during my New York City years to teach me the tools I needed to become a singer. He was and still is my mentor with all of the book wisdom he acquired.

There are brothers who just decided I was their adopted sister. Human spirits who are intelligent, creative, empathetic, funny, and adventuresome and who don't use the word "can't."

One day in 2017, New Orleans flooded. I swam home to a message that Mr. Georgia (Bob McClure) was coming to get me to witness the solar eclipse in the mountains at his lovely home. We danced with his little tribe like banshees in theatrical gypsy garb. Not to mention Bob and his partner, Don, reached out unexpectedly to offer the money needed to make my *Living the Life* album.

I remember Christopher Matson, an interior decorator, taking me in for a week and, upon arrival in New York City, getting on his knee to give me an antique ruby and gold fleur de lis ring. That gave way to eight days of gospel church, museums, long walks, and charades. Later he opened The Jungle Room, a 1940s club in Puerto Rico where I performed and he graciously had me as his guest for a month. He had previously set up a gig for a wealthy Russian couple in Cancun. We drove all around downtown in a taxi looking for a Mexican mariachi trumpet player the night before the gig. He also set up the Peace Prize Forum gig in Minneapolis, which included an adventure with Garrison Keillor.

How about my former neighbor Brandon Bergman? In New Orleans, during my lowest days in the Treme, he took me and my Frenchie into his home for tea and biscuits and talks on spirituality and Dolly Parton. He was always a bright light around the corner from the nuthouse I was living in.

How about when we came back from Russia and Daniel Nardicio promoted a sellout show at Feinstein's on Park Avenue in New York City for my band? I appreciate the years of our coffee dates and creative discussions. His newest undertaking, as of this book's writing, is a club in Manhattan called the Red Eye.

Mark Ahlman, my heart. My band and I were playing at The Supper Club in Manhattan, and he walked up like a handsome prince. How lucky could I get? He asked me if my cousin was gay. I said no, he's just metrosexual. He and I laughed so hard over the years. Where is he now? No one knows. I can't seem to find him.

I feel so lucky to have been taken under the wing of so many brothers. I love those guys. Can someone tell me where to find a straight man with the same attributes? (Christopher says all straight women say that.)

One Year Sober

I can honestly say that 2020, my first year of sobriety, was the hardest year of my entire life. The year of Covid. When I was in the ICU, I was given 29 days to live, hallucinating and seeing the light. I guess I am stubborn, and I never give up. Also, I know when it's time to surrender. When Anders Osborne came to see me, he took one look and cried. *The world needs you,* he said. *I can get you into an ace rehab center in Nashville. If you don't like it, you can leave anytime and keep drinking.*

That was the first time someone wasn't lecturing me, instead letting me make a decision for myself. I accepted. It took every ounce of energy I had to crawl into that wheelchair with a crippled leg and make my way back home with a hospital ride. I felt very few people really believed in me anymore.

I went home to Grandville at the rental on Franklin Avenue, where there was an overwhelming gas leak. Not only were we being evicted for not being able to pay the exorbitant rent, but the gas company had also come by and shut off all the gas, saying we were lucky we didn't die in our sleep and that the house didn't blow up. So, I packed all of my things and put them into storage, and prepared to go to rehab. I felt so beat up and tired of trying to survive, but I had just run out of steam and hit the end of the road.

I believe in redemption and a higher power, and I do listen to some religious agendas. I don't always agree with what I hear. The high-end rehabilitation center in the country far away from Nashville was cold, lonely, and depressing. For one month, the staff kept us so busy mentally and physically with one-on-one counseling, group therapy, and all kinds of crazy exercise. A little butch lady knocked on the door every morning when it was still dark outside and yelled in her smoky, raspy voice, *It's mindfulness time!* My roommate Jessica, a tall, funny, voluptuous blonde hairdresser from Kentucky, would roll over and say, *Na-maste right here in bed.*

We would go off campus to poor churches in Nashville, where many people shared their stories of addiction with sorrow and humor. Resources are not as abundant for some, so church becomes a place to wash up, eat, and find strength and peace of mind in a small but supportive community. I would go from fighting the good fight and doing what was asked of me to feeling so much anger that nobody really understood me. Bit by bit, they chipped away, exhausting us physically and mentally with no distractions, to the point of having epiphanies and breakdowns, realizations and removal of painful boulders of emotion that I'd spent a lifetime carrying.

With those feelings coming out, I felt as if I could breathe for the first time in so many years. I didn't realize how much my strange upbringing had haunted me for so long. I always knew it was a very hard road we were asked to travel as children, but I felt we had turned out to be strong, self-reliant grown adults.

I never missed drinking; I just felt very lost and sad. With no distractions of TV, cell phone, or reading (except a small library of expensive books on addiction), I was forced to learn to stare at the wall and think about my life and what was important to me. There are so many great things that we take for granted every single day: our health, our friends and family, and the gift to be an American and to make the choice of what we individually would like to do with our lives and our legacy.

The ladies there came from all walks of life: wealthy, poor, alcohol addicted, opioid addicted, crack addicted, but the thing that they all seemed to have in common was extreme unhappiness and being trapped in a world that they had no control over. They were quite funny and we all bonded communally. I really listened to their stories and became sympathetic to their plights. Most of them had husbands and children, and most of them had issues with being bossed around by dominating men.

By the time one month was over, I felt like I had been there for a year. I realized I didn't have a home to go back to and I didn't know where I was going to stay. I sent texts to a close-knit group of friends who I thought would be mentally healthy to be around while I went to an Intensive Outpatient Program for two months. Only one person responded. Her name is Dixie Rubin, and she was a total saint to take me (and Allie) into her home and house me unconditionally for six weeks. I will always be indebted to her for her generosity and thoughtfulness. While walking Allie in the area where Dixie lived, I found a cute home around the corner for rent, which is where I moved (and still reside as of this writing).

I never expected all of the kindness that came from so many wonderful people after I became sober. It still makes me cry to know that their generosity was because of me as a person, not an avatar; that I have value as a human being. I never felt that before, because I had been told by my father that I always must give more than I take to be valued by others. This realization made me feel like I was no longer dependent on music to be accepted.

The timing of everything is funny. In December 2019, I was half dead and seeing the light. I missed Christmas and New Year's because I was drugged up and attached to a hospital bed, hallucinating on some other planet from the medications. During Mardi Gras 2020, I was in rehab, except on Fat Tuesday, when I was standing stone cold sober at Saint Peter and Royal streets with drunken chaos around me and Covid running rampant.

In rehab we made a vision board. I placed a country home with trees and grass, healthy Indian food, fruit, animals, and my loved one and I sitting hand-in-hand on the floor with joy and love in our hearts. I also placed a gypsy riding a black horse, a Frida Kahlo character with an LV travel bag, and a billboard top 10 song (still desiring as a bucket list to make a top 10 hit even if I'm writing rather than singing it).

Be careful what you wish for because it might come true. And what I wished for did. Two dogs, a cute country style home in Gentilly that was always a mess with dishes that needed to be done, and a boyfriend who made me laugh, think, and create, and who took on sobriety a month after I did. I've heard it said that it is a miracle when two recovering alcoholics can make it together. We did it, and we aced it for a while.

I felt that I was being karmically paid back for having imposed my behavior on ones that I love, never thinking at the time that they would be affected as much as they were. So, as 2020 came to a close, I was thankful, I was sad that I ruined my health, and I was hopeful for a future as bright and adventuresome and creative as the past and its prime moments of my life had been. The beauty of being sober is the pain and the joy of real life; being brave enough to face it without fear and say, yes, I can overcome, with a clean mind and conscience.

Contender

To stay in the game, one has to make difficult decisions that are literally a question of life or death. I usually let the cards play out and the choice is made by default. So, I asked this question honestly.

Should I:

A) Get a liver transplant, which will require a lifetime of medications that can cause other health issues?

B) Attempt to solve the problem with an intense program of holistic healing, which, if it fails, could be fatal?

C) Leave it in God's hands and try to live a quality life trustingly?

I hesitated to share this on social media because the last thing I wanted was a pity party. But I believed (and still believe) that sharing my journey would be helpful for me so I would not feel so alone during that strange, isolated time. It also shines a light on what the repercussions of drinking can bring if one is lucky enough to survive it.

Two full days of tests in the hospital were eye-opening, educational, and scary, and required self-control during an emotional rollercoaster. At the end of each day, I was extremely drained after the tests and trying to learn a whole new medical language on the spot.

I had an emotional breakdown with all of the confusion in my head about what to do. The next day I woke up on the brighter side of the bed, realizing that I must move to a place of positivity and not fear.

The hospital is such an interesting world. The nurses and doctors I interacted with were positively wonderful and on their game. Some were funny, some no-nonsense. I'm sure psychology and etiquette are part of their training.

I started the first day of testing with a lot of blood being taken out of my arm. The nurse was a nice young lady with the most elaborate African hairdo I had ever seen. She couldn't get into my veins because so much blood had been taken the day before. She exuberantly yelled, "It's about to blow, it's about to blow!" I got scared and thought, is my arm gonna blow up? She said it again as she tried twice more. I had to have a good laugh with her as a dark red leak dripped down my arm.

There were lots more appointments, like a stress test artificially pumping up my heart rate so fast I thought my head and heart were going to explode without the calorie-burning benefit of an Olympic workout. The day closed out with a CAT scan after I drank the ink. The young Asian doctor was so positive and kind, and said I should do something nice for myself and go eat a good meal like Popeyes. He read my mind. I was trying to decide between Whole Foods and Popeyes. I had a little guilty pleasure tradition of getting Popeyes after a long day of checkups.

I thought, if that's the worst of it, over drinking a fifth of liquor a day, I'll take it.

Messengers of God

I guess God likes to send his messages through ladies who happen to be relatives of my very favorite old-school R&B musicians here in New Orleans. The last four ladies I've met through random luck in shopping aisles or grocery store parking lots.

I met Uncle Lionel's granddaughter, Anjel Jellie Batiste, at the Brown Derby when she paid it forward and paid for my pint of ice cream, telling me how good God had been to her. We had a real talk.

I met Lee Dorsey's daughter, Rozella Nichols, in the parking lot at Whole Foods when I complimented her car and said it looked like Allen Toussaint's but a newer version. She was awfully nice.

I met Herman LeBeaux's sister, Carrie LeBeaux, on the bathing suit aisle at Ross and we talked for over an hour about everything from the Bible and verses to opening a CBD coffee shop to the bureaucracy of City Hall.

I received the word in the face cream section at Marshalls. A woman was looking at the perfumes and not sure which one to get because they were all packaged and she couldn't smell them, so I asked if I could recommend one to her and pulled out Happy by Clinique. I told her I had been fortunate to play the premiere debut party for the scent in New York City and they sent all of us home with cases of Clinique perfume that we shared with our family and girlfriends. The smell is distinctively spring, light, airy freshness. Turned out she was Paul Barbarin's granddaughter.

We segued from her wanting to go to New York City to natural healing of the body to Bible verses in the power of God to heal. I think we were standing there for about an hour and a half. At a certain point I started feeling like my head was about to explode with all of the strange energy, and she took my hand and loudly prayed an extended prayer for me and for my loved ones. She kept mentioning that Matthew 18:19 contained the most important words of wisdom.

I guess during Covid, window shopping was the hotspot for meeting interesting people.

While I was standing there with her animatedly praying for me, a few bottles of cream down was a lady I recognized, my former neighbor's mother, who visits every year from Detroit. She is so wonderful too and spent a lot of time talking about the Bible and Jesus. I guess I must have looked like I needed a good talking to.

I've been saved three times by the Baptist Church, invited personally to church by Jehovah's Witnesses, a Seder dinner, multiple Catholic and Christian services, as well as a Hari Krishna temple on Sundays. I am thankful there are so many people who care about God and want to see me understand the power of God and Jesus and Buddha and Allah.

I have learned a lot and also came home that day with a new skin regime at a discount, including foaming cleanser from Japan, shea butter for the face from Australia, and sea salt intensive cream for the body from France.

God, Religion, and Church

I believe in God. Not as a Santa in the sky standing at a golden gate with a bunch of golden angels, but as a big, powerful source of energy. A force that dictates and moves the parts and pieces called us. I think we are all little puzzle pieces allotted to make the perfect picture. When we do our higher part and find our place, the gaps of the puzzle close and together we become one in an angelic Michelangelo mural.

My mother is Jewish, my father Christian. Both abandoned their faith to pursue Buddhism. Lay of the land for the kids: What goes around comes around. Be empathetic. Give more than you take. Say your prayers. Reincarnation is real. Keep a clean slate karmically. Always act as if someone up there is watching you. Give it all away.

I have always gone to many different churches around the world. They have been a solace away from all the chaos. Quiet and alone to think and breathe. When going to a service, I leave an ear open to the lesson.

I've met many good people in church. The ones that claim *they are the way* are unattractive to me. If we all believe in God, aren't there many religious platforms to get there? That mentality is a big reason I choose not to commit to just one avenue of understanding.

In Mexico, women are expected to wear skirts and cloths on their heads. At the Baptist super-church in New Orleans East, I was the only one in a dress. The participants in the women's empowerment conference from the ages of 12 to 65 owned the Beyoncé tight blue jeans and high heels look. I think God appreciates all respectful thoughtfulness to show up to the plate with your hair spit-combed, shoes tied, pants pulled up, and most important, a smile and willingness to participate.

I have seen and experienced powerful actions that make me know there is a higher force at work. It's not just in His house. It's in everybody's. We are all sheep and shepherds. Does God care if you wear lipstick? Does He care about the petty little things? It seems like that force is all about the big picture of goodness and love.

There are churches with straight-laced White people in Connecticut singing the European hymns with no emotion. Making quilts for the winning ticket number. Giving away thousands to the church for tax deduction purposes. It's their way to give to God.

There are multitudes of trombones playing hard and loud at the United House of Prayer for All People in Harlem, with people falling out. "Sweet Daddy" Grace had many denominations of bills thrown at him as he walked the aisle to the pulpit in flamboyant purple decor.

There are Baptist services at the Joy Theater in New Orleans with a female preacher who pulls up in a Rolls-Royce for the service, talking about the three Ts God expects of you: Time, Talent, and Treasure.

There are dozens of unassuming small brick churches in the Seventh Ward. I was invited by a preacher, a recovering addict, who chaperoned his church kids' field trip on the streetcar. I went. It was one of the few times I stood to share my marital woes.

Little Israel, the mayor of St. Bernard, insisted I go to church with his grandma and his brother Ishmael. That was the smallest room I'd ever been in. He laid his 12-year-old head on my shoulder. There were a lot of confused faces.

The White Girl Rehab Brigade went to every Black church in East Nashville to understand our addictions through their journeys. The shuttle took us from a fancy safe center twice a week to churches where all they had was the church, community, and strength of will power. In the middle of sharing their horror stories of addiction, we would always find the hilarity and go to town to the point where the whole circle of Black and White were rolling on the floor.

The most memorable churches to me are the ones in Greece and Scotland. Greece's for its hourly incense burning, bell ritual presented by a somber, robe- and pocket watch-wearing preacher. Scotland's for its size and grandeur. History is ensconced in its walls. Thousands of years of weight can be felt in the air.

The closest I've come to a godlike experience was on a Greyhound bus when I was 16. I went from my mom in Texas to my dad in New Orleans. There was one seat left. It was next to a very dirty, smelly Black man holding a full garbage bag. He was nice. Quiet. He asked me if I believed in God. I said yes. He pulled an old well-worn bible out of his garbage bag and began to read me verses. After each verse, he turned to me to explain it. His eyes were glowing radiantly, and he had a halo around his head, brightening his dirty face. I felt tickles in my stomach and a huge calm come over me. He departed the bus with a smile halfway through my trip. I hadn't noticed before that he was wearing bright red brand-new tennis shoes.

Merely a Mortal

I wear my mortality with an air of grandeur. It is a starched suit that lies under the coat of armor fashion called the front face facade I present to the world. There is a bit of pompousness that I walk around with, the mindset of invincibility. Walking a tightrope of taking chances without a net. No matter how much scurrying away from the subject, it will absolutely happen to you. *Splat. Kerplewy.* Funeral parlor.

The poker game is over. You've lost the final hand to death. He's become bored with your monotonous ways. He puts his cigarillo out and lays down his full-house hand, as you lie in the coffin in your perfectly starched suit. Loved ones and enemies with white hankies cry or smirk under them.

What did you spend your mortality time clock on? What was your legacy written for posterity?

The beauty of choice.

No matter your mindset, whether it be fear, peace, or narcissism, you will never escape that ball and chain carried around daily until your final garb is removed. You are merely a mortal after all. So get off your high horse and make that pilgrimage to Mecca.

MELD Score

"What is a MELD Score?" I asked the doctor. (MELD = Model for End-Stage Liver Disease)

"It is a way to determine your liver disease by bloodwork," he said. "The normal range for most people would be 8 to 10. When you left the hospital, you were 38. At 40, you're dead. You are holding now at 26, which isn't good enough to not need a liver transplant."

The horrible thought of being cut open and having somebody else's liver put into my body seemed so unbearably painful, I wanted to just pass out, die, run away, and think this was not real but some sort of bad dream that I would wake up from or that the gods would say yes, you can heal yourself.

The nutritionist told me to purify myself, to remove all toxins from my body. When everything is in order, the body will work properly and heal itself. Even knowing that, I couldn't stop myself from getting a Sprite or a Popeyes once in a while. What kind of a Darwin award would I get if I died because I had Popeyes? I did give it 90 percent of my very best effort, but it still was not good enough to get my score down to a 21.

In May of 2020, my head surgeon and the board of surgeons looked at my case and determined I needed a liver transplant. I carried a heavy weight of impending doom on my shoulders all day and all night. I was morose, looking at the world through the eyes of someone whose days were numbered.

I couldn't continue to exist in that state: going to the hospital to remove 22 pounds of fluid from my stomach every two weeks, barely able to walk, looking yellow, scaring people, morbidly depressed, dragging, lacking energy. That was the way it would be for a period of time until my liver just gave out. There was no way to know when that would be.

Stage 4 cirrhosis. It sounded bad. I gratefully and hesitantly accepted to be on the list, still praying a miracle would happen. It took a year of enduring tests like a guinea pig to find out if I was worthy to be cut open to receive someone else's liver — someone who wasn't lucky enough to live.

I hated myself for ruining my perfectly good liver. I hated myself for all the pain I had caused my family and friends, especially my mother and my daughter. Putting pressure on the hospital system. People who were actually sick for a reason other than something self-imposed could have received the benefits I was getting. The amount of money that was going into my body to be able to live caused so much guilt I almost couldn't take it.

When I got out of rehab in February of 2020, I thought it was all going to be okay. I had no idea that I had destroyed my body to the point of no return.

Finally, the doctors said I was strong enough and I was cleared to get a new liver. The dual feelings of thankfulness and slow impending doom cannot be overstated. I was on the list. I had the right to turn down a liver if I thought it was inappropriate. Well sure enough, God threw many balls my way. There was a prisoner/drug addict, no thank you. A Hep B/Hep C liver that could be cured out of surgery, no thank you. All the options were made of toxic energy, toxic lives, toxicity that had killed these people. I didn't want a wounded liver to be put into my body. I couldn't stand the thought of living with something like that. No, no, no.

* * * * *

After a couple of months, the head nurse said, "Ingrid, we're going to have to take you off of the list if you don't say yes to any of these options."

That very day the hospital called with two liver transplant options. I was asked to be number two for both of them. I thought, *okay, the pressure is on. If I play my cards right, go sit and wait for hours at the hospital like I have done multiple times, then I will be allowed to go back home and still be on the list.* I went into Ochsner and within half an hour the nurse said, "You're going into surgery in 30 minutes."

Holy shit! I couldn't believe it. The first feeling was utter sickness in the pit of my stomach with a massive adrenaline rush and fear. God, I wanted to run away, the other part of me let her distract me so much that I realized I hadn't made a will. I had a couple of minutes, so I wrote it on a loose-leaf piece of paper, photographed it, and texted it to my mother, daughter, and sister. The nurse witnessed it. Then I met the anesthesiologist team that was going to put me to sleep. I said hello to them and the lights went out.

I woke up with big tubes in my throat that felt like they went all the way down into my intestines. The nurses were trying to yank them out like some sort of exorcism. I couldn't breathe. I was scratching frantically trying to get them out. They wouldn't take them out until I was breathing on my own. I felt like I was throwing up the birthing of an octopus alien that had attached its tentacles to my insides and wouldn't let go. Finally, with clumps of blood, she came for breath. That harrowing feeling when you're under water barely coming up to breathe overwhelmed my being.

I was beat up, with metal Frankenstein rods in my neck, a freak who couldn't move. Shock, numbness, confusion about where I was until... *Oh my God, I can't believe it, I'm alive*! I was a broken piece of machine having to be put back together again. Slowly, patiently, slowly, patiently. *My God, how much patience do you want from me?* Unbearably slow, I did it. Here I am, able to tell the tale. I was crying so hard because for the first time it was all coming out. The quiet sorrow, regret, pain. The tears in my eyes, the words from my mouth, the pounding in my heart. It felt cathartic.

I made it because the system paid over $1 million to keep me alive. I never paid a penny. Granted, I didn't have a penny. My promise to myself in return for that labor of love and investment into me is to never drink again.

What These Eyes Have Seen

From the Colorado mountains,
To the Mojave Desert,
And Baja beaches,
Displaying sharks below,
From train stations to hitchhiking,
Many landscapes
Fast and slow.

From city action to jazz band clubs.
Cobbled streets of Belgium,
Switzerland, Russia, Mexico,
These feet have tripped the light fantastic
Also crawled so very slow.

From circuses with straw floors,
White bulb string lights,
Showgirls behind stage curtains,
Are shadows in the night.
12-year-olds dance in the night.
Dark-eyed handsome boy,
Whose looks make your stomachs drop,
Using you up, leaving you blue.

Pale white sands of Puerto Rico,
Crystal clear grey blue water
With rocks below in Greece,
Mississippi River so muddy,
You can't see below your knees.
Showboats made of wood,
Every ghetto neighborhood,
Movie star premiere nights,
Walk the red carpet
Full of fear and excite.

Swing dancing from New York to LA,
Watch the aerial swing flips,
As she glides between his legs.
Rock stars, movie stars,

Famous faces,
Who've made their mark,
We've met so many,
They've told me stories,
From their open heart.
From bums on streets,
Shared smile and a word,
To the white picket fences
Of families well learned.

From tradition and values,
To proletarian ways,
From beatniks to hipsters,
Elder statesmen
Who shared their joy and pain.

Mentors with wisdom
Take me under their wing,
Learning how to glow,
Learning how to sing.
Learning how to critically think,
Chess, music, love, literature,
The mind, heart, and soul,
Are filled up to the brink.

From shuffling the streets,
Dancing the blues,
Bob Fosse jazz hands paying the dues.
Busking the corners
To earn a dime,
Dinner for family,
Mercado finds.

Musicians with stories,
Musicians with notes,
musicians with lessons,
Musicians who gloat.
Music all day,
Music in every way,
Music eaten up
To earn dues paid.

From a little girl's feet
Walking the desert,
In the bright blue moon glow,
Looking for turquoise,

Indian arrowheads
In the distance
Banshees moan.

First love in plazas
Of Mexico,
Virgin touches bring marriage,
And a baby to grow.
Home in New Orleans
Play Jackson Square streets,
Family memories
So hard and so sweet.

Whoa.
Brothers and sisters
In black and white,
Teaching them to dance,
Bang the bass drum,
The sound makes them prance.
The beat makes them come.

Good people,
Crazy people,
Smart people,
Beautiful people,
Narcissistic people,
Talented people,
Don't matter 'bout the money,
I've met them all.

Hamptons,
Vogue covers,
Celebrity weddings, see,
German Academy Award performances,
Russia for a day,
Red Square, tea and freeze.

Singing with Zippers,
The Big Time galore,
Old-fashioned theaters
Sold out once more.
Mercedes-Benz Sprinters,
Five-star hotels,
The same show nightly,
Burned out in jail
For a short spell.

These eyes have seen it all,
Every detail noticed,
Enthralled.
Cheap sequins,
Metropolitan styles,
Charlie Chaplin bombs,
Ballerinas jete glide.

Elephants, monkeys,
Talking parrots that say "fuck"
Horses and burros we ride,
Bicycles peddling
For miles and miles.

Singing mariachi
At Christmas in bars,
Thousand peso notes thrown,
Christmas dinner in the family car.
Feliz Navidad, Feliz Navidad.

Shuffle ball change,
Slide, sway, swoop,
Belt out a song off key,
Take one for the troops,
Bring home the candy.
Reading literature,
Voltaire to Anne Frank,
Marilyn Monroe, Hitler,
Trixie Belden made bank.
Libraries as babysitters,
Across every state
Large and small,
Dewey Decimal System,
Let this girl eat cake.

Love, love, love,
Star eyes I have seen,
Dropping stomach,

Touching skin,
Young, wild, and free.
Christian boys in Texas,
French kisses in Mexican streets,
New Orleans players,
You never know who you'll meet.
New York artists with class,

I've kissed them all with eyes wide open,
Shadows of faces in dark theaters
Make memories that last.

Death of a daddy in cardboard,
Pink fuzzy blanket with class,
Second line for your father,
All musicians play brass,
Stately family tribute,
Blow heart-filled notes as they pass.
Passing of loved ones,
Open casket and closed,
Stuffy aired dark
In funeral homes.

Ridiculous laughter,
Nervous at the macabre,
Gut-wrenching laughter with kids
Over silly things you can't stop.
Smiles, tears, from many faces
They are etched forever in your mind,
Will always stay forever
In this heart entwined.

Tap dancers under shiny lights
Illuminated on stage,
Brilliant costumes glitter,
Notes flow above you,
Audiences on display.
Glorious Broadway
To Mexican discotheques,
Then subways below,
Even in treehouses,
Put on the greatest show.
What these eyes have seen
Are one million amazing things,
A kaleidoscope of fantastical scenes.

As I tumble through this life,
I keep my eyes wide open all the time.
A snapshot of a moment
That will never away,
Collages of months and years safely locked to stay.
In my mind's eye
Images are magnified with time.
Every blink a movie poster

With humor, horror, awe, and sublime.
What these eyes have seen
Has ignited joy and pain.
These lenses keep busy searching
For their new snap refrain.

As the Hospital Turns

After my liver transplant surgery, I made a little video. I was actually quite surprised at how energetic I felt, even in pain.

Every day after that I had been dragging more and more. Strange changes were morphing daily to the point of me wondering if the distortion of my body was permanent. "It's all normal," said the head doctor, "you're doing really great. Better than most," he said, as my eyes were getting puffy and the scar was oozing and getting gorier looking. The worst was that certain parts of my body were turning into a bloated mess. *Oh my god! Who's ever going to love me again?*

The surgeon had a smile on his face and said it was normal. Actually, sometimes men's body parts blow up to the size of horses as he pointed at my ice water tumbler. All of a sudden, an odd visual came into my head I did not want to see right then, maybe ever... He also patted himself on the back for the steroid trick that makes patients feel invincible.

I felt like a puppet being controlled physically and emotionally by the chemical equations of a mad scientist whom I was forced to trust completely, as turning back was not an option. All I knew was that I was very lucky to be alive. I watched myself and saw my body reconfiguring its new equations.

I was advised by a woman named Catalina to name my liver and imagine healing colors. She was able to overcome breast cancer by practicing this technique. "Iris" was like a baby not quite ready to activate. Okay, the doctors said, let's stimulate her. Open, prick, stick, swallow, open mouth, vitals check, insulin check, gauging pain. Blown veins, spurt spurt spurt.

How do you feel on a scale of one to ten, as they gauged how much pain killer to give. I felt like there were a thousand hot nails hammered into my side, nauseous, headache, discombobulated, and I sounded like Joe Pesci. *Will I ever sing again? I can't worry about that right now, and there will not be any more renditions of "Happy Birthday" being sung for anyone for a while.*

I certainly didn't want to become a pill addict. Another Pandora's box wasn't invited. Instead of being honest that my pain number was a seven, I said it was a five and got half the dosage, so I ended up white knuckling the day away.

I woke up wondering where I was. It happens when you're on the road in back-to-back places with quick turnarounds. *Am I at the Venetian in Las Vegas? It looks like the sun is coming up on the desert. Or am I at Mama Stella's patio overlooking the ocean in Greece?*

It took a few minutes to get centered and realize I was in a hospital in Jefferson Parish. What I was viewing was not water or desert, but empty concrete parking lots covered by an oppressive, grey, sweltering sky.

The nucleus of a hospital is an intriguing beehive of intricate workings that go hand in hand precisely and effectively. It's the greatest show on earth, and you're a living specimen inside a big glass jar in the freak show tent.

From the top to the bottom. No one ever meets the enigma of the wizard behind the curtain. Regardless of their status, every single person working was kind, thoughtful, sharing, and wise. Watching the same medical routine through different Florence Nightingales, some slow and methodical, some fast and jerky; some verbal, some non-; some so doggone full of character. *Sweetheart, this machine just won't listen to me,* as she with a Dolly Parton nail flicked the insulin line to my vein.

Overall, the nurses were like well-trained athletes, looking like they had just run the Olympics, glowing with health. There were two in particular I really bonded with. One actually did my photo shoot in the room with me.

My honorary uncle, Rodger, drove for four days straight from Santa Rosa, California, to be one of my caretakers. He came straight to my hospital room.

The tribe of nurse assistants looked like New Orleans Bounce stars. The hair, makeup, nails, shoes, full she-bang showtime. One of my favorites was Ashley. She was vivacious and outspoken. We bonded when she complimented my haircut. I told her about the barber in Gentilly who cut it for $25. He went to school with Grandville. He did such a perfect job, but he kept yanking at first, double checking it wasn't a wig. He said he had never cut "White girl hair" before.

Ashley had long, luxurious hair. But she kept hitting the back of her head with her whole hand. She said her scalp was itchy underneath her wig. Anyways, there was Rodger, musty, dusty, hot, and sweaty looking like the red-bearded wood hunter with a hippie tie dye mask, standing next to her in the room. Ashley kept giving him "the look," then out of her back pocket came a spray can of candy cotton sparkle rainbow room deodorizer. She sprayed it all over him and then all over the room, leaving everyone choking.

I got it. He was *stanky.*

I told everyone about what a hero he was for driving straight through from Albuquerque, and she was in complete awe at the concept that he slept in his van at truck stops.

Finally, she said, "Wow! My butt would hurt."

It's hard to imagine *that* possibility.

On Sunday, she talked to me in the dark room. I couldn't sleep. I couldn't do anything. It all hurt. She asked me about my music and story and relationship. I told her my candid feelings, fears, hopes, and sorrows. She looked right at me and said, *talk to God.* I guess I was feeling emotional. She gave me a big hug, hit the back of her head again, and walked out.

Sunday breakfast: one plain prebaked biscuit, one scoop of plain grits under fancy lid covering. No butter, no salt, no jam. The nurse felt bad. She said one of her patients had been in Angola for 20 years and when he saw that breakfast he was served, told her he was better fed there. Two amazing friends, Laura Anderson and Dixie Rubin, snuck in healthy fruit, snacks, and Indian food.

I know that Eastern and Western medicine both have powerful benefits. For them to work together is the ideal. At least in my new world of learning, they've been working very well for me.

My liver donor was a younger person who'd had addiction problems. Her liver was completely healthy. She slept with a drug addict. That's all I know. I was allowed to write her family a thank you letter in six months, after they'd had some time to mourn.

To lose the one you love, enabling another to have a second chance at life, must be so emotionally confusing. I know this gift of a liver must be protected. Taken care of with love.

I also know that the amount of faith, belief, effort, and support that was put into me by so many thoughtful people doesn't allow for backpedaling mistakes. It's a non-negotiable caveat in the unwritten agreement when given this amount of trust.

Not one swig with the idea of a quick buzz can ever replace the enormity of how much goodness has come into my life.

What's next, Iris?

I think this is the beginning of a beautiful new friendship.

* * * * *

Demigod Doctors

Every bit of love from your healing hands to mend a body broken by simply being human. A heart, a mind, and a soul are no good without a body for the brain. Your disciplined wisdom gave me life again.

All the years of toil you paid to learn your craft without complaint. Unconditional love stitches, nurture and will, has me on the mend. Thank you isn't a powerful enough word to say what I feel for your 20,000 hours of study to help me heal.

A miracle it is, and every single one of you is a saint, committed to the mission of making people well again. My life was in your hands, the night shift drill, everyone a team with a voice of solidarity saying, "I will."

My new liver and I will forever be thankful to a team of heroes who came in and saved my life.

Thank you, Ochsner Hospital.

Rodger That

Gifts come in unusual packages.

Uncle Rodger is my caretaker, handyman, driver, family, and peaceful, wise comedian. This could be a successful business idea. Live in everything man. That takes a lot of pressure off boyfriends and husbands, so they can do the fun things.

As a family band, we played the Halifax Buskers Festival in Nova Scotia. My sister-in-law Priscilla had met Rodger previously, so we stayed at the hostel he was running. He joined my father's Work Group and graciously got his booty kicked into gear by my father to learn different skill sets and adventures for life.

He has been through thick and thin since I was 16. He was the sailor for the first family and historical raft trip to cross the Atlantic from Newfoundland to Ireland.

He was the road manager on The Flying Neutrinos' first major tour through Europe under my leadership when the band was signed to Fiction Records. Among many other unique undertakings, such as many years with the Red Cross aiding in national catastrophes, Rodger married my honorary Auntie BellaDonna, making him my honorary uncle.

I have a photograph of them that I took in Las Vegas in a Del Taco. The look of two people so happy, giddy, and in love after 20 years is enough to tear anyone up.

He may not wear a nurse's uniform, but I couldn't ask for a more perfect person to see me through to health stability.

Gratitude Letter

My mentors at Cumberland Heights suggested I write a gratitude letter.

I am grateful for everything.

To be fortunate to be alive today and see spring blossom.

To have a circle of the most positive, kind, intelligent, humorous people in my life. It is a very solid feeling for which I am very grateful.

I am grateful for every moment with my family. And for their unconditional forgiveness after all the worry I put them through.

I am grateful for my mother. She is the very best example in every area of life. I am so lucky I won her in the birth lottery.

I am grateful for the financial space to have a home and food without hustling underpaid gigs while recovering my health in sobriety. Thank you, Ferrero Rocher, for picking my song!

I am grateful to not want to drink anymore and have to white knuckle it or dance around the fire of desire.

I am grateful for the little spontaneous adventures, the beauty that results from new impressions and food for thought. I don't take them for granted anymore.

I am so very thankful to know what I was born to do and to be gifted the basic talent to grow with hard work. Having something to call my own, with the freedom to express it and share it is everything. It can never be taken away no matter what my position in life or who comes and goes.

I am thankful for my musical family, who have let me lead them into the dream while teaching me the vocabulary and technicalities of music to be a contender, not just a hobbyist.

I am thankful to be me, with all the ding, dangs, imperfections in progress, striving to ascend incrementally.

Specifically, apart from my family and many good friends, I am thankful to the New Orleans Musicians' Clinic for being saints, especially Catherine Lasperches, Bethany Bultman, and Megan McStravick; Medicaid for covering a year of exorbitant hospital bills; MusicCares for covering the cost of rehab in

Nashville; and to the fans who delivered food to the front door during Covid with their good will.

I am grateful for my little doggie tribe to come home to.

I am more grateful than ever to be alive.

Road Trip

Every road trip should have a Stuckey's pit stop with a Mexican blanket, corn dog, and a Big Gulp — necessary lagniappe. And every road trip should require a few off-highway excursions.

From deserted coal mining towns to Navajo Indian arrowheads in the desert, to the dusty carnival that came to a small Texas ghost town, to meeting the man who invented Jiminy Cricket at a McDonald's, you never know who or what you'll meet.

You might even get a marriage proposal at 15 from the son of a Christian radio station owner. You don't have to accept it, you know. That most certainly would be the end of the line.

I love road trips (when I'm not rushed or evacuating from a monster hurricane). That's when dramedy really unfolds.

Motel 6s, holding evacuees in Walmart, slippers, jammies, and head curlers, gunshots in the night, leaking waterfall walls, banging on the door and low men's voices yelling for Latisha at 4 a.m., fucking so hard in the room next door the bed frame and the wall are banging, leaving you feeling like you're involved as a threesome by default.

A caravan is not always ideal. Everybody goes different speeds and has to potty at different times. That's when the rule about no Big Gulps comes into play. Everyone gets mad because they all want to see different sights. Why wouldn't everyone want to climb through the mud to see Patsy Cline's gravestone lit by a full moon at midnight in Winchester, Virginia? They just don't understand what they're missing.

Sleeping in your car at truck stops. You wake up with the sun pounding on your face, sweating. Your mouth is so dry there's a saliva line around your lips like a low tide foam at the beach.

HEY! Did you see the billboard for the biggest cinnamon rolls in the world attached to the used DVD store? It's the next exit!

Hurricane Ida

August 29, 2021. Sixteenth anniversary of Katrina. Batten down the hatches again. We've got a storm coming. There will be garbage floating down the streets. There will be strange creatures walking to the doors and coming through every crack possible in the old houses of New Orleans. There will be darkness, so light your candles and say a prayer that Entergy and the Sewerage and Water Board will be there.

The trains are blocking the roads, the ships pounding their foghorns. The lines at Walmart are long. Cornbread will be gone. Now is the time to prepare to lock down your masterpiece, make love, bake cookies, live this day as if it were your last glory.

For tomorrow there will be more leaves and branches, so retreat and save your energy to survive in the trenches. Someday there will be a second line, hold the fort my friends, there will be king cakes and hurricanes, a cocktail, and kindred spirits sharing laughter with new friends. For the newbies who have arrived during the dark pandemic time, know that the banshees very soon will come out and shine.

Bring it on, bring it on, show us what you got, we can do better; as they say, we are stuck in our resilience.

* * * * *

Country Bumpkin Evacuees

Lucy, you got some 'splainin' to do…

Three weeks after my liver transplant, we arrived in Houston at Clay and Katia Conrad's upscale home looking like the Beverly Hillbillies. My mom, Uncle Rodger, two doggies, and myself in my best gypsy dress trying to fit in with Rodger's hippie boho traveling red band van. We were hot, sweaty, tired, grumpy, and stressed.

We were very well received; it was a gift to have a haven where we could regroup and wait out Ida. The Conrads' home has a combination of gadgets that are The Jetsons *très moderne*. It took my mom and me 20 minutes to figure out how to work the remote control for the light in the bedroom. The coffee machine configuring reminded me of the time I was a nanny to a little boy in Provincetown. He insisted he knew how to work the VHS, so we believed him as he jammed the tape in and started banging every button. He was only three. My mom put his dinner into the microwave with Saran Wrap. It melted in the food and we fed it to him not knowing better. I place that one all on her.

We started pressing every button on the fancy machine with shots, foaming milk, and chaos ensuing to present a perfect cup of coffee. In fairness, I'd never encountered machines like this anywhere else in the world.

Then there was the Romani bum look as we transferred my belongings to my mom's SUV. Grocery bags with rhinestone necklaces thrown in at the last minute, dog crate, Marshalls bag with sound gear for gigs, if need be, two massive suitcases full of performing clothes. Huge Muscle Milk container. What kind of freaks had arrived? The neighbors asked us to move our vehicles from the front of their house. What the heck was I thinking packing all this crap? I had Katrina PTSD.

Gigs for me weren't dere no more. Where would we go? What would we do? Rodger was leaving the next day for Albuquerque, with all my pills and doctor's appointments now on us.

Albuquerque is more important? Come on, Rodger, take one for the team. Oh, wait, you already did.

* * * * *

Where did five weeks go? I couldn't believe it had been that long since my liver transplant.

Part of me felt sad that it was the end of an era in New Orleans as things were slowly getting stripped away from its unique spendor bit by bit. The culture bearers were becoming a dying breed. The jazz players were smaller in numbers as a tribe. The unique thriving pulse of action slowly was going into arrested development, a state of gentrification and stagnation with Covid.

Every storm brings questioning of one's commitments to a long love affair with the city. But like having an affair in a solid marriage, the thought of moving to a new city felt disloyal. Sure, she lets you down sometimes. But she's like a huge, rusty cargo ship that just keeps plugging and creaking with slow solidity. You might fall in a rusty pothole, but you're not going to go down with her ship.

Maybe given a hall pass, it might be nice to go a-visiting. A horse ranch in Texas with my friend Lady Tommie, an invite to come to Nashville.

What did they do way back when before modern conveniences as they sweated in their corsets by candlelight, using outhouses with gators and snakes around? We're pretty lucky to be alive today.

What's fun in the dark? Apart from where a carnal mind might be going, telling stories is actually really fun. We used to trade sentences and make them up on the spot when we were kids.

During Zeta, Grandville and I wrote some really good songs together in the dark while the wind was banging the walls. I was thinking of all my friends while sitting in the hot dark night and feeling for them.

Special thanks to our hosts for taking us in at the last minute. There should be an adopt a musician and their family program. We come with a pineapple, and, when the welcome is over, the pineapple representing proper etiquette disappears, so do we.

*****

"You Can't Be Serious, Spock"

On the way home to New Orleans after 12 days, there were no hotel rooms available in Lafayette, Baton Rouge, or every little port along the way. They were sold out. I thought it was a stroke of luck to reserve two rooms at a FEMA hotel. While waiting in the lobby for two and a half hours for them to figure out how to use my registration number, they realized that they booked all the rooms for the Entergy people.

Meanwhile, eight New Orleanians behind me, women no less, were putting out a big old chirp-chirp-chirp for us. Yes, this was a very serious matter. It was getting dark, we were tired. We had two and a half hours to go to get home, but it seemed oh so far away.

Need gas, Spock. Gas stations are sold out. What, seriously, if there's no gas in Lafayette, would there be gas in Baton Rouge?

Yep, but hey, I'm an eternal optimist and yes, vacation was right around the corner. I heard from my good friend that New Orleans was a ghost town. I planned on becoming Howard Hughes, writing, recording, reading, staying away from people with the cooties.

Whipped Cream and Cherries

Boobies, ta-tas, chi-chis, vavooms, mangos, oranges, whatever you may call them. It had made me so sad that they had disappeared along with my derrière. Maybe there was hope for them to reappear with the help of a trainer?

Grandville had told me I looked like one of the African women in *National Geographic*. That made me sad. I used to look at those magazines as a child. In the first nude photos I ever saw, the physical changes of a nubile baby making youth breasts to the sagging used ones of the elderly who'd had the life sucked out of them by their seedlings. The sacrifices of the woman's body to procreate were harshly judged by the male eye.

Torture of women for men's pleasure, be it in Africa with bronze rings around the neck, one added each year of life to stretch the neck so the elderly stateswomen could be painfully forced to proudly stand tall while their breasts sagged to the ground. Or the foot binding in China to make a smaller shoe size cropping the ability to walk properly.

As a dancer I had them and didn't want them; as a singer they were lagniappe to be Jessica Rabbit; as a mother, it was painful to be Dolly Parton while nursing three years. As a liver transplant newbie, I was thankful to have them blossoming back.

Ambassador of Love

The grey clouds roll with the white ones, trying to decide whether to rain or shine. The humidity in the early fall makes me think the latter. The birds are frantically chirping from the swaying oak trees that a storm is coming.

She sits by my side on the broken swing suspended by two milk crates on the disorganized raised porch. She is dying. I sit next to her in stagnation, knowing the right thing to do but selfishly wanting to hold every second possible with her. Tricking myself into thinking that maybe she is still enjoying life. After all, she is still eating with interest. She sits in full position swaying from side to side with her labored breathing.

My heart hurts just thinking about it and tears well up in my eyes. This girl has been with me through every tumultuous moment of my life these last six years. My very best friend. Every ward, every eviction, every glorious moment from when there was steak to when there was just barely a can of Alpo.

She is an ambassador of love.

Everywhere we walked, she would bring people together with her joy and beauty. She even agented a few bookings. A club owner would see her, find out in conversation that I am a singer, and book me some dates. She knows where the bacon nation is in every ward. A treat and a rub from a nice person. And she always intrinsically knows her way back to her home for that day.

Pain isn't enough of a word to describe witnessing her in it. Yet I don't know when to be the determiner of her final peaceful rest. Take her to the park, take her to see her old chum Jelly Roll, take her for her favorite Whopper Jr.... Is it me wanting that for her as she can barely walk and for the first time ever peed the bed this morning?

I knew what I had to do, and it broke my heart.

* * * * *

Then that day came...

Dear Allie, you were a one-of-a-kind Frenchie. I love you from the deepest place in my heart; thank you for being my best girl on this journey. Please forgive me for trying to do what is best for you. No more pain. I love you so much.

"And I know we'll meet again some sunny day."

Mortality

In two months' time, three friends died. Way too young. Even if you're 100, you may never say goodbye. Because to never see you again breaks my heart.

I'm the worst at accepting the inevitability of death. No one in my rascal tribe is allowed to go away. Never see you again? Incomprehensible. Like my dad, I hate goodbyes. If I love someone, I love them forever.

My dad hated to lose ones he cared about. He believed in reincarnation. For someone who was a nomad dragging his family through endless adventures and journeys, he was terrible at goodbyes. It was always "Ciao." Therefore, I was his father reincarnated. My sister was my father's best friend, Trent, reincarnated. And while he did test his theories on us and we psychically passed the test, it was hard to wear a dress and believe I was my own grandpa. Or that my sister was a hardcore sailor my dad met in his beatnik days in San Francisco. We both agreed we felt like men in drag.

Why did you always make us say goodbye when you were so bad at it? Every town, port, and country, you get attached, and then it's time to move on.

Somebody up there has a strange game plan I can't understand, as much as I try to rationalize or figure it out. Please stop taking everyone in threes. One at a time is hard enough to digest.

Some believe that we are recycled, just like the rest of the elements in the universe. Water from the river turns to rain, turns to fog, turns to the ocean, turns to the clouds again, and so it goes... Something like that. If that's true, as my grandma would say with her delicate, soft hands on my face yet again, another goodbye, "There are no endings that are not also a beginning."

The list keeps getting longer up there. I sure hope you all are working on your tambourine playing to start an orphan band, 'cause when I see you, I'm gonna crush you with my love. Until then, proceed forward.

There Is No Ending That's Not Also a Beginning

I can't get it out of my head. It follows me everywhere I go. The utopian idea that dreams come true with hard work, people are good with discernment, karma is very powerful, to always have a clean bill, the idea that one can achieve whatever they desire in this life with the right tools learned to get there.

It wasn't true.

We were raised outside the grid. Inside the grid was quite a different story. Having to fit into a complicated social structure didn't seem to be an easy transition for myself or any of the kids in the group. None of the grid made sense.

My sister Jessica went to college without one single day in public school. She graduated magna cum laude in journalism and was the only student in her class to get a job in it. She has navigated three major newspapers since then, working her way up from reporter to deputy editor at *Honolulu Civic Beat*.

Every kid in our family has aced the dreams they pursued. Granted, there were so many things we didn't feel comfortable growing up with. We never really had a childhood. Somehow most of our world made sense to us then. Somewhat. Trying to navigate life in the real world became sailing through an ocean of chaos. Why wouldn't a boyfriend want to be in a polygamous relationship with me with two other men involved?

Why would anyone want to be in a relationship where the other person wants to suffocate them? Nobody owns anybody else. I never did and still don't have a clue how to build and run a household. We were never on a hamster wheel to pay bills. We lived rent free our whole upbringing. We also didn't have running water or electricity. Nine-volt batteries to read by were a luxury; crapping in buckets or the river or hidden locations or fancy hotel lobbies became the norm.

Washing our hair in a McDonald's in a sink in Nowheresville became a solution. River bathing with a bottle of joy. Reduced materialism so that the laundry washed every three weeks or so was manageable financially.

I became a chameleon, trying to fit into other people's families. Watching how they made food, going through their drawers, intrigued by what they had, why they had it, and the way it was put in order.

We never had furniture. We lived out of our bags, which were kept ready to go so if at a moment's notice in case my father decided to make an extreme redirect, give our boat away and say we were going on a bicycle trip. We were ready to go.

For my 18th birthday, as a gift, my father made everyone in the group give away everything they owned to the Mexican circus we were traveling with.

It wasn't very well received by anybody in the group, which had so little to begin with. We were trained to carry a fire extinguisher and a machete to protect ourselves on the streets. It made sense to us, but upon witnessing the absurdity of it through the eyes of others, it felt completely humiliating.

Wearing lingerie and tutus seemed normal until I was laughed at by others. Freedom to dance, viewed with awe and laughed at by others. Don't wear those items, and definitely don't dance. Sleeping on train station floors. Horrifying to others, but normal for us. By the same token, their worlds didn't make sense to me.

While taking care of people's animals in the beginning of my independent New York City days, I would do a full exploration of their space. I borrowed a book on Kiki De Montparnasse from a fancy Soho art gallery owner's bookshelf. I took *The Sun Also Rises* with a big striped beach towel to Coney Island.

Why were people living lives that were a facade to cover their real lives up? At least they looked normal instead of the compass-less being I openly presented.

No matter how hard I tried, I couldn't feel like I fit in. I did try so hard, but none of it felt second nature. We were told to sleep when we were tired and wake up when we were rested. The idea of being on one's natural timing was of dire importance. God forbid you should wake the sleeping tiger called our father. The warrior would be on full alert sending a yell out of nowhere that would make you jump out of your skin.

So many things in both worlds made no sense. I was stuck in the middle trying to navigate them. Succeeding on the outside but not so much on the inside. Wondering why I didn't fit in but was accepted for my novel way of being. I've heard that we always go back to what we remember as a child for nurture. Even though it's not rational; it can be painful or even detrimental to one's physical and mental health as we know that kind of love to be real.

My mother supported my father while he dreamed and created his vision. I supported my husband so he could have the space to be an artist, but he chose not to, which was disappointing to me. The feeling of complete loneliness if you didn't have the whole tribe sleeping in one room together made it very difficult to function as a lone wolf.

On the hunt down the dirty brick road for The Big Time, I never realized until it was gone, that The Big Time was happening my whole life in search of this nebulous dream that seemed to promise nirvana. A three musketeers' family who were loyal to death. Adventures galore together as a dysfunctional family unit. The ability to go to Front Street to work on the dream learning by error.

In retrospect, I realize I was pursuing something so aggressively with a single-mindedness that I thought would give me complete acceptance by the real world. It has dominated my whole life from the time I was four.

You are an ugly, laughed at, dirty nothing as a human being, but you are God's gift when you entertain people and make them happy.

I loved that feeling so much, it drove my whole life, bulldozing over the ability to live a multidimensional life that held other potentials for joy.

As I am in recovery from drinking myself almost to death, as my brother and sister did, and my paternal grandma and grandpa did, I have been told multiple times by many who are helping me heal unconditionally, stating the reason is that I have a value as a human being.

I cry to my core every time someone says that. It pains my mother today to not have interjected a change along the way in my upbringing. How could my mom know at the time, the consequences of being raised the way I was?

Every person in the group had a right to leave. It was required by my father that all the kids had an eighth grade education and know how to paint signs. All the kids left the group between the ages of 12 and 14. Todd and Jessica came to live with me as a segue to beginning their own lives.

The neurosis only came out later as a burned-out jaded adult who had been taken complete advantage of in personal and professional relationships because she was told adamantly to never give up. Ever.

Still, I wouldn't change a thing about my upbringing because it made me the person I am. Others seem to appreciate the uniqueness that only now, I am trying to appreciate myself.

The constant message in recovery from many is that in order to break through you have to break down. Nothing of value comes easy; it takes intense work on yourself to grow. It's harder than opening for Porno for Pyros to thousands of screaming fans.

In retrospect, I've come to realize with bittersweet sorrow, like Dorothy clicking her ruby red heels after her adventures in Oz, "There's no place like home." The Big Time sought daily by my father and me was there the whole cacophonic while.

The Drinking Game

People ask me if I am tempted to drink. I am thankful that I'm not.

I make a point to look at the bottles of liquor at the grocery, or people sipping away, I think about that first firewater shooting through my throat, opening up my chest and igniting the dream state in my brain. That temporary moment isn't worth letting down all of the people in my world who have invested their faith in me. It costs too much to fall to the bottom and it's too hard to get back to the top.

One drink. That's what everyone says is all it takes to fall back down the rabbit hole. That's a terrifying thought. I've seen it happen right in front of my eyes. It broke my heart to witness my whole dream of a sober relationship being thrown away to a Skol bottle as I maintained sobriety while preparing for a liver transplant.

One drink for me equals death. I dream about drinking every night. It's an awful same dream with different settings and casts of scolders. I am wandering, trying to see my loved ones. When I do, I always have a bottle or cocktail attached to my being. I'm not drinking, but nobody believes me and I am ostracized from the safe haven of home.

I dream about the man I was with. He is in that hazy shadow background with the same reputation attached to him, watching me quietly from afar. We got together when we were drinking. But the moment I saw him one afternoon with his gentle doe eyes and tall lanky shyness, I saw lightning bolts of love. We were kindred spirits who understood each other. Going through drinking and sobriety together bonds two people more than a marriage. You become like one. Every time for four years I would think of him and he would call.

Having Grandville in my life when no one else wanted to have anything to do with me was a gift from the heavens. Was it love? Was it understanding? Was it loneliness? I attached myself to him like the never-ending lifeboat. What really is love? I believe it was the first time I was ever really taken with anyone.

He got sober first. I kept drinking. He fell off and we drank together again. I almost died and got sober. He went to rehab a month after I did. We spent a Covid year isolated inside together, sober. We had the best time. Laughing, learning, playing chess, making love, which is something I was afraid to do sober. Then he fell off the wagon during the holidays and I stayed sober. It broke my heart to not be able to communicate with him as he was destroying himself and us and me.

Then it all fell apart. Now we're both sober separately. I finally got to understand what I had put the ones I love through. It was torture.

The drinking routine. I had my first official night of drinking wine at 24. I was so sick the next day. My girlfriend, who was a pro, told me to stuff my face with a big hearty breakfast and a glass of milk. It worked. I became a red wine with ice cube drinker, but only rarely.

There was the night my boyfriend stood me up to be with another girl. We were living together. I was so mad. I chug-a-lugged his warm vodka bottle and immediately puked my guts up.

Alcohol was not the focus of my life when I lived in New York City. Becoming a winner was. There were cocktail hangs at the gig and socials, but it never was a habit or a problem.

I was unable to justify going out to be with friends because it would be a bad look and irresponsible. I kept gigging, doing shows for drunk people who didn't care about what I was sharing. Drink some more. Take the back street home. Drive carefully and make sure the headlights are on.

Slowly I started to come up with a routine to cover up how much I was really drinking. *Always know where your keys are. Always try hard to not look or act inebriated.* The gum was often forgotten. Then bathrooms became my solace with my bottle. Gig breaks. Grocery shopping. Even in my own house. Hiding bottles. My favorite was Baker's bourbon. That was way too expensive for a habit. So it was Wild Turkey 101. Why waste time; may as well get to that high with the first swig.

Then there were my gin and tequila periods. They were cheaper. But they didn't taste so good straight and warm. Making a perfect cocktail went out the window. Drinking in view of others versus drinking in secret limited my options.

After being kicked out of my own home, rejected by my daughter, and losing everything that I supported for 12 years, I switched to cheaper booze. Somehow landing in Gentilly, with the Brown Derby a few blocks away, I ended up with the old Black grandpas buying pints in the morning. That store was the typical fried chicken, liquor, and smokes store. That became my normal.

Every neighborhood I landed in had a corner store with your two for five. What did drinking all day and night feel like? A constant dreamy way of viewing the world. No hard edges. Nothing affected me. Not the bad. But with that, not the good either. I rarely was hung over. Somehow, despite being broke, there always seemed to be money for liquor. The oddity is that I never blacked out, never had a DUI. I toured out of the country, and somehow I kept it (mostly) together. So I didn't think I had a problem. Even getting up to a bottle of booze a day. Russia, Greece, Norway, London, Puerto Rico, Mexico, Canada, and all of the United States on a major tour as the lead singer of the Squirrel Nut Zippers, I was able to do all of it. But not to my best abilities.

I justified not having a problem. Everyone just didn't understand me. They were cruel for canceling me out of their lives while they still continued to drink. How could they drink in front of me? I might embarrass them. Which I had done in the past from time to time. I live in a drinking circle. We've all seen each other at our worst. Why was I being ostracized?

What about drinking was more important than anything else? It was my safety net. My career was disappointing, my marriage was disappointing. The back-to-back deaths of my dad and brother were devastating.

I couldn't depend on anything except that definite comfort zone that made everything feel alright regardless of the state of affairs in my world that I had no control over. Liquid courage, a friend called it. The bravery to be the person you want to be without judgment. Or so you think. All the drinking had some hilarious moments that make for great big fish stories. In the brotherhood of musicians, it also makes for some tragic ones, friends dying way too young.

I was part of the boys' club called jazz. I felt if I could drink any of them under the table, I would command equal respect. Who knew a female body can't handle that amount of alcohol the way a man's can? Until the day it couldn't.

The thought of giving up the bottle gave me massive anxiety attacks. Facing the real world without a buffer seemed impossible. Liquor and I were like a marriage. We laughed, we cried. I was in a codependent relationship. But liquor didn't care. There was no emotional reciprocation. Just a silent, hard bottle of liquid.

There was an elephant in the room while I was trying to have a real relationship with another person. Gauging their mental state, unable to objectively gauge mine. I can't imagine all of the experiences around the world without the presence of alcohol. It is the watering hole for gatherings bonding all souls in solidarity.

I don't miss it. I've drunk enough bottles to have funded a liquor store. I feel bad for my (former) liver. She was literally in a toxic relationship with me and had absolutely no power to speak up until she just died. No one ever plans on having a drinking problem, but then there you are. It just started to roll like an out-of-control vehicle speeding toward a cliff. I feel so lucky to have jumped out of the car before it crashed into the cliffs below with a massive explosion called death.

It was promised by those in sobriety that a whole new amazing world awaited. I didn't believe them. But you know what? They were right! My life is full of people who are doing impressive things with their lives, all with a sober view of the world.

I have to say throughout the whole nightmare, there were a few who stood beside me, much to their chagrin. My mother was there for all of it firsthand. For that I am so thankful and sorry for what I put her through. No one deserves to spend Christmas in the ICU wondering if their daughter is going to make it.

A 25-year relationship has come to an end. I can honestly say, I'm so ready for the next chapter.

Meet Me Under the Chime Tree

Meet me under the chime tree
I'll be waiting for you,
Where the wind blows,
Each chime's melodic hues.

While the world whizzes by,
Under it,
I sit alone, once blue,
Listening to nature's voice
Play its orchestral tune.

Meet me under the chime tree,
I'll be waiting for you.
With a picnic basket
Of love mixed with food.

As the wind blows,
Chime notes flow,
Green grass,
Watch the rowboats row,
Lovers kiss,
Best laughter of little kids.

Under the chime tree,
A dreamy bliss,
Why can't every day in life
Be exactly like this?

Other Works That May Be of Interest:

Baja Journey by Maxine Pearlman

The Happiest Man in the World by Alec Wilkinson

Random Lunacy Documentary by Home Team Productions (available on YouTube)

The Work Group Tools, floatingneutrinos.com

The original draft of this book was typed in the Notes section of an iPhone 7.